# BALANCING
# ACTS

# Twayne's American Thought and Culture Series

*Lewis Perry, General Editor*

# BALANCING ACTS

*American Thought
and Culture in the 1930s*

TERRY A. COONEY

*Twayne Publishers*
*An Imprint of Simon & Schuster Macmillan*
*New York*

*Prentice Hall International*
*London • Mexico City • New Delhi • Singapore • Sydney • Toronto*

*Balancing Acts: American Thought and Culture in the 1930s*
Terry A. Cooney

Twayne Publishers
An Imprint of Simon & Schuster Macmillan
866 Third Avenue
New York, New York 10022

Library of Congress Cataloging-in-Publication Data

Cooney, Terry A.
   Balancing acts : American thought and culture in the 1930's /
Terry A. Cooney
       p.    cm. — (Twayne's American thought and culture series)
    Includes bibliographical references and index.
    ISBN 0–8057–9060–8 (alk. paper). —  ISBN 0–8057–9069–1 (pbk. :
alk. paper)
    1. United States—Civilization—1918–1945.  2. United States—
Intellectual life—20th century.    I. Title.  II. Series.
E169.1.C765   1995
973.917—dc20                                                        94–23610
                                                                         CIP

The paper used in this publication meets the minimum requirements of American National Standard for Information Sciences—Permanence of Paper for Printed Library materials ANSI Z3948–1984 ♾

10 9 8 7 6 5 4 3 2 1 (hc)

Printed in the United States of America

*For my parents*
*Richard H. Cooney and Marcia L. Cooney*
*who were there*

# Contents

# Illustrations

# *Foreword*

The American Thought and Culture Series surveys intellectual and cultural life in America from the sixteenth century to the present. The time is auspicious for such a broad survey because scholars have carried out so much pathbreaking work in this field in recent years. The volumes reflect that scholarship as well as valuable earlier studies. The authors also present the results of their own research and offer original interpretations. The goal is to bring together books that are readable and well informed and that stand on their own as introductions to significant periods in American thought and culture. There is no attempt to establish a single interpretation of all of America's past; the diversity, conflict, and change that are features of the American experience would frustrate any such attempt. What the authors can do, however, is to explore issues that are of critical importance to both a particular period and the whole of American history.

Today the culture and intellectual life of the United States are subjects of heated debate. While prominent figures summon citizens back to an endangered "common culture," some critics dismiss the very idea of culture—let alone American culture—as elitist and arbitrary. The questions asked in these volumes are directly relevant to that debate, which concerns history but too often proceeds in ignorance of it. How did leading intellectuals view their relations to America, and how did their compatriots regard them? Did Americans believe that theirs was a distinctive culture? Did they participate in international movements? What were the links and tensions between high culture and popular culture? While discussing influential works, creative individuals, and major institutions, the books in this series place intellectual and cultural history in the larger context of American society.

*Balancing Acts* is one of several volumes dealing with a single decade of the twentieth century. Terry Cooney keeps a tight focus on intellectual and cultural life in the decade of the Great Depression and New Deal in the United States and rising totalitarianism and impending world war overseas. He analyzes a variety of intellectual engagements with Marxism and artistic treatments of misery and heroism among working-class Americans. But he does not present the decade simply as a time of conflict and radical transformation. Without overlooking the serious problems that shook confidence in American institutions, he discusses the resilience of liberalism, the persistence of conservatism, and the emergence of ideological positions that are not easily classified. In a decade of recurrent debate over what values are fundamentally American, few were willing to advocate that the nation turn its back on all traditions. Instead, as Cooney shows in discussions of films, music, paintings, and architecture, as well as a wide range of written expression, Americans favored "balancing acts" that blurred distinctions between old and new and deepened faith in an ongoing national identity in the midst of unprecedented challenges.

A book on a short period must face the issue of continuity. *Balancing Acts* looks back in every chapter to events and movements before the 1930s, and it takes proper note of the artistic and intellectual currents that surfaced in the 1930s and became more prominent thereafter. But Cooney takes the issue of continuity to another level by showing just how earnestly Americans of the 1930s struggled to hold onto meanings from their past and to see themselves, with all their heterogeneity, as a single people moving forward in time. *Balancing Acts* ends with advice to consider in our own time as we encounter challenges to privileged notions of what constitutes American culture.

LEWIS PERRY
*Series Editor*

# *Preface*

Reviewing in 1938 three of the guidebooks produced by the New Deal Federal Writers' Project, the British journalist D. W. Brogan suggested to his European audience that the guides illustrated "the richness of American life which the casual visitor too easily dismisses as monotonous and fundamentally dull." Brogan found a wealth of curiosities and surprises in American culture that were anything but monotonous, and he quietly marveled over the tensions and contradictions that the guides seemed able to accommodate. Tone and content were not constrained by government sponsorship, as they would have been in Britain. Announcing that gambling was "strictly speaking illegal," the *New Orleans City Guide* also provided directions to gambling resorts and specified their hours of operation. Brogan wanted his readers to grasp a fundamental insight: "America is a tradition-minded as well as a tradition-breaking country."[1]

Efforts to preserve and to escape tradition represented only one of the balancing acts characteristic of the 1930s. Individuals, groups, and communities regularly weighed competing values and ideas on a sensitive scale, adjusting meanings, explanations, and commitments within a society under pressure. If the experience of economic depression raised questions about family relationships and individual success, it led at the same time to a broader contemplation of the nation's development and of American identity. If intellectuals of the thirties entertained ideas about the radical reconstruction of society, they worried as well about liberties and legacies that might be lost. If people confronting crises at home and abroad searched for emblems and ideals of national cohesiveness, they also edged their way toward a wider acceptance of difference and toward more complex models of American culture. In many cases, not just the content but the framing of the question was at stake. By the end of the 1930s, more than one pattern for thinking about social, political, aesthetic, and cultural order had gained a sustaining vitality within American thought and culture.

Any effort to explore the history of a richly variegated period will encounter the limits of inclusion and the problem of choice. In surveys of American history and in public memory, the economic and political issues linked with the Great Depression and the New Deal hold pride of place in discussions of the 1930s. Such issues cannot be ignored in an examination of thought and culture, but neither can they be central. Thus, the legislative history of the New Deal, the vivid saga of labor organization in the thirties, the multifaceted story of agricultural change, the shifting patterns in the power and distribution of industries, and related economic and political concerns do not receive sustained attention in the discussion that follows.

Within the realms of thought and culture, a greater emphasis on intellectuals and their ideas might have justified increased attention to a cast of prominent individuals or to developments within specific academic disciplines. Similarly, a greater emphasis on popular culture might have called for prominent treatment not just of the topics discussed but of others, including the comics and professional sports. The approach taken here seeks an intermediate path that addresses a range of questions important to the intellectual and cultural life of the 1930s, giving roughly equivalent weight to the overlapping spheres of formal and public ideas. The discussion does not pretend to be comprehensive.

In 1941 Eugene Lyons characterized the 1930s as *The Red Decade*, and radicalism has held prominent place in studies of the period ever since. Lyons greatly exaggerated the influence of the left and served up a polemical condemnation. Others during the postwar decades have turned to various forms of thirties radicalism to explain an attraction no longer vital, to celebrate an impulse continued or revived, to unearth the seeds of later activism, or to examine the political and intellectual limitations of an older left. Yet radicalism is but one voice of the thirties, and it is not necessarily the loudest. Scholars have put forward a number of organizing themes for the cultural history of the decade, each of which tends to reduce the others to a supporting role at best. These themes include the cultivation of nationalism, the discovery of the concept of "culture," the impact of "modern" media, the preoccupation with past or future, and the pursuit of an ideal of commonality.

The interpretation found here is less concerned with asserting the centrality of one impulse than with thinking about the tensions within and between values, ambitions, ideas, and circumstances. The desire to move in more than one direction at once, to have it both ways, to live with or to resolve contradictions, appears during the 1930s in the most broadly public spheres as well as in the narrower territories of individuals defining their beliefs and families furnishing their homes. Discussing these tendencies and tensions neither excludes those with single-minded commitments nor denies the importance of unifying programs and myths. It seeks to expand, not contract, the domain of reflection. A closer attention to the balancing acts of the 1930s may help us to appreciate not simply the limitations but the creativity Americans showed in responding to the dilemmas of their period, and it may remind us that the answers they gave have relevance for our own.

# Acknowledgments

A work of synthesis is dependent on the efforts of many previous scholars; those to whom the debt is most direct are acknowledged in the Notes and the Bibliographic Essay. Support from the National Endowment for the Humanities helped get the project off the ground. Lewis Perry, as general editor for the series in which this book appears, provided encouragement and useful comment at several points along the way. Thomas A. Davis, academic dean at the University of Puget Sound, complicated the writing somewhat by asking me at an early stage in the process to serve as his associate dean, then helped sustain the work through his understanding and interest. As is often the case with families, Denise, Haynes, and Evan did their own balancing between patient acceptance of energies directed elsewhere and a proper insistence on contributions to the common pool.

*one*

---

# Challenge and Persistence

Remembering the moment 35 years later, the woman's voice broke, and her account was marked by tears of anger, frustration, and helplessness. She had maintained a relatively privileged position during the Great Depression, continuing her university training until graduation in 1933 and then quickly getting a job as a county relief case worker. The job paid well, giving rise to feelings of guilt even as she worried about being laid off herself. She had majored in social service administration, but because her teachers were still preparing students to work with immigrant families, she knew little of the unemployed. At 21, she found herself, unnaturally it seemed, an authority figure for people often much older than herself: people who felt a "terrible dependence" on case workers for food or a meager income; people who directed both gratitude and blame toward these bearers of their fate, though the case workers might feel there was "little we could do."

The father in one of the first families the young woman visited was a tall, graying railroad worker left jobless by the economic collapse. She had been instructed that she must actually witness the effects of poverty, that she must look to see, for example, if a family needed clothing. This mandated invasiveness shaped the moment that could lay waste her composure even after 35 years: "He let me look in the closet—he was so insulted. He said, 'Why are you doing this?' I remember his feeling of humiliation . . . this terrible humiliation. He said, 'I really haven't anything to hide, but if you really must look into it.' . . . I could see he was very proud. He was so deeply humiliated. And I was, too."[1]

This experience was painful not because either person acted improperly or with ill will, but because the depression put customary values under strain and created cultural tensions and conflicts that were not easily resolved. The rail-

1

road man may well have been an exemplary citizen who had worked hard, provided for his family, valued his self-reliance, and lived up to every standard of American respectability. Yet a failure in the entire economic system had left him unable to find work, unable to provide, unable to defend his independence, and needing an assistance that his values made it mortifying to receive. Many in the larger society, and even in the relief office, would have been happier not to give him that assistance. The young woman noted that "quite a few" case workers believed that "some of the people weren't looking hard enough for work" or were "loafers." Judging joblessness and need as moral failings helped to maintain particular value constructions and to avoid doubts about the economic system. For the larger number who acknowledged that indeed the system had broken down at least temporarily, and that aid to those who deserved it was appropriate and necessary, anxieties remained. To demonstrate that a worker deserved aid, they invaded the dignity and self-respect that, by their own lights, most made the worker worth aiding. The young woman's experience suggested other complications as well: a disturbance of assumptions about generational order and sexual roles during the depression; the ironies of looking to expertise to deal with problems about which few were expert; the tension between compassion and efficiency; and, less directly, the strain placed on principles of limited government by the demands of omnipresent need.

The economic crisis that accelerated this testing of values did not descend over the nation all at once. The stock market had crashed toward the end of 1929, offering a convenient historical marker for the beginning of a long downward slide, but conditions in 1930 provoked little sense of urgency among either the nation's leaders or their most avid critics. President Herbert Hoover used the word *depression* to describe what most assumed would be a short-term slump to avoid the more extreme implications of traditional terms like *panic* and *crisis*.[2] By 1931 the mood had changed, and it had become clear that the deepening depression was not just national but international. Shelters hastily made from wooden boxes and scrap metal accumulated into urban encampments of the homeless dubbed "Hoovervilles": Portland, Oregon, had two such villages, and the one in St. Louis claimed a population of over 1,000 people.[3] In a coal industry already plagued by overproduction, the depression brought reductions in jobs, workdays, and pay. When a group of Pennsylvania miners tried to strike in self-defense, they were ejected from company housing and left to eat weeds, with no local doctor willing to risk the ire of the company by treating them. Between 1929 and 1931, in the mining region of Harlan County, Kentucky, some 231 children joined many from Pennsylvania in dying from what a contemporary observer called "those providential diseases which enable welfare authorities to claim that no one has starved."[4] Daniel Willard, a railroad president speaking in March 1931 to a university business school audience, declared, "I would steal before I would starve." However much this may have said about the perception of worsening social conditions and about Willard, it underestimated the obstacles even to stealing for those in the Hoovervilles and Harlan County.[5]

By 1932 agricultural prices had reached extraordinary lows. The impact was particularly severe in areas depending primarily on a single crop, whether it was wheat, corn, cotton, or tobacco. Corn was being burned for fuel in the Upper Midwest because it had virtually no market value and proved cheaper than coal. Protesting farmers, some of whom were organized by Milo Reno and his Farm Holiday Association, dumped milk and eggs on highways and blocked the transportation of crops in attempts to force up prices. Angry crowds blocked foreclosures and turned sales of debt-ridden farms into "penny auctions" at which the only bidder would offer a penny and return the farm to its previous owner. Nature added to the burden of falling prices when drought robbed beef cattle of their natural fodder on the ranches of the mountain states and turned the Great Plains region into the "Dust Bowl."[6]

Cities faced a comparable economic crisis: those most dependent on single industries were the hardest hit. With the collapse of the booming automobile industry of the 1920s, the number of workers employed by the Ford Motor Company in Detroit fell by more than two-thirds, and unemployment for the city in 1932 was estimated at over 50 percent. Southern cities faced a pattern of wage-cutting and futile strikes in the textile industry, while those in the Pacific Northwest suffered through regional declines above 50 percent in lumbering and wood products as construction fell nationally by three-quarters.[7] In Chicago there were reports of 50 men fighting over a barrel of restaurant garbage; Chicago teachers who went unpaid for months in 1932–33 were sometimes not much better fed. Although the city managed an exposition to mark a century of progress in 1932, the Chicago Public Library was enduring its third year without book funds. Libraries had taken on a special importance in the context of the depression because they were warm and free. Philip Rahv, who would become an important editor, a major literary critic, and a professor at Brandeis University, was then a young man without a high school diploma, sleeping at times on park benches, and educating himself by day in the shelter of the New York Public Library.[8]

Gross statistics told one version of the nationwide story. Net farm income had declined from over $6 billion in 1929 to just over $2 billion in 1932.[9] The gross national product in constant dollars dropped by 31 percent from 1929 to 1933.[10] Investment fell from $17 billion in 1929 to $1.1 billion in 1932.[11] Unemployment had been 3.2 percent in 1929; it rose to a not yet shocking 8.7 percent in 1930, to 15.9 percent in 1931, and to approximately 25 percent in 1932 and 1933.[12] Unemployment figures for the period, however, must be taken with a lump of salt. The Hoover administration did its best to insist on making estimates as low as possible, and techniques for gathering such data were not well developed. Many people who had stopped looking for work or never started were not counted. Suffice it to say that at least 13 million people were unemployed in the winter of 1932–33. This figure left a large majority

"Jobless men lined up for the first time in California to file claims for unemployment compensation." Dorothea Lange demonstrates here her exceptional sense of composition and a skillful use of light. The broad impact of the depression is suggested in this photograph by the varieties of clothing found in the unemployment line, by the range of caps and hats, which can be associated with differences in social standing, and by the span of ages, from the gentleman with light hat and cane to the young man with slicked hair. The jobless in this photograph include no women, however, nor any discernible ethnic or racial mix. *National Archives*

still employed, a fact it is important to remember in considering the experience of the 1930s. Yet many who were working faced reduced hours or days, sometimes adding up to less than half the normal work for the year. The effects of unemployment and underemployment reached well beyond the people who appeared in national statistics, justifying by 1933 the judgment—fundamental to the intellectual and cultural outlook of the period—that this was not simply a depression but, indeed, a "great depression."[13]

A range of circumstances affected the way each person reacted to joblessness or economic stress, but millions of individual cases created a number of discernible patterns. Between 1929 and 1932, for example, the suicide rate per 100,000 rose from 13.9 to 17.4, an increase of 24 percent.[14] Men and women making less drastic decisions during the first years of the 1930s reduced the birth rate by 10 percent (quite typical internationally as well) and the marriage rate by 20 percent.[15] Whether because of the cost involved or for other reasons, the divorce rate also fell. Perhaps surprisingly, given the realities of physical suffering and the vivid images of depression breadlines, the death rate per thousand moved downward from 11.9 in 1929 to 10.6 in 1939, and life expectancy rose over the decade from 57.1 to 63.7.[16] Explanations for this pattern seem somewhat speculative. For those who lost their jobs, the quality as much as the amount of food they ate seems to have declined. Yet especially after relief efforts were in full swing, certain groups among the traditional poor may actually have been better able to keep malnutrition at bay than they had been under "normal" conditions of poverty. The majority who continued to work, meanwhile, benefited from falling prices and may have improved their diet and living conditions. Like the prosperity of the 1920s, the depression of the 1930s was distributed unevenly; in its cultural as well as its economic impact, it followed no single pattern or rule.

Psychological responses among those who had lost steady employment did have similiarities across a number of cultures in Europe and the United States. As John Garraty notes in summarizing a range of studies, the newly unemployed first looked energetically for a new job. "If nothing turned up, they gradually became discouraged, perhaps emotionally distraught. But after some months of idleness, they either sank into apathy or adjusted to doing nothing, in either case leading extremely circumscribed existences in apparent calm."[17] Such a pattern should not be allowed to obscure the many protests among the American unemployed, limited and short-lived though most of them were. The "distraught" and the truly apathetic (as distinct from those who "adjusted") were perhaps no larger a segment than the roughly 5 percent of the jobless who participated in the sharper forms of protest at their height.[18] Most of the jobless continued to want work, and many resisted the idea and the habits of relief: in a study conducted in New Haven, Connecticut, E. Wight Bakke found that no matter how far they had been pushed toward destitution, about half the unemployed stuck to their sense of themselves as self-reliant workers and refused to seek aid. Established values and desires persisted among those hit hardest by the depression, whose reactions to adversity conformed neither to the hopes of radicals nor the fears of conservatives. The relative cultural stability among unemployed workers thus confounded the assumptions of more than one social thinker in the early 1930s.[19]

The behavior of the unemployed and of people beset by continuing economic insecurity could defy expectations in other ways as well. Even for many living on a shoestring, hardship did not eliminate all possibility of cultural and financial choice. Like jobless Belgians who took up pigeon-raising and hungry British families splurging on sweets and tea, Americans looked for something to relieve the debilitating effects of want, idleness, and gloom. They went to movies by the tens of millions weekly. They followed sports closely and boosted their own participation. They played and invented games that, in the face of a systemic crisis, held out the opportunity to compete and the hope of winning within a stable framework of rules. (Roosevelt's promise of a "new deal" in the largest game of all evoked a response far greater than any he had anticipated.) While commentators proclaimed the death of capitalism, the board game "Monopoly" rushed to an extraordinary popularity by allowing all comers to accumulate property, to take a "Chance," to dream of building a hotel on Boardwalk and collecting exorbitant rent. In the midst of economic depression, such patterns suggested a stubborn resistance to psychological depression and to the abandonment of familiar values.[20]

Both the challenge to, and the persistence of, cultural expectations and behaviors were particularly evident in the experience of women during the depression. The thirties inherited the assumption that women would normally marry and stay within the home. Even so, the number of wage-earning women had grown steadily during the 1920s to reach 10.6 million, or 21.9 percent of the entire workforce, in 1930; about 25 percent of all women over 15 were working, but less than 12 percent of married women, as compared with 50 percent of single women.[21] The depression brought widespread assertions that women ought not to hold jobs when men were out of work, both on the argument that they should be trying to strengthen the home and on the fallacious assumption that men's income supported families while women's did not. A particular campaign against married women whose husbands also worked caused a slippage in professional and governmental positions. In something of an ironic twist, however, traditional patterns of job segregation and lower pay based on assumptions about women's social role now provided a degree of protection against depression challenges to women's employment based on those same assumptions. Men were reluctant to enter fields that had come to be strongly identified with women—clerical and office work, for example, where recovery was more rapid than in industrial employment and where an explosion of federal agencies and programs contributed to an expansion of jobs after the early thirties. Moreover, as the process of mechanization leapt forward in some industries under the incentives of the depression and the New Deal, jobs usually held by men involving a traditional skill or heavy labor declined, while relatively light jobs tending new machines went in greater part to women who could, by custom, be paid less. The proportion of women in the total workforce inched upward to about 25 percent by 1940, and the segment of married women working climbed above 15 percent (or perhaps more indicatively, 13.8 percent of those with husbands present).[22] After considerable turmoil, both the ideological assertions of women's proper role, and the trends toward increasing employment that stood in tension with those assertions, seemed to have been reinforced.[23]

In the labor organizing campaigns of the 1930s, women workers, like members of some minority groups, were included primarily when their concentration in particular industries made them impossible to ignore. As Alice Kessler-Harris has remarked, unions were for most women workers "reluctant benefactors" at best.[24] On a wider scale, labor activism involved many women who were not workers themselves but who were married to workers. Women played an important role in major strikes during the decade by establishing channels of supply for men "sitting down," by demonstrating themselves, and by joining women's auxiliaries. Although this involvement could be justified on traditional grounds, it sometimes pulled women into new roles and provided a taste of organizing, politics, and power that became threatening when too thoroughly enjoyed. Union leaders, as in the 1934 Minneapolis Teamsters' strike, sometimes used arguments based on women's domestic responsibilities to urge them into active support of their striking husbands and then tried to restrain women who became too fully involved. Labor activism during the depression sometimes stretched established conceptions of women's roles, but organizers sought primarily to take advantage of prevailing norms rather than to change them.

Within the family or household, the relationship of a husband and wife might be strongly affected if suddenly the man was not working or if the depression otherwise undermined established expectations. The sharpest role reversal occurred if a woman moved into the man's traditional place as primary breadwinner, although statistically this could have happened in only a small proportion of households. Yet any case in which the husband was unemployed or the family faced hardship opened the prospect of increasing influence for women as guardians of the domestic economy. Whether this constituted a fundamental shock depended on the circumstances. Financial pressures and shifting viewpoints might strengthen or sour a marriage, depending on the personalities involved and the structure of the relationship. Religion, ethnicity, and social class all played a part in shaping a family's capacity to deal with change and stress.[25] Even gross statistics suggested different circumstances and experiences. Among married women, a higher proportion of native-born whites than of foreign-born were in the labor force in 1930, while married nonwhite women had a participation rate more than three times that of whites—33.2 percent to 9.8 percent. The proportion of white married women at work rose during the 1930s and lifted the rate for all married women, but the rate for nonwhite married women fell during the decade by almost 6 percent.[26] The particular stories growing out of the depression would have varying narratives and conclusions. Nevertheless, a general social assessment can only conclude that the depression tested the strength of a sizable number of American families and marriages without altering significantly the shape of these institutions or fundamentally restructuring men's and women's roles.[27]

For a few women, the circumstances of the 1930s opened up opportunities for public service and access to positions of power for which there was limited precedent. Republicans were swept out of office in 1932; the Roosevelt administration brought a range of new people to Washington; the New Deal's rapid expansion of federal offices and programs created a fluidity more open to unconventional appointments than were established bureaucratic structures; and in the social welfare fields related most directly to relief efforts, women were well represented. The most exceptional woman who rode to public prominence on the Democratic tide was Eleanor Roosevelt, who through her own public activities, her network of friends, and her special relationship with the president, expanded the prospects for other women in public life. Franklin Roosevelt appointed Frances Perkins to serve as his secretary of labor, the first woman in the cabinet, and Molly Dewson wielded considerable political influence as head of the Women's Division of the Democratic party. Roosevelt also named women to serve for the first time in other important positions: Marion Glass Banister as assistant treasurer of the United States; Ruth Bryan Owen as an ambassador; Florence Allen as a judge on the U.S. Circuit Court of Appeals. Although sensitive to questions of opportunity for women and the needs of women on relief, the many women who served under the New Deal did not, for the most part, concentrate primarily on policies affecting women; they did not work from or seek to construct an intellectual framework of particularist advocacy; and they did not attempt to create lasting organizations and structures devoted exclusively to the interests of women. The depression and the New Deal created a climate of crisis and opportunity for people with interest, experience, and training in social welfare policies. The challenge of shaping general social reforms and making them work claimed priority for most women in the New Deal, with the assumption that this process would be most effective when it recognized and addressed the needs of women within a larger framework.[28]

The depression, then, did not collapse the dominant designs within the American cultural web, but it did provide both need and opportunity to nudge them around a bit. Patterns of basic values, including those shaping the social identities of men and women, demonstrated considerable flexibility in the uses to which they could be put even as they also proved to have a striking durability. On specific matters of both practical and symbolic importance, change could sometimes occur readily when circumstance and desire coincided with the power to act. Roosevelt had the authority to break precedents and to encourage new directions with his appointments and policies, and he used that power many times. Particular groups and individuals likewise took advantage of choices within their own spheres. Taken together, such decisions may have altered the flow of deeper historical streams. Efforts to construct new frameworks of meaning and behavior, and efforts to maintain the vitality of established values and outlooks, would unfold in the 1930s as a series of struggles between the power of cultural inheritance and the impact of changing circumstance and singular events.

## The Promise and the Threat

Many of the darkest cultural visions of the 1930s owed their birth to the years between 1931 and 1933. The bleaker works in film and fiction during this period seemed intent on destroying every ray of purpose or hope in the stories they told. Anxieties over the essential structures of American government and society led to scattered notions of dictatorship or cataclysm. As economic conditions continued to deteriorate, Herbert Hoover did not fail to act, but he slipped more and more into a sour defensive posture behind promises of eventual recovery that did not convince. In the summer of 1932, when as many as 20,000 depression-battered World War I veterans came to Washington seeking early payment of a bonus already promised by Congress for 1945, what began as a peaceful petition ended with Gen. Douglas MacArthur leading an ignoble military campaign to drive away the veterans and their families and to teargas and burn their encampment at Anacostia Flats. The White House was sealed off in midsummer by chains and guards; the veterans were accused of being Communists and crooks; MacArthur made unfounded claims of having saved the country from revolution; and administration officials denied that the army had done what newsreels clearly showed it doing. Exaggerated fears of an upheaval from below seemed to be producing panic, instability, and violence from above.

One person's fears in the early 1930s might stir another's hopes. Among intellectuals drawn toward analyses of American society, the depression crisis was often a stimulant to the journalistic dissection of what had gone wrong and to dreams of setting things right within a quite different societal framework. Upheaval from below was for some liberal and most radical intellectuals a consequence to be anticipated and welcomed. Generalizations simplify what was often a fluid and multi-sided debate among strong-willed people, but generalizations are necessary. Convinced that the depression marked a critical point in the history of capitalism and American society, social thinkers on the left sought to look toward the future through harsh criticisms of the past. American values were too rooted in experiences that were no longer viable: they were too agrarian, too bourgeois, too individualistic, too self-seeking at the expense of the public interest and the values of community. The corporate economic system had created concentrations of power that arrogantly resisted change even after their own breakdown. Big industry through mechanized production had rushed to deliver more goods than Americans were able to consume; a narrowly conceived drive for efficiency had produced the tragic wastefulness of want amid plenty; private property and private profit had nourished extremes of wealth and poverty. The current crisis, in revealing vividly the social injustices and failures of corporate capitalism, called into question not only economic structures but also the liberal ideas and institutions that had been counted on to limit, manage, and humanize a system of which they now seemed too much a part. For some, the depression undermined the notion of representative government, the hope for legislative reforms, belief in reasoned argument, confidence in the processes of education, and even a commitment to basic civil liberties. No limits from the past were to be allowed to constrain forceful action in the present.[29]

One significant body of intellectuals on the left emphasized the importance of planning, of technical expertise and social engineering, in producing a more just, efficient, orderly, and humane society. Particularly in magazines such as *Common Sense*, the *New Republic*, and the *Nation*, as well as in a variety of books, people like Adolph Berle and Gardiner Means, Stuart Chase and George Soule, Freda Kirchway and Max Lerner, Thurman Arnold and Rexford Tugwell, argued for the virtues of a rationalized society managed by experts who would serve the public interest. In general, they hoped to move toward this society (which some were happy to label "socialist") through democratic electoral politics, although they were not entirely successful in confronting the tensions between a commitment to democracy and the top-down control of planning by a trained elite. Often they worked from an assumption common in the 1930s that the nation's economy could no longer be expected to grow and that the problem was to introduce central controls over a more or less steady-state society for the benefit of all.[30]

Another cluster of intellectuals, generally considered further to the left in the early 1930s, were more attracted to visions of conflict and class power, to glorifications of action, to the idea of revolution. Their condemnations of liberal ideas as inescapably attached to corporate capitalism and bourgeois culture were correspondingly more extreme. The title of John Chamberlain's 1932 book, *Farewell to Reform*, emphasized the antiliberal militance of his call for a fundamental attack on "the price and profit system."[31] The central problem for Chamberlain was how to wrest power from a ruling class that would not relinquish its grip peacefully. Intellectuals who had been radicals before the depression often expected the economic crisis to create the kind of swift historical turn their varying beliefs demanded. Like many others on the far left, James Burnham and James Rorty accepted the commonplace radical claim that the United States had to move toward socialist revolution or slip into dictatorship and fascism. Lewis Corey insisted in 1935 that the salaried employees and white-collar workers of the evolving middle class were rapidly being "proletarianized," so that a revolution shaped by their alliance with blue-collar workers was virtually inevitable.[32] The Communist party offered a version of Marxism-Leninism tightly yoked to the policies of Joseph Stalin and sought to claim ideological leadership of the revolutionary cause. Younger literary intellectuals were perhaps the most inclined to invest their faith for a time and to borrow the Communists' rhetoric and their promise. Yet even when powerfully drawn toward Marxism and the mystique of the young Soviet Union, the more substantive social thinkers of the thirties seldom allied themselves for long with the Communist party.

A brief look at four intellectuals who gave sustained attention to radical ideas and who were influential over time in shaping the perceptions of others may help illuminate an important moment in American intellectual culture. People who made ideas a central preoccupation struggled with conflicts between values, and with values pinched by circumstance, as did relief workers and the unemployed. Along with other Americans, intellectuals wrestled with questions of what in their inheritance was worth saving, what changes were demanded by logic and circumstance, and what, indeed, their range of choice might be. More so than most groups, intellectuals tried to answer questions posed by the depression not simply for themselves but for the society and culture as a whole.

John Dewey by 1930 had already had a long and distinguished career as a philosopher of education and an advocate of philosophical pragmatism. At 71, he might well have retired from public debate with grace; some who associated his outlook with a liberalism they were now seeking to disclaim may have wished that he would do so. Instead, Dewey wrote several books and dozens of magazine pieces during the 1930s, and his involvement in intellectual and political affairs left little doubt as to his vigor. Dewey had come to believe that private control over major industries had to give way to new social forms harnessing the economy to the benefit of all, and this belief made him a radical. At the same time, he refused to reject all liberal values, finding ideas derived from liberalism fundamental to the practice of democracy. If the existing political and economic systems did not always meet his democratic tests, Dewey often saw the prospect of equal or greater abuses in radical doctrines and organizations.

In 1934 Dewey contributed a piece entitled "Why I Am Not a Communist" to a *Modern Monthly* "Symposium on Communism." Dewey offered four major objections to Communist party ideology and American efforts to ape the Soviet model, articulating in the process his own guiding principles as well. First, he observed that American Communist ideology rested "upon an almost entire neglect of the specific historical backgrounds and traditions" of the United States: the attempt to transfer an "autocratic" Russian tradition to America was "nothing short of fantastic." Equally oblivious to distinctions, the cultural philosophy of "official Communism" lost force through its "absurd attempt to make a single and uniform entity out of the 'proletariat.'" Second, Dewey complained that the "monistic" Communist philosophy of history simply failed to comprehend American issues, politics, and values. American problems flowed, Dewey insisted, from the "failure to introduce new forms of *democratic* control in industry and government consonant with the shift from individual to corporate economy." In the effort to move toward democratization, other groups had to be allied with workers to achieve significant change.

11

Communists were blind to this possibility, just as they ignored to their peril "our deeply rooted belief in the importance of individuality" (by which he did not mean economic individualism). Third, Dewey declared himself "profoundly skeptical" that class war was the only path toward genuine social improvement. Indeed, he declared, revolution in a modernized society would produce only chaos, and some presumptive radicals would be quick to reject official communism if it were in America "much more than a weak protest or an avocation of literary men."

Dewey's fourth point was deeply felt and demonstrated clearly his struggle for balance. The "emotional tone and methods of discussion and dispute" that Communists seemed to encourage struck him as "extremely repugnant." Here his continuing respect for certain elements of liberalism became apparent: "Fair-play, elementary honesty in the representation of facts and especially of the opinions of others, are something more than 'bourgeois virtues.' They are traits that have been won only after long struggle." The Communist willingness to deny civil rights to all but proletarians, to destroy political parties, to constrain "the rights of freedom of speech, press, and assembly," represented threats that were compounded by Party eagerness to curtail the reasoned debate essential to democratic culture. The "hysteria" of Communist denunciations, the "character assassination," the "misrepresentation" of opposing views, and the "apparent conviction that what they take to be the end justifies the use of *any* means" added up to a method and outlook "fatal" to the achievement of any new society worth having.[33]

Dewey not only wrote but acted to defend such views. In 1937, as he approached 80, Dewey agreed to head the Commission of Inquiry into the Charges Made against Leon Trotsky in the Moscow Trials, a task that required him to make a tiring trip to Mexico, where the exile Trotsky could give his testimony. Dewey knew the position would make him a target of abuse from Stalin's sympathizers, who could not credit the mounting evidence of Soviet purges, and Dewey accepted Trotsky's politics no more than Stalin's. But he saw the opportunity to affirm the importance of a fair hearing, balanced inquiry, and basic decency—even, or especially, for radical politics. A strong critic of state centralization as well as of antidemocratic practice, Dewey in 1939 stood prominent among a group of intellectuals who infuriated the Communist camp by linking Soviet Russia and Nazi Germany as repressive states at a time when Communists were trying to claim precedence in an international campaign against fascism. Throughout the 1930s Dewey pursued the idea of a new political party to build an alliance in support of radical democracy, generally voting for the perennial Socialist presidential candidate Norman Thomas for lack of a better alternative. He was never able to create a potent radical force, but in electoral terms, neither was anyone else. The strength of Dewey's example lay in his steadiness of principle, his ability to distinguish ideological dispute from personal rancor, and his model of sustained thought and action, traits that were far from commonplace among politically engaged intellectuals in the 1930s.[34]

Sidney Hook had been a student of Dewey's at Columbia before joining the Philosophy Department at New York University in 1927. During the late 1920s, Hook did research in the Soviet Union and helped bring out English-language editions of some of Stalin's writings. Publication of *Towards the Understanding of Karl Marx* (1933) and *From Hegel to Marx* (1936) made Hook the leading American scholar of Marxism. Hook's *Understanding* held that a properly conceived Marxism could be merged with precepts from Dewey's pragmatism without doing intellectual injustice to either. Marxism involved, according to Hook, a complex analysis of all the social and historical forces shaping human life, and it asserted the profound influence of class origins and social environment on individual perception and behavior. Yet it insisted as well that human choice and human action to bring about change were both possible and necessary, and it saw the future as indeterminate and difficult. Hook's Marxism rejected claims of inescapable laws or inevitable revolutions and presented itself as an open-ended philosophy distinguished by its scientific approach to society. The unity of Marx's thought, Hook argued, lay "not in his specific conclusions but in his method of analysis." It was thus entirely proper (and often convenient) "to dissociate the Marxian method from any specific set of conclusions, or any particular political tactic advocated in its name."[35]

In 1932 Hook seemed prepared to accept the Communist party as a legitimate vehicle of Marxism, and he publicly declared his support for the Communist presidential ticket. By 1934, however, the Party had become one of those "particular" claimants from which the philosophy of Marxism needed to be separated, though Hook continued to advocate a communism divorced from the Stalinist corruptions of "mistaken theories and tragically sectarian tactics." Writing for the same *Modern Monthly* symposium as Dewey, Hook set out to explain "Why I Am a Communist," qualifying his affirmation with the subtitle "Communism without Dogmas." Hook offered five positive arguments for communism that defined his radical hopes: (1) an "argument from efficiency," which emphasized the present evidence of capitalism's "necessary economic waste" and its "waste of human resources"; (2) an "argument from democracy," which insisted that true communism would not support a minority revolution but would seek revolution only when "general discontent with capitalist rule" extended to a majority, making force justifiable as part of the "fulfillment" of democracy; (3) an "argument from morality," which declared that the freedoms of inquiry and discussion about which Dewey and others had been concerned were unequal and abridged under capitalism, and that communists, to succeed, would need to be exemplars of "the highest ideals—the most important of which are courage, intelligence, and honesty" (unfortunately, the official Communist had "abandoned the true communist position in this as in other matters of behavior"); (4) an "argument from art," claiming that a communist society would "break down the false separation between aesthetic significance and utility"; (5) and an "argument from necessity," which found in communism the only viable way to oppose the drift

13

toward fascism that was a "natural outgrowth" of capitalism and was visible even within the early New Deal. The logical conclusion was that a new communist organization was urgently needed. Independent radicals kept looking for new beginnings.

Even as he made his positive case for communism as an ideal and a set of principles, Hook went on immediately to set forth at greater length his critique of the "dogmas" that made the "official representatives of communism" a fair target for those who assumed they spoke for Marxism and for radical ideas. What became clear through this process was the degree to which Hook's rejection of the Communist party shared fundamental political and intellectual precepts with Dewey's more general critique. Hook took the question of democracy as a touchstone (though he was more inclined to rationalizations of "transitional" necessities than Dewey). He insisted on the importance of reasoned analysis and debate and mocked the "superstition" that there was a "class-view or party-line in all branches of science and art, and presumably even in logic." He warned against the "dogma of the 'collective man'" and argued that true communism was only "hostile to individualism, as a social theory, and not to individuality, as a social value." And perhaps most fundamentally, he held that it was "impossible to make a sharp division between means and ends"; hence, current tactics reflected the kind of society an ideology might actually produce.[36]

Through both his positive assertions and his critique, Hook was trying to hang on to an ideal of communism that might ultimately attract "thousands of intellectuals and professionals" with left sympathies rather than drive them away, as he believed the Communist party was doing. In the context of the 1930s his effort was doomed: distinctions between communism in theory and practice could be maintained by a few intellectuals for a time, but for most people the Communist party provided the visible face of communist and Marxist ideas. Harsh Communist attacks had their effects on Hook himself. His opposition grew ever sharper as the decade progressed, with a concomitant erosion of his positive case for communism. In the 1930s and beyond, Hook's intellectual and organizational efforts would make him one of the Communist party's most prominent foes. There was something more significant than irony in the fact that the author of "Why I Am a Communist" and the period's leading scholar of Marxism should come to be best known as an anti-Stalinist (or in the terminology that would mark the loss of distinctions, an anticommunist).

Among the intellectuals attracted to Marxism in the 1930s, one scholar has concluded, there were only "two who made distinctive contributions to a reexamination of social thought." One was Sidney Hook, the other Edmund Wilson.[37] Wilson had established himself by 1930 as one of the leading younger literary critics in the United States, though little in his work of the 1920s recommended him as a scholar of Marxism or of social ideas. Yet the stock market crash in its symbolic significance provoked a strong reaction in Wilson, and he turned eagerly toward the prospects for radicalism and the idealistic promise of the Soviet experiment. When Herbert Croly's death prompted a struggle over editorial policy at the *New Republic*, Wilson took the more radical side in "An Appeal to Progressives." The capitalist system had tumbled down and crumpled the American faith in moneymaking as it fell, Wilson believed. Now was the time for public advocacy of socialism with the hope that Americans might put their "idealism and their genius for organization behind a radical social experiment." Wilson tried to boost the Russian example as a challenge and an inspiration, comparing the Soviet five-year plans (somewhat naively) to Liberty Loan drives. Even so, like Dewey and Hook, Wilson understood the importance of a specific context and was no supporter of a prepackaged politics. American progressives, he argued, needed to "take Communism away from the Communists" and create a program of their own.[38]

Wilson was stirred by the sense that he was living at a historic moment, by the thought of intellectuals becoming actors in history, and by the possibilities of inspiriting a movement of profound significance. He sought a radicalism distinctly rooted in the national culture, and he hoped that Americans would draw on their pioneer experience to seek out a postcapitalist frontier. From relatively early in the decade, Wilson's sometimes passionate engagement with the historical romance and idealistic promise of revolutionary Marxist ideas fed an impatience with political behaviors that violated his conceptions of an American movement, of the intellectual's role, and of radical standards. Although he gave formal support to the Communist ticket in 1932, he also complained about the Party's habit of "manufacturing martyrs" and of "using" intellectuals. By 1934 he was wading into a study of the socialist intellectual tradition running from its wellsprings in the eighteenth century, through Marx and Engels, and up to the brink of the Russian revolution. Wilson learned German to read texts in their original language; he traveled to the Soviet Union to gather materials and pay homage to Lenin; and from 1934 onward he published parts of his emerging work as essays, adding their voice to the ideological jostling of the period. His full study appeared in 1940 as *To The Finland Station: A Study in the Writing and Acting of History*, a book both of celebration and attack.

Wilson celebrated the aspiration of the radical socialist tradition and the thinkers in whom art and politics seemed one. Marx and Engels, Lenin and Trotsky, he once remarked, were "poets themselves in their political vision," men whose strength came from the "intensity of their imaginations" and the "skill with which through the written and spoken word they were able to arouse others to see human life and history as they did." Such heroes of mind and purpose were not in all ways exemplary; Wilson took pains to find a full measure of human frailty and to suggest that their achievement sometimes came at the expense of those around them. Yet there was no mistaking his admiration for the powerful political and moral ideal he found in their work: the desire to eliminate privileges of birth and wealth; the impulse toward a

15

cooperative society; the ambition for people to exercise a conscious and imaginative control over their own social relations and conditions. Sherman Paul can thus conclude that Wilson's book "celebrates the human will to overcome the injustices of existence."[39]

Yet as another reader notes, *To the Finland Station* presents a "highly critical account of Marxist theory."[40] Indeed, it is impossible to miss the debunking tone apparent in Wilson's treatment of the "Marxist Dialectic." Influenced in part by Max Eastman (who had engaged in a running dispute with Sidney Hook over the "scientific" nature of Marxist analysis), Wilson labeled the dialectic a "religious myth." The triad of thesis, antithesis, and synthesis that Marx had borrowed from Hegel was simply the "old Trinity, taken over from the Christian theology, as the Christians had taken it over from Plato." Along with other mistaken theories and an excessive dependence on the proletariat, the reliance on this "mythical and magical triangle" had led to problems in Marx's thought.[41] These root difficulties were dwarfed, however, by the waywardness of contemporary Communists, with their "Church" of the "Dialectic" and their "History" raised to a "semi-divine principle" of inevitability that eliminated the human need for either thought or action. The gap for Wilson between creative intellectual tradition and entrenched Communist doctrine was wide. In adjacent sentences, he could refer to Lenin's conception of politics as "one of the great imaginative influences of our age" and reduce Stalin to a "Georgian bandit-politician, who started on the road to power with a few Marxist texts in his head."[42] If Wilson still hoped to keep alive a radical ideal at the end of the 1930s, it was an ideal that refused definition by Marxist theory and encouraged hostility to Communist practice.

Reinhold Niebuhr's path through the decade followed an evolution of intersecting ideas about religion and politics characteristic of his thought. Niebuhr had built a reputation in the 1920s preaching social reform from a Detroit pulpit before moving to a faculty position at New York's Union Theological Seminary, where he would remain for 30 years. In 1929 he joined the Socialist party, which under the leadership of the former Presbyterian minister Norman Thomas gained a reputation for being both militant and responsible, and by 1930 Niebuhr was standing as a Socialist nominee for the New York State Senate. Having visited the Soviet Union briefly during the summer of 1930, Niebuhr, like Wilson and others, had seemed to hope that some of the energy and purposefulness he sensed there might appear in an American radical movement as well. His overwhelming defeat by both Democratic and Republican candidates in the fall could not have nourished his optimism. Yet the depression was deepening from month to month, and through 1931–32 Niebuhr predicted social upheavals, led by "the disinherited," from which society could only be saved by thoroughgoing socialist transformation. He met with Dewey and others to contemplate a new political party, discovering in the process how sharply leftist intellectuals of their ilk were cut off from any significant political base. Sticking with the Socialists in 1932, he accepted a nomination for Congress.[43]

In the months before he turned his energies to the fall campaign, Niebuhr completed the bulk of *Moral Man and Immoral Society*, which would appear within weeks after the election.[44] Socialist candidates, like Communists, did poorly. Niebuhr himself fell short of the vote received in 1930 by the Socialist nominee in the same district, and he was left complaining that Americans seemed "inert" in the midst of suffering. On the heels of this radical display of electoral ineffectiveness, *Moral Man* appeared bearing passionate preelection assertions that affronted many of Niebuhr's religious and political friends. In the effort to overcome "social inertia," Niebuhr declared, reason and analysis could only produce failure; "science" could not inspire workers to the emotional commitment necessary for success. Dewey was dismissed as dull and ineffective, though Niebuhr had allowed Dewey to speak for him during his campaign. Rejecting nonviolence as an ethical limitation, Niebuhr argued that the use of violence might be necessary and morally appropriate in certain situations—if, for example, the proletariat was in a position to make its revolution quick and complete, which Niebuhr clearly stated in 1932 it was not.

Niebuhr's positions on reason and violence aroused the most direct response. Yet his challenge to the religious and intellectual traditions from which he was departing reached toward a more fundamental level. Liberal and left Christian social thought, and to some extent American reformism more generally, had looked toward the gradual emergence in history of a "cooperative commonwealth" or a "beloved community," anticipating that progress toward this ideal of social justice and harmony would occur, variously, through reason and disinterested expertise, through the inspiration of artistic vision, and through the power of religious love. In *Moral Man* Niebuhr dismissed the entire vision as one that would never be realized. Society was an arena of unending conflict, and Christian love was not sufficient to battles over institutions and power. Even so, Niebuhr closed by praising as a "valuable illusion" the idea that humans could collectively achieve "perfect justice," allowing that the "sublime madness in the soul" thus inspired might encourage "terrible fanaticisms," but suggesting that reason could "control" the illusion once its revolutionary work was done.[45] Not alone on the left in the early thirties, Niebuhr vested an extraordinary responsibility in intellectuals. They would encourage illusion, myth, and propaganda to spark a radical social movement yet presumably remain sufficiently detached from the ideas they fed to the masses, and sufficiently in control, to pull in the reins when "fanaticism" grew dangerous. The reasoning power that was insufficient to lead a revolution would be necessary to save it.

In the course of responding to sharp criticisms of *Moral Man*, Niebuhr labeled himself a "Marxian"; but his work from that point onward more clearly led away from an endorsement of proletarian revolution than toward a further insistence on its urgency. Still a critic of liberalism in politics and religion, Niebuhr increasingly acknowledged a valuable side of the liberal tradition as well. The rise of German fascism prompted him to declare liberalism's insistence on "human rights which transcend any particular rights" of "race, class, or nation" to be no illusion but part of an "ageless culture."[46] He proved wary of dogmatism and absolutes (at least those that could be humanly known), and he turned against claims to an exclusive social virtue, placing greater emphasis on individual ethical consciousness. By 1935 Niebuhr was turning his ire against the moral pretensions of the proletariat and seeing a "demonic element" in all who presumed that they could end worldly injustice.[47]

Theologically, Niebuhr was drawn toward the concept of Original Sin and the myth of the Fall: Judeo-Christian tradition for him taught the interrelatedness of seeking to do good and doing evil unavoidably in the process. The views for which Niebuhr would come to be best known—his preachments on the need to act politically yet with a humility rooted in the knowledge of inevitable failings—were beginning to emerge. He launched the periodical *Radical Religion* in 1935 in an effort to distinguish religiously based radicalism from Marxism, and in its pages he moved toward the "realistic" choice of defending Western democracies against fascism. Though not yet comfortable with such a choice, Niebuhr would support Roosevelt in 1936 as a lesser evil.

Radical ideas were not new to American thought in the 1930s, but the magnitude of the depression gave sharp critiques of American social and economic institutions a far wider intellectual currency, encouraged debate over the meaning and applicability of socialist, communist, and Marxist ideas, and allowed the belief for a time that fundamental political transformations might be at hand. Intellectuals who gave sustained attention to social thought, including Dewey, Hook, Wilson, and Niebuhr, tried to answer foundational questions about the goals and the process of radical change. Such efforts at various levels of sophistication provided a way in which a particular group of Americans could respond to the evidences of the depression, to shifting economic relationships, and to wider cultural tensions. If in one sense the process turned their attention toward American society and encouraged them to fulfill their role as critical intellectuals, in another sense an engagement with radical ideas allowed them to turn away from immediate social needs and prospects to invest themselves in a political thought more abstract and speculative. Perhaps it would go too far to suggest that radicalism could sometimes stand in relation to depression experience as an intellectuals' equivalent to filmgoing or pigeon-raising, but radical social thinkers at times appeared reluctant to confront their own situation or to pay responsive heed to their own injunctions and results.

Although many called for a radical ideology responsive to the American context, little systematic thought of lasting significance seemed directed toward producing the requisite ideas. Perhaps Dewey, who had limited use for Marx, tried as hard as anyone in the 1930s to construct a radicalism connected to an American framework. Many on the left found him insufficiently radical. Hook and Wilson invested themselves heavily in the study of Marxism and maintained their differing versions of a positive radical faith. But neither spent much time trying to construct, from Marxist or other resources, a sustained radical analysis of the United States. Efforts by others to examine long-term patterns of institutional development and social experience were sometimes insightful, yet such commentaries were frequently led astray (especially in the early 1930s) by an eagerness to prophesy imminent revolutionary transformation. The common left-wing presumption that a depression-battered citizenry would quite naturally turn toward radicalism became an emblem of just how poorly radical social theory understood the American populace. Strong leftist opposition to, and even contempt for, the New Deal—at least through 1935— did little to explain why the New Deal could assemble the coalition of workers, farmers, ethnic minorities, middle-class people, and professionals that radical thinkers had been able only to imagine.

More striking, upon reflection, than the effort to construct an American radical ideology in the 1930s was the rediscovery or reassertion among certain intellectuals on the left of values and principles many had earlier taken for granted. The issues of Communist tactics that had troubled Dewey at the beginning of the decade, and to some extent Hook, Wilson, and Niebuhr, were no small matter. Communist behavior, domestic and international, produced a pattern of incidents in the thirties that drove left intellectuals away from the Party and, in varying degrees, from the positive exploration of radical ideas. Many onetime Party allies moved into critique and resistance after confronting the need to defend such liberal notions as free speech, open debate, and the right to a fair trial, and after measuring their own reactions when abusive tactics and manipulative methods were used in the name of a radical cause. Perhaps no "lesson" learned in the 1930s was more commonly cited by radical (or ex-radical) intellectuals than the principle that means must be related to ends: elevated goals could never be achieved through a tainted struggle that would alter and corrupt the very idea of what might be accomplished.

Reservations about Communist belief and practice merged with wider concerns over the nature of centralized dogmatic movements as fascism gathered force during the 1930s. Through 1939, a good many liberals and leftists looked to the Soviet Union and the Communist party as major bulwarks against fascism. Yet important clusters of intellectuals on the left drew a different conclusion, increasingly coming to link Hitler's fascism and Stalin's communism under the new label of "totalitarianism." Try as they might to resist the implications at first, the dangers they perceived on the left and right made their own society look a good deal better. Perhaps more consciously, though also later than many other Americans of the era, left intellectuals found themselves at the end of the thirties trying to construct some equation of old and new, trying to sort out which ambitions for a radical society they could still embrace and which values from their inheritance they were committed to preserving. For intellectuals, it was less the radical enthusiasms of the 1930s than the consciousness of their dangers that provided the more powerful legacy.

## *Looking Forward, Looking Backward*

In every period efforts are made to erect against the jarring realities of the present an imagination of better and more stable worlds tied to the past or future. Religious systems of thought have regularly posited a harmonious existence from which humans have departed or toward which they should aspire. Both conservative and radical ideologies have appealed to notions of justice and the right ordering of society rooted in a hallowed past or linked to a future not yet achieved. Such broader frameworks were clearly at work in the 1930s, but the desire to critique or evade the present was often manifest in ways far less sweeping or systematic. Visions of a past recovered or a future transformed might offer at times little more than escapism. Yet the manipulation of future and past might also provide interpretation and choice, helping people contain the tensions of the present in ways both abstract and mundane.

In the winter of 1932–33 a search for explanations and solutions merged with hokum and fantasy during the brief heyday of "Technocracy." The Technocrats argued that the progressive mechanization of work in modern industry had displaced human workers and caused unemployment (an argument in which they were not alone); they insisted, however, that this negative result could be turned to positive benefit through proper planning. Promising an expert analysis of every phase of society summed up in some 3,000 charts, the "consulting technologist" Howard Scott asserted the happy results without waiting for any completed study: efficiently ordered production could provide every American with an affluent existence with people working only four hours a day and retiring at 45. (The similarity to Edward Bellamy's vision in *Looking Backward* (1888), written more than four decades earlier, was unmistakable.) Current leaders and institutions had to somehow give way so that Technocrats could exercise complete authority and usher in the golden age. The pseudoscience and the simplistic explanations, the promise that only a few obstacles to proper planning blocked a gushing forth of progress and prosperity, won a very considerable attention—until it was disclosed that Scott's statistics and his claims of expertise were themselves manufactured. Technocracy suggested how rapidly efforts to analyze the present might gallop into fantasies about the future, and how eager some would be for the run.[48]

A different version of the implications and potential of mass production emerged through the work of an energetic group of industrial designers who were warming to their purpose as the thirties began. Coming from backgrounds in commercial art, stage production, advertising, and the crafts, the newly self-conscious industrial designers preached the wide application of a style they associated with the modern, the efficient, and the unified. At its center was the concept of streamlining, inspired especially by the airplane and the imagery of flight. Sharp corners or abrupt protrusions would give way to extended lines and fluid curves that, along with the frequent use of newer materials like aluminum and chrome, would create a feeling of aerodynamic smoothness and easy motion. Advocates acknowledged both commercial and psychological objectives. The streamlined style would convince consumers of the wonders of progress, prompt new buying that would combat the depression, and provide conscious control over the influence of mass-produced goods on everyday experience. Industrial designers also claimed aesthetic merit for a thoroughgoing application of streamlining, though some critics questioned whether the style made sense if the objects involved were never in motion. (The Museum of Modern Art in its 1934 exhibit on "Machine Art" emphasized a contrasting functionalist aesthetic that embraced industrial products not consciously designed.) At its extreme, the promotion of streamlining found even a nationalist angle in the claim that this particular version of modernity was establishing a distinctly American taste and style.[49]

Industrial design appeared by nature to be tied to the immediate and the tangible, yet conceptually it seemed unable to restrain its practical ideas from floating toward deeper and darker waters. The designers often accepted an image of the machine as a model of achievable perfection and beneficent harmony. That same harmony, they suggested, could become the social norm if progress took the form of applying the principles of the machine to society as a whole. Thus, the curved lines of streamlining, when embodied in architecture, might guide people's gaze and perceptions, draw attention to important doorways and passages, and help human traffic flow more smoothly. Such practical claims led onward for those rising to the lure of wider social implications. Because streamlining conveyed a sense of smooth operation and lack of friction, curved surfaces and fluid lines could suggest that social and institutional processes were functioning effortlessly and efficiently, under the guidance of reliable and sure-handed leaders. Visions of future harmony through technology and design played an important role at the New York World's Fair of 1939, both in the tightly planned urban environment of the "Democracity" exhibit and in a number of more loosely related corporate displays. Yet industrial design's aspiration toward coherent control and machine-like perfection would fade rather than flourish after the 1930s. Such ambitions would run distinctly against the grain during a period of intense anxieties over totalitarianism. And more subtly, certain of the appeals implicit in streamlining would lose force with the depression's end.

Jeffrey Meikle has argued that industrial design contained at its core two opposing but paired suggestions: the aerodynamic, bulletlike form that found its most compelling symbol in the streamlined railroad locomotives introduced with great fanfare in the 1930s suggested a rushing forward; the carefully designed interiors of cars on the same trains (and, indeed, the whole infatuation in streamlining with curved lines that implied circular completion) suggested a stable environment that was, contrarily, protected from the rush of change. Meikle has detected in these paired ideas important psychological implications:

Two sections of an oil mural painted in an octagonal room at Stamford High School by James Daugherty for the Connecticut Art Project strive to create a coherent impression from an energetic mixing of diverse symbols and elements. One section, concentrating on music, places African-Americans at the center surrounded by images suggesting jazz, folk, classical, and military music. Other figures represent different styles of dance, while the area containing Native Americans and a log cabin (along with the central figures) offers ties to the American past. In another section of the mural, the images suggest work and progress—an urban world of skyscrapers, motor vehicles, telephones, and traffic lights. Yet while airplanes and dirigibles float above, the partially streamlined modern train in the upper center stands beside one of the earliest nineteenth-century steam engines in an assertion of continuity and compatibility with the past. Especially with the remaining sections taken into account, the mural as a whole creates a striking assertion that the character and vitality of American culture are rooted in its heterogeneity. *Connecticut State Library*

> The streamlined style expressed not only a phallic technological thrust into a limitless future. Its dominant image, the rounded, womblike teardrop egg, expressed also a desire for a passive, static society, in which social and economic frictions engendered by technological acceleration would be eliminated. Streamlining was paradoxically a style of retreat and consolidation as well as one of penetration and forward progress.

Seen in this light, the paired modernistic symbols of the New York World's Fair, a three-sided pyramidal tower rising to a point 700 feet in the air and a large abstract sphere standing beside it, embodied "the contradictory associations of the more ordinary streamlined architecture around them—the 'Trylon' representing limitless flight into the future, the 'Perisphere' controlled stasis."[50] The celebration of streamlining may thus have reached its height in the 1930s because it suggested simultaneously two quite different ways of stepping out of the present and looking past depression realities. Without any consciousness of contradiction, Americans could imaginatively

embrace both a promise of rapid change and the attractions of a fixed stability (a combination that was also found in some radical versions of impending revolutionary transformation and the classless society to follow). If the depression boosted the appeal of such ideas, its end would have tended to undermine them.

A present filled with frustration and confusion could also be set against visions of a more cohesive, more romantic, or more purposeful past. The restored colonial capital of Williamsburg in Virginia opened to visitors in 1935 as a "living community" demonstrating eighteenth-century crafts and customs. With slavery largely invisible and dirt and disarray suppressed (these features were themselves later "restored"), Williamsburg attempted in the eyes of its sponsors to depict the "moral and spiritual values of life" deemed to be of "lasting importance to all men everywhere," including a firm belief in individual rights, self-government, responsible leadership, and opportunity. Such an emphasis suggested that there was both critique and refuge in a reconstructed and sanitized past that resolved modern anxieties about the fate of the individual and the restriction of opportunities.[51] Historical romances offered a different kind of contrast with the present. Bulky best-sellers, from Hervey Allen's *Anthony Adverse* (1933) and Kenneth Roberts's *Northwest Passage* (1937) to the most popular of all, Margaret Mitchell's *Gone with the Wind* (1936), offered an extended relocation into worlds of dramatic events, controlled sexuality, and colorful heroes and heroines—all generally tied to the epic of nation-building.

Historical topics and themes provided the most frequent subjects for the 1,000 or so murals created for federal buildings across the country under the auspices of the Treasury Department and for the approximately 2,500 produced through the relief efforts of the Federal Art Project. Many of the murals depict events in local history or show familiar scenes in different eras. One commentator on these works has suggested that the disorienting force of the depression naturally encouraged a "turning back to the past when men presumably did things right."[52] Taken as a group, the murals emphasize patriotism and progress: settlement accomplished; ideals of freedom attained; opportunities turned to achievement through work, cooperation, and faith. Noting the scant depiction of depression realities in the murals, it is easy to conclude that they represented a widely shared impulse toward finding in the past an escape from present concerns.

Yet this would be too simple. If the murals did not address the present directly, neither were they irrelevant to it. To the extent that they depicted and upheld treasured American myths, the murals may have spoken to depression anxieties about social breakdown and threatened values; they may have constituted, as Karal Ann Marling has argued, a "ritual act . . . invoking a community gestalt to insure psychological and physical survival."[53] More concretely, the mural artists made it their clear objective at times to suggest or demonstrate continuity. The historical record in America, and in particular locales, revealed a pattern of challenges being met and trials overcome, offering reassurances that present difficulties, too, would surely pass. Alfred Haworth Jones has described an intellectual reframing of American historical writing in the 1930s that sought neither to condemn nor to flee to the past but to examine "usable" national traditions with a "meticulous attention to authenticity." In the grand biographies that were a particularly notable product of 1930s scholarship, myth and message were as intertwined as they were in the murals. Looking to "other eras of crisis" for lessons to be learned, scholars constructed an American past filled with testing and turmoil. They stressed characteristics deemed central to American democracy, including a pioneer habit of tackling problems head-on. And they allowed people to respond, as Jones would have it, "to the highest incarnations of themselves." At the summit of the process stood Abraham Lincoln as a symbol of American values and national survival, lauded in a multivolume biography by Carl Sandburg, in a Pulitzer Prize–winning play by Robert Sherwood, and in two major films.[54]

Images of the nation's history and character, then, were both mythic and practical; their content provided a way of looking beyond the realities of the 1930s and a way of speaking to them. Assurances of continuity could be found in the emphasis on national and local traditions that was missing both from radical visions of upheaval and from technological dreams of a world remade. The past could bind the immediate to a wider context, draw attention to lasting values, and encourage community affirmation. Yet the relationship of past, present, and future for Americans of the 1930s was seldom simple. At any given moment, many impulses were possible, and an accommodation of variety and contradiction proved a stronger cultural need than unity of outlook and imagery. Appropriately enough from this perspective, the symbols of the New York World's Fair included not only Democracity and the futuristic Trylon and Perisphere, but also an iconographic statue of George Washington, whose inauguration 150 years earlier provided an official reason for the celebration.

Examples both public and private of the tendency to look in more than one direction can be traced once again through design. Industries based on public entertainment and leisure recovered more quickly from the depression in the mid to late 1930s than did traditional manufacturing sectors. New fixtures and construction embodying current notions of design were especially evident in the restaurants, lounges, and theaters built or redecorated in the second half of the decade. Such facilities threw off movie-palace pretensions to luxury, now associated with excess and failure, and abandoned the illicit speakeasy world that had made the nightlife of the 1920s seem too liberated, disreputable, and uncontrolled for many Americans. They embraced instead the presumably broad appeal contained in the curved lines, the shining aluminum and chrome, and the openness and flow of streamlining. Nightclubs in the 1930s, Lewis Erenberg has argued, were "legitimated and integrated into the

American fabric" in part because the streamlined style "sought to balance the emphasis on luxurious consumption with attention to values of production." With persuasive self-contradiction, the materials and design of the leisure world provided a testament to work, technology, and progress; the avid pursuit of pleasure was situated within an environment of smooth control.[55] Nightclubs had widened their cultural appeal by allowing Americans to read mixed messages into the imagery of entertainment.

The glamorous nightlife of New York and Los Angeles might have been little more than a fantasy in most cities and towns, but the interplay of values, styles, and cultural meanings could be as alive in local settings as in metropolitan clubs. As contemporary observers noted, the decor appearing in restaurants led many ordinary Americans to identify the designs and materials of streamlining especially with eating and drinking. The act of eating out and the environment in which it was done merged as an emblem of the modern. Conceptions of modernity themselves were thus enmeshed in the accommodation of contrasting values inherent in the streamlined style, and diners were free to construct their own understandings of what participation in the modern might mean.

The interplay did not stop there. If the more visible emphasis in the public sphere fell on being (safely) up-to-date, the balancing process at home had different results. Products reshaped by streamlined design found their way primarily into kitchens and bathrooms, and they were usually purchased individually rather than as part of a complete remodeling. A new appliance thus suggested technology and change even as it was itself "domesticated" by the familiarity of all that surrounded it. And clearly there were significant limits on how far most people would go. Living rooms and bedrooms remained dominated by traditional styles, as did magazines of home decoration. Even the "Town of Tomorrow" at the New York World's Fair placed the newest consumer appliances in houses shaped primarily by traditional architectural design.[56] Especially in the private sphere, older commitments of style and meaning were as potent as the "modern," and older cultural balances vied with the new. American values and American lives were parts of a complex cultural mosaic under continuing construction.

## Technology and Science Applied

The materials emphasized in streamlined products, the ideas associated with their design, and the circumstances of their use underline the ways in which technologies shape and are shaped by particular cultural settings. The plastics that were appearing ever more widely during the 1930s, from steering wheels and tableware to dice, reflected organized research efforts within a commercial framework. Modern technology and its products needed to be "sold," as they were in part through design. The Du Pont Company developed the most important of the new multiple-use plastics—Nylon, number 66 of nearly 100 "superpolymers" produced by a special research team. Nylon soon replaced silk in women's stockings; catgut in tennis rackets, musical instruments, and surgery; steel in machine bearings; and varying materials in wire insulation, umbrellas, and parachutes. The metals of streamlined design claimed special association with the airplanes from which the style took essential inspiration. Cloth-covered planes withered away in the 1930s before the strength, size, speed, and power of the new all-metal craft, first the Ford Trimotor and then the Douglas DC-3 and the Boeing 247. A range of technological developments, in the air and on the ground, sustained the extension of commercial aviation; but no technology was more important than the sense of modern adventure and the visions of social improvement that created a "winged gospel" around the idea of flight.[57]

It culture and technology could work jointly to shape an industry, however, their combination was not always enough. In the case of the famous streamlined locomotives of the 1930s, the metallic imagery seized imaginations more than pocketbooks. These conscious representations of speed and power carried, ultimately, an ironic connotation: bigger, faster, heavier equipment helped make the railroads less flexible economically than the truck and bus systems that were moving aggressively to take over their business. Material, technology, design, and context came together with uneven results.

Scientific research and technology fed the creation of techniques, the spread of applications, and the elaboration of entire cultural spheres during the 1930s. In agriculture the interwar period saw a number of innovations: the hybridization of food crops, including the development of corn hybrids that produced high yields and stood up to machine harvesting; the use of genetic manipulation to develop new breeds of cattle and swine, with the new technology of artificial insemination ensuring their commercial viability; and the spreading use of agricultural chemicals, both to enhance growth and to kill. Radio and film, with the help of an expanding technological base, shouldered their way into the center of American culture. Medicine delivered the first sulfanilamide drug, Prontylin, in time to save Franklin D. Roosevelt, Jr., from a streptococcus infection in 1936, promising a new age of miracle drugs. These technologies depended in part on the work of the past; other quiet developments in the 1930s would have a similar resonance for the future. Howard Aiken, supported by Harvard and IBM, and John V. Atanasoff at Iowa State College had both begun work on early versions of the computer by the end of the decade, and Bell Laboratories had launched a research group that would create transistors. Each form of technology accumulated from origination to full implementation its own history of interacting contexts. Some, like radio and film, prompted almost immediate debate over the nature of their cultural impact. Others stirred over time concerns about social reconfiguration, environmental impact, and equitability of access. Significant technological change posed new questions of cultural balance.

After 1920, according to some scholars, a newer conception of "system" took hold that emphasized "interdependence of relationship" and assumed parts "closely integrated as a whole."[58] Such ideas "blurred distinctions between technology and other endeavors and made it conceivable to seek technological solutions to social questions."[59] "Human engineers," in this view, would blend the possibilities made available through electricity (supplemented by the automobile and telephone) with careful planning, drawing inspiration from wistful visions of country towns, from models of efficiency and experiment, or from ideas like Lewis Mumford's notions of a "biotechnic," organic regionalism. In the 1930s private proposals gave way to public projects, most notably, perhaps, the Tennessee Valley Authority (TVA). Under the TVA, the generation of electricity became for a time an integrated part of a broad planning scheme in which social and technological issues were understood as interdependent.[60] Yet the more common pattern, toward which the TVA itself had migrated by the end of the decade, was to expect that electricity would indeed benefit society without considering very closely just what or how positive results might occur. The federal government undertook huge hydroelectric projects during the 1930s involving the construction of massive dams, and with the help of the Rural Electrification Administration after 1935, it sponsored a rapid spread of electrification to farms. Battles over public versus private control of power accompanied every step. The results suggested "interdependence" but not the comprehensive control of "system": the dams were more effective in the production of electricity than the generation of social solutions.

Contributions from science and technology were generally set before the public in the wrapping paper of progress. Yet Americans were not of one mind in the 1930s about the implications and results of science or about the authority of scientists. The depression fostered new doubts and reinforced older ones. Reflecting on the vogue of technocracy, William E. Wickenden of the Case School of Applied Science suggested that the average citizen was not "quite so cock-sure as he used to be that all this science is a good thing. This business of getting more bread with less sweat is all right in a way, but when it begins to destroy jobs, to produce more than folks can buy and make your wife's relatives dependent on you for a living, it is getting a little too thick."[61] If the average person struggled to balance the benefits and the costs of technological change, a number of religious leaders weighted their assessments quite clearly on the side of doubt. John Haynes Holmes, a liberal Protestant clergyman, declared that "science is wonderful, but also terrible . . . for the reason that it has no values," and a mixed group of religious and secular intellectuals revived a 1927 proposal to halt scientific research for a time, with G. K. Chesterton telling an American audience that there was nothing wrong with electricity "except that modern man is not a god who holds the thunderbolts but a savage who is struck by lightning."[62] Intellectuals on the political left had their own sensitivities about the proper limits of science, and the *New Republic* questioned vigorously whether scientists could claim "authority on all social questions."[63]

Yet there was also an undeniable fascination with science, and it ran deeper than a quest for immediate technological and social applications. A group of science writers followed science meetings, one observer claimed, like "sports writers follow baseball and football teams," with one group, called Science Service, having links to 100 newspapers. In the depression year 1934, scalpers could charge $50 a seat to hear Einstein lecture in Pittsburgh.[64] Einstein carried, of course, not only his individual prestige but also the appeal of the most intriguing scientific frontier of the period, modern physics. The United States would become the central locus of that frontier during the 1930s. Between 1920 and 1932 the annual number of Americans taking Ph.D.s in physics more than tripled, and thanks to expanding fellowship support, at least 50 of the total of 1,000 or so who earned doctorates in these years continued their study in Europe, where they could mingle across national lines with Niels Bohr, Enrico Fermi, Edward Teller, John Von Neumann, Hans Bethe, Leo Szilard, and others. After 1932 there could be little doubt that American physicists had arrived. Five Nobel Prizes were eventually awarded for work done during that year, three of them to Americans: Harold Urey received his for proving the existence of the hydrogen isotope deuterium, which had great significance for developing theories of nuclear structure; Ernest Lawrence provided a fundamental experimental tool in the particle accelerator, or cyclotron; and Carl Anderson demonstrated the existence of a new particle, the positron, again with fundamental theoretical importance. Physics was now focusing on the structure of the nucleus as its most urgent question.

By 1936 *Newsweek* could proclaim, "The United States leads the world in physics."[65] If disagreement remained, it was rapidly dissipated as Hitler's attacks on Jews and deteriorating conditions in Europe drove leading scientists toward the United States. By 1941 American universities were employing more than 100 émigré physicists, including eight who had won or would win Nobel Prizes.[66] Many of the recently arrived physicists were concerned that atomic scientists remaining in Germany would push toward the development of a bomb; in 1939 Eugene and Leo Szilard had convinced Albert Einstein to send a letter to President Roosevelt warning of the danger and urging an American project toward the same ends. By 1942 the Manhattan Engineer District, or Manhattan Project, would be under way. In its more famous aspects, the project brought together a remarkable collection of scientists, including many of those with whom American physicists had studied in Europe more than a decade before, to devise at last an atomic bomb in the desert of Los Alamos, New Mexico. Yet the project also fit within the ongoing development of "large production systems": its relationships among "scientists, engineers, and managers . . . were in many ways analogous to the relationships . . . at innovative production companies," and it depended on extended facilities at Oak Ridge, Tennessee, and Hanford, Washington, the first drawing power from the TVA and the second from Grand Coulee Dam and the Bonneville hydroelectric projects.[67]

This Margaret Bourke-White photograph of Fort Peck Dam under construction in Montana was chosen as the cover for the first issue of *Life* magazine in 1936. The monumentality of the project is dramatically apparent, suggesting the contemporary emphasis on large-scale undertakings in engineering and technology (as well as in the social and economic spheres). Hydroelectric projects of regional scope were among the most ambitious of federal ventures and served to substantiate the idea that the New Deal was responding to the depression with energy and creativity. The pillars of the dam stood as monuments to the strength of the nation and the spirit of its people, as the editors of *Life* made clear in their accompanying story. Bourke-White's penchant for striking angles is evident in the photograph itself, and its evocative qualities help explain her early success as an industrial photographer. *Margaret Bourke-White*, Life Magazine, © *Time Warner*

Few examples could match the production of the atomic bomb in demonstrating the importance of context for the directions in which scientific knowledge would be applied. The bomb was a triumph of science, a marvel of technology, a major organizational accomplishment, that could be delivered by political and military judgment in a modern metal airplane to destroy two Japanese cities and astound the world. The excitement and accomplishment of American physics in the 1930s led in part to the atomic bomb; the bomb led back into questions about the relationship between science and values, about the desirability of technological "progress," and about the capacities of human judgment. Perhaps for those who knew little of the science or technology involved, it led back, or forward, to a challenge with which the culture of the thirties was continually engaged: the challenge, and the necessity from day to day, of finding a balance between confidence and caution, upheaval and root-edness, hope and fear.

Commentators at different times have labeled the 1930s both a radical and a conservative decade. Either claim may be defended; neither alone is adequate. Women were sometimes drawn into unfamiliar roles in families, in labor demonstrations, and in politics and government that challenged common assumptions about their "place," yet the framework of those assumptions showed little evidence of decay. Leading intellectuals identified themselves with calls for radical change, yet most at the same time wanted to preserve political, intellectual, and moral values derived from established traditions. People looked to the future and to the past. The appeal of rushing ahead was balanced against the appeal of stasis. The unmistakable allure of the new drew strength from an ability to incorporate the familiar.

Even in the absence of economic collapse and international crisis, Americans of the 1930s would have confronted evolving problems of cultural definition. They would have wrestled with the relationship between cultural disparateness and national identity, with the implications of modernity and the "modern temper," and with the efflorescence of what would soon be called mass culture. The Great Depression and the developing threat in interna-tional affairs changed the context within which most problems could be con-sidered and brought politics to the fore, adding a special twist to cultural and intellectual concerns. Gradual transformation and immediate experience, established practice and changing needs, older values and new interpretations, combined to shape the ways Americans individually and collectively sought to structure their institutions, their understandings, and their identities.

*two*

---

# New Deals and Old

During the 1930s it was hard to escape the reach of politics. Much of the intellectual discussion of the period was drawn in one way or another toward the problems presented by the depression, toward the adequacy of recovery and reform measures, and toward the competition of values and ideologies at home and abroad. Programs born in the nation's capital touched the lives of individuals and communities throughout the country, making a previously rare influence seem common. Federal action began to redefine the place of at least some economic and social groups, and federal dollars became a major force in the arts. All of this activity meant change but seldom upheaval. What did and did not happen in the politics of the thirties provides an important set of readings on the development of American culture.

A variety of movements operated outside the two dominant political parties or sprang up on their fringes during the depression. There can be little doubt, however, that what stood at the center of political life in the 1930s, and what left the greatest mark on American society, was the administration of Franklin Roosevelt. The very idea of what "government" implied, the images conjured up by the term, and the effects on people's lives that its use assumed, were significantly altered by the New Deal. Before Roosevelt came to office, as William Leuchtenburg has reminded us, local communities in normal times had only limited contact with national government:

> If you had walked into an American town in 1932, you would have had
> a hard time detecting any sign of a federal presence, save perhaps for the
> post office and even many of today's post offices date from the 1930s.
> Washington rarely affected people's lives directly. There was no national old-age pension system, no federal unemployment compensation, no

aid to dependent children, no federal housing, no regulation of the stock market, no withholding tax, no federal school lunch, no farm subsidy, no national minimum wage law, no welfare state.[1]

By the end of the 1930s, most of these programs would be in place and communities would have been touched by many relief measures that would not outlive the depression.

An altered relationship between government and the economy reshaped experience on Main Street. Before the 1930s, business and financial leaders were largely free to make important economic decisions as they saw fit. Despite the clamor surrounding antitrust campaigns and early twentieth-century regulatory legislation, and despite the brief period of extensive federal controls during World War I, the national government had taken explicit economic actions within quite limited contexts, mostly in conjunction with efforts to protect or aid private business interests. Out of the New Deal grew a revised balance of public and private that would soon earn the label "a mixed economy." Now the stock market would be regulated by federal laws and by the Securities and Exchange Commission, which sought to establish some minimal level of financial and ethical probity. Fiscal and monetary policy would come to the fore as more conscious tools of economic adjustment. Labor-management relations would develop within a legal framework that established minimum wages and maximum hours for many workers and defined guidelines for union organization and collective bargaining under the oversight of the National Labor Relations Board. And agriculture would be supported through an extensive array of federal subsidies and loans. As some commentators have put the case, the United States had developed a national economy during the first third of the twentieth century; the New Deal created a political framework to match the scale of this economy and to provide at least some mechanisms of management and support.

Whether from the perspective of a corporate boardroom or a bungalow kitchen, the winds of change in the 1930s seemed to honor Franklin Roosevelt as their Aeolus. Roosevelt, through the force of his personality and actions, created new expectations for the presidency and became himself something of a cultural phenomenon. With Roosevelt's arrival, the White House began to tremble with ideas, legislative proposals, and executive pronouncements that issued not as occasional breezes but in gusts and gales. This storm of activity gained its limited measure of coherence from the simple fact that it was identified with the president, and during the thirties even legislation that Roosevelt supported only weakly or late became inextricably associated with his name. Roosevelt was *the* symbol of the enlarged scope of the federal government, the new colossus of the Democratic party, whose appeal helped bring about one of the major political realignments in American history as the Republican party was unseated from the position of general dominance it had held since the 1850s.

In this political cartoon by Edwin Marcus, which appeared in the *New York Times* of 18 November 1934, Franklin Roosevelt is a master of two strategies and two outlooks. The violin as an instrument of classical music representing aesthetic culture and an established order provides a symbol for conservatism. The saxophone, powerfully associated in the 1920s and 1930s with jazz, popular music, and youthful liberation, suggests the venturousness of bold policies. The cartoon indicates clearly that the two-sidedness of Roosevelt's political appeal was recognized early in his presidency. And Uncle Sam was not alone in responding favorably to the balancing of tradition-oriented continuity and reform-minded activism. *By permission of Donald E. Marcus*

35

The president also put himself in the forefront of the news and of the nation's political consciousness. Roosevelt welcomed reporters to the White House twice a week, calling them by name and bantering with them as he turned their questions to his own advantage. Similarly, he saw the potential in the still-new medium of radio and used it masterfully to win support for his leadership and his program. People heard a warmth in his voice and felt a new kind of personal contact with this president. (Before radio, only a limited number of people could ever have heard a president's voice). During Roosevelt's first year in office, the daily mail brought ten times as many letters to the White House—some 6,000 to 8,000 per day—as had arrived in peak periods during the Hoover administration, and an era of mass political letter-writing was born. Such remarkable public appeal carried lasting cultural force. John Garraty has pointed out that though there was significant social reform and more substantial economic recovery in Great Britain than in the United States during the 1930s, the period entered that nation's cultural memory as "a time of inactivity and decline—the Great Slump." No political figure was able to move the British people or to rouse enthusiasm for a campaign against the depression as Roosevelt did in this country.[2] In making himself the dominant American political figure of the thirties, Roosevelt also shaped the way the period would be experienced and understood—as a time of action and energy, not of decline and drift. Americans of the 1990s, worrying over the decaying infrastructure of a troubled American economy, have reinforced that positive perception in looking frequently to the federal projects of the 1930s as a model for the concerted action they believe necessary.

The instincts and choices that combined to form Roosevelt's cultural and political style were plainly apparent in his response to the new administration's first major test, the banking crisis of 1933. Unlike the banking system in most industrialized countries, American banking depended not on a few centralized institutions with many branches but on thousands of independent banks whose ability to establish branch offices was severely restricted. Generally small, subject only to varying state regulations, and often without adequate reserves or security for deposits, most banks were ill prepared to face the economic pressures brought on by the depression. When funds loaned to finance stock speculation disappeared with the drop in values, when farmers and small businessmen could not make payments on their mortgages and loans, the assets of weaker banks fell dangerously. And as some institutions collapsed, worried depositors demanding their money launched "runs" on other banks that quickly exhausted the currency available. The problem became acute late in 1932 and reached a panic stage by February 1933 when the governors of Michigan, Maryland, and other states felt compelled to order a temporary closure of all banks. On Roosevelt's inauguration day, 4 March 1933, with banks in 38 states already shut down, the governors of New York and Illinois added their states to the list, and the New York Stock Exchange closed its doors. This was crisis indeed.

Roosevelt did not hesitate to act. On the evening of his first day as president, he instructed the secretary of the treasury to have a new banking bill drafted within five days. The next afternoon he called for a special session of Congress to convene on 9 March, stopped all movements in gold (which had been leaving America for Europe), and declared a bank "holiday" throughout the nation. The financial emergency was so apparent that when Congress met, it was more than ready to follow Roosevelt's lead. In the early afternoon of the ninth, a banking bill was read to the House from the one copy available; within an hour it had been approved on a voice vote without dissent. With minor opposition, the Senate endorsed the bill in the early evening, and the president quickly signed it into law. The Emergency Banking Act of 1933 expanded presidential authority over transactions in gold, established procedures for the reorganization of banks, provided for new supplies of currency through the Federal Reserve System, and organized the reopening of stronger banks. On 12 March Roosevelt delivered the first of his "fireside chats," explaining what had been done and offering reassurance that citizens could now depend on their banks once more. When stronger institutions opened again on Monday, 13 March, more money was deposited than withdrawn. The banking emergency had been brought under control.

Failing banks and frozen assets conveyed more than an economic threat for those who regarded savings accounts as emblems of their virtue, status, and security. Communities and neighborhoods across the country felt the blow, and they knew that deliverance from further disaster had come at the hands of the federal government. The Emergency Banking Act had taken immediate steps; within the first "Hundred Days" of the New Deal, other reform measures followed. Among these was the establishment of the Federal Deposit Insurance Corporation (FDIC), putting the authority of the federal government behind the security of deposits in member banks up to a specified limit. Between 1929 and 1933 the number of banks in the United States had fallen by more than 10,000, with the number of bank failures rising from 659 in 1929 to 4,004 in 1933.[3] With the reforms of the New Deal, the number of failures dropped to 61 in 1934, and the number of banks remained stable for the next four decades. People almost certainly did not think about the FDIC or other banking measures on a daily basis; other federal programs of the thirties claimed more continuing attention. Yet saving local banks and offering guarantees for millions of modest individual accounts delivered an important double message. These steps promised continuity by building buttresses for existing local structures and values; at the same time, they pledged corrective change, providing an early signal of an expanded federal presence and a new governmental interest in protecting individual citizens (especially, perhaps, the kinds of citizens who had savings accounts).

Some had expected more radical action. A few had thought that the president might call for the nationalization of banking and were disappointed when

In John Steinbeck's *The Grapes of Wrath*, small farmers driven off the land by drought, poverty, and tractors migrate westward to California. The Joad family, which stands at the center of the tale, endures a string of hardships, finding their best haven for a time in a migrant camp run by the federal government. In this scene from the movie version of the story, local authorities closely tied to powerful state interests seek to intimidate the migrants but are restrained by the intervention of the camp's manager, a figure resembling Franklin Roosevelt who asserts federal authority on the side of the common people. Regardless of the observer's perspective, government presented more than one face in the 1930s. *Museum of Modern Art/Film Stills Archive*

he did not. Surely if Roosevelt had been inclined to seek a fundamental economic restructuring, the circumstances in March 1933, including the receptivity of Congress, offered a unique opportunity to do so. But Roosevelt sought no revolution. In a speech to the Commonwealth Club of San Francisco during the 1932 campaign, Roosevelt had described economic control by government as a "last resort, to be tried only when private initiative, . . . with such assistance and balance as government can give, has finally failed."[4] There had as yet been no such failure, as he saw it, because there had as yet been no proper attempt to remedy the current difficulties. Roosevelt had no desire to destroy the private economy; rather, he declared his confidence that much of its structure could be preserved with the help of government. The notions of "assistance and balance" could have quite different meanings for different people, but they clearly implied that new economic institutions or controls would rise beside older forms, not as a replacement for them.

The banking crisis also helped demonstrate the difference that an individual leader could make. Roosevelt had already shown that he understood the techniques of gaining public attention to deliver the cultural and political messages he wanted heard. When nominated by the Democratic party, Roosevelt had flown dramatically through wind and storm to deliver the first convention acceptance speech in American history, rejecting the expectation that a candidate should feign ignorance of his nomination until officially informed weeks later. Lest anyone miss the point, Roosevelt declared his own action "symbolic" of the intent to break, not all traditions, but "absurd traditions" and "foolish traditions" in attacking the nation's problems.[5] In his inaugural address the president declared that "the only thing we have to fear is fear itself," a claim that was neither new nor entirely true. Reflecting a widespread appreciation that the depression was not just an economic but a psychological condition, Roosevelt's assertion announced, more than anything else, that *he* was not afraid, that *he* was ready to act, and that *he* expected popular support. Biblical imagery and patriotic references rooted the address in familiar cultural traditions, but firm language proclaimed that the nation was about to take a new course. Roosevelt began to break the gloom of depression by providing an opportunity for hope, and the stream of letters to the White House began.[6]

The fireside chat on banking thus came within a context of symbolism and promise that Roosevelt had already established, yet it added elements of its own. In taking to the radio, Roosevelt was not speaking to the public through some immediate audience at a convention or inauguration but addressing people directly in their homes. His tone was not formal, anxious, or awkward, but comfortable and familiar, conveying a confidence rooted in his own secure sense of identity. He explained in simple language how banks worked, what had created the crisis, and what steps the government had taken to resolve it. Now, with the machinery of restoration in place, "it is up to you to support and make it work." Only those Americans "who have not recovered from their fear" would make withdrawals. People and government together would triumph. Roosevelt was suggesting that Americans could do much to overcome the depression simply by believing that they could; he was making his personality an instrument for direct political appeal to an entire population; and he was attempting to construct a close sense of contact between the people and their *national* government. Moreover, he was once again both emphasizing a change in the direction of the country and assuring Americans that "there is nothing complex, or radical, in the process."[7]

The New Deal would measure up as one of the most important periods of social reform and economic adjustment in American history. Frequent assertions that no fundamental upheaval was taking place served in part as a form of public reassurance, providing a degree of political protection. Yet these same assertions reflected accurately the assumption of most New Dealers that they would regulate some institutions, make others work more effectively, and construct programs of their own within the general framework of the existing political and economic system. The new would rise beside the old. Business executives would continue to make important economic decisions, but they would not hold such power alone. Wall Street would manipulate capital, but financial authority would now rest at least as heavily in Washington. Change would serve the end of long-term stability. From the distance of several decades, a fundamental concern with continuity is easy to discern. Yet at the time, the New Deal seemed to some a betrayal of the most basic American principles, a radical threat to the nation's identity and character. The values and ideas at stake seemed worthy of the most passionate response.

## Responsibilities Individual and Social

The most powerful opposition to the New Deal during the 1930s came from the right of the political spectrum, from those who thought that government was doing too much. In 1933 this opposition was restrained. Although Roosevelt had faced resistance in his pursuit of the Democratic nomination, and although a sizable share of the voters in 1932 had supported Hoover (as is true for the losers of even lopsided elections), the situation bordered closely enough on the desperate by early 1933 that few sought to stand in the way of vigorous presidential action. The New Deal rapidly changed the nation's mood and put many Americans back on the road to political confidence. Within months after the legislative blitz of the Hundred Days, various groups began to complain about the consequences of specific programs, to demand more, or to challenge the direction of the New Deal in general.

By 1935 the New Deal was being pushed toward bolder legislation by rising labor activism in the industrial unions that formed the Committee for (changed in 1938 to *Congress of*) Industrial Organizations. The CIO would continue to provide both a support and a leftward prod for Roosevelt. Other popular movements were constructing more ambiguous political identities. Francis Townsend's pension-plan movement made older Americans a political force and helped spur social security legislation in 1935, but the movement rapidly came apart over internal corruption and sullied alliances. Father Charles Coughlin, the "Radio Priest," built a mass audience supporting the early New Deal before turning against Roosevelt. In 1936 he attempted disastrously to form a new party with Townsend and the fascist sympathizer Gerald L. K. Smith, who attacked African-Americans, Jews, atheists, and "communists in the Roosevelt administration" while referring to the president himself as a "cripple."[8] After 1938 Coughlin, too, descended entirely into bigotry. Louisiana Governor, then Senator, Huey Long became an audacious political force challenging Roosevelt with his "Share Our Wealth" program and a style that made some fear dictatorship. Long was stopped by an assassin's bullet in September 1935, leaving some of his followers to trail off behind Smith. Alan Brinkley has argued that the Long and Coughlin movements, whatever the quirks of their leaders, represented neither antidemocratic uprisings nor a progressive tide but rather a powerful "urge to defend the autonomy of the individual and the independence of the community against encroachments from the modern industrial state."[9] A declining localist tradition thus blended hope and resentment in its challenges to the New Deal. Community values both included and excluded, and the same localism that spurred opposition to centralized and impersonal power could embrace anti-Semitism or racial caste.

Different intellectual foundations supported a more enduring resistance to the New Deal that was quite consistently identified with the political right. The prospect and reality of expanding governmental activity appeared for conservatives of both major parties a threat to their entire understanding of the world. That understanding often began with an assumption at some level that the economic universe functioned according to natural laws that were beyond human control. These laws were regarded as absolute truths, as parts of a right ordering of social activity that carried strong moral implications. As Adam Smith had argued in 1776, economic responsibility should rest with the individual, who in pursuing his or her own self-interest within a free competitive framework, helped create the greatest advantage for all under the guidance of an "invisible hand." The law of supply and demand, when allowed to operate freely, guaranteed long-term progress. Because the properly functioning system was driven by individual initiative, ambition was to take the form of hard work, which made the best use of time and resources, prevented dissipation, and resulted in greater productivity. All effort was thus shaped by a personal character able to resist the blandishments of the world and to uphold, in the ideal at least, high standards of integrity and conduct. From this perspective as well, a system of unrestricted capitalism was inherently just because people got what they deserved: the rich had presumably earned their favored place, while the poor were responsible for their own fate through deficiencies of ability and effort. On such premises, it was easy to confuse the existing social hierarchy with a moral one.

By the 1930s this individualistic outlook had come under considerable pressure as developments in the American economy undermined many of the assumptions about opportunity and fair competition on which it was based. Yet it had also demonstrated a stubborn resilience. Individualist values helped make the idea of private property rights almost sacred, and the relationship between individualism and property proved adaptable and subject to indefinite extension. Using a legal fiction defining the corporation as an individual, for example, the Supreme Court for decades had turned the 14th Amendment to the protection of business interests, in ironic contrast to precepts limiting governmental intervention.[10] Conceptions of rights based on local community practice and on long experience in the assertion of "states' rights" joined with and reinforced individualist tenets. The mingling strains had in common their strong distrust of an activist government that might restrict the powers of property, challenge the moral assumptions of individual responsibility, or disturb the social arrangements of town or region. And their advocates took the principles and privileges they defended to be the very essence of American constitutionalism and democracy.

Limits on the range of acceptable policy were posted at the beginning of the thirties. Hoover's secretary of the treasury, Andrew Mellon, and many leading economists argued not simply that the depression must be left to cure itself by natural correctives but that the process would have beneficial effects, providing just punishment for the sinfulness of waste, poor quality, and excessive wage scales while making room for the stronger, more hardworking, and more efficient. President Hoover himself did not equate virtue with inaction or deny all governmental responsibility; indeed, he did more than any previous president to respond to depression. Yet Hoover's actions constantly confronted the limits set by his principles. Because the character sustained by "American ideals and American institutions" had to be preserved, drought, hunger, and suffering could be addressed only in "the spirit of charity and mutual self-help through voluntary giving and the responsibility of local government," not through national action.[11] Businessmen could be urged to take voluntary steps to maintain employment and wages, but for government to act directly was to risk a "centralized despotism" that threatened "not only our American system but with it our progress and freedom."[12] Hoover did bring himself to accept by 1932 the creation of the Reconstruction Finance Corporation (RFC) to make stabilizing loans to certain banks, businesses, and lower levels of government, but to the lasting detriment of his reputation, he rejected any form of direct federal relief to the millions of unemployed and the destitute. Lines of principle embodied fixed truths, the bases of all values.

Franklin Roosevelt's attitudes were by this standard shocking. "We must lay hold of the fact," Roosevelt said at one point, "that economic laws are not made by nature. They are made by human beings." To this a conservative Boston newspaper responded in dismay, "Two more glaring misstatements of the truth could hardly have been packed into so little space."[13] For those who embraced the precepts of natural law and economic individualism as the only "truth," it was difficult to accept a leader who suggested that people and governments could act to shape their own truths. Indeed, to its own most passionate adherents, the integrated system of automatic adjustments, assured progress, just hierarchy, and limited government seemed remarkably vulnerable. Moving away from the individualistic view of the world even a few steps brought cries of calamitous danger and gross betrayal.

The expansion of the federal government under the New Deal became, by these lights, a radical abandonment of American political principles and a leap toward centralized authority and collectivism. The newspaper publisher William Randolph Hearst helped set the tone in late 1933 when he assailed the

National Industrial Recovery Act as "absolute state socialism" and "a menace to political rights and constitutional liberties."[14] A year later such themes became the rallying cry of a new organization dedicated to Roosevelt's political defeat, the American Liberty League. An organization founded mainly by a circle of conservative, often wealthy Democrats, including the former national party chairman John Raskob, two members of the Du Pont family, and two previous Democratic presidential candidates, John W. Davis and Al Smith, the Liberty League attracted more than 100,000 members and spent over $1 million assailing the New Deal between 1934 and 1936.

The president of the league, Jouett Shouse, in a radio address of mid-1935, defined the organization's purposes as defending the Constitution and protecting "personal and property rights" in the face of an ominous threat. The Roosevelt administration had broken with established tradition, Shouse complained, by preparing bills at the White House and sending them to Congress "with orders that they should be passed without change" and without adequate debate. Roosevelt had criticized recent Supreme Court decisions overturning early New Deal legislation, demonstrating, as Shouse would have it, that both the laws and the criticism were parts of a calculated assault on the proper limits of national and presidential authority. The "dangerous un-American and undemocratic authority of the appointed bureaucrats" who were for the moment in "absolute control" had led to administrative actions that "veered from the extremes of fascism to the limits of socialism." Indeed, Shouse claimed, the legislation of the early New Deal better represented the platform of the Socialist party than the Democratic. To the Liberty League, the changes taking place boded a revolutionary overthrow of individualism and democracy, of freedom and opportunity, that violated the very meaning of the United States as a nation.[15]

Writing some years later, Herbert Hoover demonstrated in his memoirs that the battle to control the meaning of the New Deal was still being waged. In addition to advancing once more the argument that the depression would have ended sooner if natural economic processes had been allowed to run their course, Hoover did his best to condemn the steps taken under Roosevelt not simply as unwise but as alien to American tradition. The guiding phrase for the New Deal, according to Hoover, was "Planned Economy." This phrase had no legitimate native roots, for it was an "emanation from the caldrons" of "all three European collectivist forms"—"Communism," "Socialism," and "Fascism." With a "typical collectivist torture of meaning," the expression "Planned Economy" served as a "disguise" for "governmental execution and dictation" and "centralization of power." Scholars of the period have sometimes criticized Roosevelt for not building a strong reform organization; Hoover insisted that the New Dealers had tried to construct "a traditional 'mass movement'" like those accompanying "Russian Communism, German National Socialism, and Italian Fascism."

True Americans, Hoover suggested, looked only to ideas that were certifiably "American," not to products of some European witches' brew; to individualism, not to collectivism; to a democracy of independent voices and limited government, not to a system of mass politics and centralization. Hoover had known from the start that "the character and purposes of the men coming into power were not those of traditional America." Fortunately, the "schemes" of New Deal politicians, the "attempt to revolutionize the American system of life," had been at least partly thwarted by the "traditional American love of freedom and devotion to constitutional processes." Hoover made it his purpose to affirm "the rightness of the American manner of life" that had been betrayed during the "disaster" of the New Deal.[16]

Those who spoke from a perspective like Hoover's nearly always assumed that what constituted *the* American way—the one acceptable framework of values and policies—was clear and indisputable. Without such a fixed conception of what "American" meant, a term like "un-American" made little sense. Those who became New Dealers, by contrast, tended to find such definitions cramped and narrow-minded; their own arguments generally assumed a more complex and more open conception of what had been and might be "American." It was not that the architects, supporters, or even friendly critics of the New Deal lacked commitments to particular views of the nation's purposes or to particular values; these they had aplenty. Rather it was that both the nature of these views and the number of competing ideas under the same political roof encouraged diversity. In their variety as well as in their specific content, the assumptions and the claims of the New Deal challenged the fixed truths of individualism and their hold on national tradition. The political battles over the meaning of the New Deal, both at the time and since, have contributed to a continuing struggle to define American identity.

Those who supported substantial reform in the early 1930s took it for granted that individualism as a comprehensive outlook was outmoded and in need, at the very least, of major revision. The historian Charles Beard put the case with characteristic intensity in 1931: "The cold truth is that the individualist creed of everybody for himself and the devil take the hindmost is principally responsible for the distress in which Western civilization finds itself. . . . Whatever merits the creed may have had in days of primitive agriculture and industry, it is not applicable in an age of technology, science, and rationalized economy."[17]

Beard's remark touched on several related notions. One held that though the pursuit of self-interest might have served under the economic and social conditions of a previous era, the tenets of such a system could no longer apply. Reflecting the contemporary influence of Frederick Jackson Turner's emphasis on the settlement of new land as central to the American past, many pointed out that the frontier had now disappeared and with it the wide-open opportunities and rapid economic growth that had supported individualist values. Some gave the new confrontation of limits a worldwide perspective, suggesting the winding down of a cycle of rapid changes promoted by industrialization. European imperialism and American "pioneering" had claimed most of the lands susceptible to their control; the natural resources that had been opened up were now being used up; the integration of the world through rev-

olutions in transportation and communication and the development of enormous business and financial organizations could not continue at the pace of
the last century; even rapid population expansion seemed to be slowing down.
By the early 1930s there were "ominous signs," as Frederick Lewis Allen put
it, "that the great age of inevitable expansion was over," requiring adjustments
in economic institutions as well as in the "mental habits" of Americans.[18]

The emergence of large corporations seemed to undermine the system of
individualism on other grounds as well. In a landmark study in 1932, Adolph
Berle, Jr., an early Roosevelt adviser, and Gardiner C. Means argued that
major American industries had generally come to be dominated by a few large
firms quite capable of interfering with any capacity of the market to regulate
the volume of production and the level of prices. They also pointed out that
a considerable gap had opened up between traditional notions of ownership
and the big-business pattern of control by corporate executives with the bulk
of the shareholders (the presumptive "owners") kept at a safe distance. As a
leading work in business history has emphasized, this "managerial revolution"
implied an economy shaped less by the "invisible hand" of natural law than by
the "visible hand" of corporate managers. Moreover, the large scale of modern businesses meant that employers seldom knew most of their employees,
that the idea of establishing individual contracts and recognizing the merits of
individual workers had become something of a myth, and that mobility from
factory floor or clerical desk into upper management was extremely rare.
Bureaucratic organization demanded predictability and obedience; below the
level of the very few corporate leaders, Berle and Means concluded, "individual initiative no longer exists." Both the model of the economy and the standards of merit on which the individualistic outlook relied seemed out of touch
with contemporary realities.[19]

These judgments were reinforced by the belief, as Beard expressed it, that
the creed of individualism was inappropriate to an age of "science" and a
"rationalized economy." What these terms meant was, of course, subject to
dispute. Herbert Hoover had an engineering background and encouraged
economic rationalization during his tenure as secretary of commerce in the
1920s, but he would never have accepted Beard's conclusions or his concept of
science. What "science" suggested to many sympathizers with New Deal
reform was a growth of knowledge that allowed humans to take intelligent
control of economic and social life. There was no longer any need to rely on
millions of individual decisions presumably disciplined by the invisible workings of suprahuman law. A rationalized industrial economy had already been
extensively shaped and structured by human agency; the point was to turn
that economy consciously to the benefit of the whole community. For many
reformers, individualism as a creed denied the capacities of science applied to
society and blocked the changes adequate to the needs of the present.

What then did New Dealers propose? The answer must be that they
offered not one unified program with a single justification but a series of

responses supported by different arguments. As Thomas McCraw has point-ed out, accurate statements about the New Deal may appear quite inconsis-tent with one another: the agricultural programs of the New Deal included the first attempts to help farmers in poverty, yet the largest farmers benefited most from the New Deal, with tenant farmers and sharecroppers gaining least; the New Deal did much to help banks and leading corporations, yet most bankers and business executives hated Roosevelt and worked against the New Deal.[20] The New Deal simply refused to obey any intellectual god, and before the smiling acceptance of Franklin Roosevelt contradictions fell power-less to dissuade. To those who saw themselves as advocates of a consistent pol-icy based on firm principle, the absence of system and center was itself a cause for alarm. In the 1930s, as Richard Hofstadter noted many years ago, it was not the reformers but the opponents of reform who dominated the "traffic in moral absolutes" as they decried the conglomerate mix of the New Deal.[21]

Perhaps in part because their opponents turned moralistic, and in part because reformers had learned something about the risks of idealism during previous decades, New Dealers tended to avoid righteous or sentimental appeals while emphasizing the practical, the specific, and the realistic. Roosevelt deliberately adopted a plain style and a common language in his pub-lic speeches. His supporters placed their emphasis on economic problems, not moral reformation; on institutional adjustments, not utopian ideals; on the details of work projects, not the trials and hopes of the workers. No pathos intervened when a New Dealer declaimed the tons of cement and sand in Grand Coulee Dam, for this was indeed concrete reality. This bias, and a sometimes ill-considered faith that good information would lead to good poli-cy, gave a considerable boost during the 1930s to the collection of social and economic statistics. Certainly New Dealers aspired to raise the quality of human life by improving the social and economic environment—and this itself was a form of idealism. But the ethos of the depression, the desire to appear tough-minded, the fascination with mechanism and detail, meant that social ideals would seldom be deployed in the rhetorical front lines of the New Deal.

Faith in the human ability to shape social conditions did find expression in the activism of the New Deal, in the emphatic rejection of the notion that peo-ple must suffer depression quietly. By contrast with Hoover, who had come to seem (whether fairly or not) incapable of action, Roosevelt identified himself with the vigorous pursuit of new policies from the start. During his presiden-tial campaign he had called for "bold persistent experimentation," and his astute sense of the need for bustling activity on the part of government was evi-dent in his remark: "It is common sense to take a method and try it: If it fails, admit it frankly and try another. But above all, try something."[22] As the New Deal unfolded, advocates of reform spoke of the practicality, not just the desir-ability, of eliminating slums; abolishing child labor and sweatshop conditions; helping people buy houses or hold on to their farms; and providing aid to needy children, the disabled, the aged, and the unemployed. The very fact of frenetic governmental action, as well as the particular measures taken, ran counter to basic individualistic assumptions and sharpened ideological lines in the 1930s.

So, too, did the idea of planning, as Hoover's attack on the New Deal made clear. In the early 1930s talk of social and economic planning was widespread. The concept was versatile enough to respond both to the conviction that the industrial system had grown too rapidly, with resultant imbalance and waste, and to the sense that an increasingly complex and technologically sophisticated economy required conscious integration and guidance to develop smoothly. Planning promised to provide the best allocation of limited resources and to ensure a balance between production and consumption. Because it would necessarily entail special knowledge, sophisticated thought, and careful calculation, the idea of planning appealed especially to intellectuals and professionals—groups that had been drawn into government by the New Deal as never before—who might be expected to play a major role in the process. Some concept of the public good as a controlling compass lay behind most notions of planning, and it was usually taken for granted that the general interest could be readily determined and that objectivity would flow naturally from knowledge and expertise.

For those furthest toward the left in the New Deal spectrum, an emphasis on gains for the society as a whole through a centralizized management of resources made planning a direct ideological challenge to individualism. In 1932 when vague talk of planning was winning much positive attention in a nation growing desperate for solutions, Rexford G. Tugwell—one of three Columbia professors who belonged to Roosevelt's early "Brain Trust" and later assistant secretary of agriculture—warned that true planning would require "fundamental changes of attitude, new disciplines, revised legal structures, [and] unaccustomed limitations on activity." Because it would introduce "order and regularity" into economic life, planned production represented "the deadliest and most subtle enemy of speculative profit-making which could be devised." When it was discovered that planning entailed "something not unlike an integrated group of enterprises run for its consumers rather than its owners," Tugwell predicted, many giving lip service to the idea would dive for cover. They wanted only gains not sacrifice; yet any economic planning, as Tugwell saw it, had to restrict the advantages of those most privileged for the sake of a broader distribution of benefits.[23] Tugwell and others who shared his attitudes toward planning did not seek government ownership of industry, but they did seek an economic reorganization that went well beyond what most Americans were ready for. Their ideas had a piecemeal influence on the New Deal, producing planning efforts in agriculture and in programs of limited scope such as the Tennessee Valley Authority, but they wanted far more sweeping changes in the thirties than they ever achieved.

A different conception of planning prevailed among other administrators and advisers in the New Deal camp. Raymond Moley, another member of the Brain Trust, wanted cooperation between government and business, with primary economic leadership left to business. Gerard Swope, the head of

General Electric and a progressive among businessmen, was enamored of trade associations and the idea of a national economic council that would produce a harvest of "studies" to bring greater economic predictability and security. The National Recovery Administration (NRA) directed by General Hugh Johnson offered a major opportunity for this kind of business-led planning. Under governmental auspices, each industry was supposed to construct a "code of fair competition" for itself in an atmosphere of cooperation that took into account the interests of labor and the public. The codes generally called for limiting production and raising prices, but what they often raised most effectively was the level of conflict between manufacturers and consumers, management and workers, large businesses and small, until the NRA was finally undone in 1935 by the Supreme Court, which objected to its broad delegation of legislative power. Nevertheless, the idea that government must cooperate with existing economic interests rather than attempt any basic restructuring remained of major importance to the New Deal.

Both Tugwell's notions of national planning and those that looked toward business accepted large-scale organization and giant corporations as permanent parts of a modern economy. In this they showed their sympathy with the side of progressive thought, associated in particular with Theodore Roosevelt's "New Nationalism" of 1912, that held that corporations had grown large through greater efficiency and that unfettered competition had become wasteful. A rival progressive tradition, linked especially with Louis Brandeis, who had exerted some influence on Woodrow Wilson, insisted that many large firms had gained their power not through economic superiority but by using unfair methods to destroy their rivals. Because concentrations of wealth and power were inherently dangerous, oligopoly and monopoly should be broken up to restore the possibility of fair competition, and Wall Street should be kept under necessary control. The Harvard Law School professor Felix Frankfurter, who later joined his friend Brandeis on the Supreme Court, sent a stream of his former students into the Roosevelt administration. The influence of this circle was felt particularly through the regulatory actions of the Securities and Exchange Commission, where the future Supreme Court justice William O. Douglas served, and in a vigorous antitrust campaign toward the end of the thirties that was cut off by World War II. Even so, the movement did little to slow industrial concentration.

Those who sought the breakup of overlarge corporations and strict securities regulation did not demand progress beyond individualism as the planners did; rather, they claimed to be its true defenders. Adam Smith had never dreamed of economic behemoths that could easily distort the relationships between independent units that were fundamental to his thought. The New Deal was working to restrain the corporate powers that were the real enemies of individualism, to restore the possibility of true economic competition and true opportunity, to encourage and sustain individual initiative. Such views, apparently so much at odds with the commitments of either the centralized or business planners, in fact existed side by side with them in the intellectual mélange of the New Deal. The different outlooks shared the conviction that the current economic and social arrangements required adjustment and the belief that government had to play an active role in bringing about change. Within any major program, each viewpoint could find expression in particular measures or through the control of specific agencies. The differences meant contradiction and conflict, a struggle over the definition of policies that went on throughout the decade. Yet lines were not always so sharply drawn nor issues so clear as it might seem.

During the 1930s reformers of various stripes looked upon the values of individualism with far more ambivalence than their sharper statements of position might suggest. Even within the context of trying to ensure a new level of support, protection, and security for Americans, they were more likely to debate how best to preserve individual initiative and responsibility than to discount these concerns altogether. In the same essay in which Charles Beard assailed the "individualist creed" and declared that to its loudest supporters it meant little more than "getting money," he also allowed that individualism would "always have its place in any reasoned scheme of thinking": "Individual initiative and energy are absolutely indispensable to the successful conduct of any enterprise, and there is ample ground for fearing the tyranny and ineptitude of governments."[24] Many of those administering the New Deal held an even stronger sense than Beard that their policies must preserve individual responsibility and the dominance of private relationships in the economy.

The operations of the various programs of work relief put on display the contest between values going on in the minds of many New Dealers. Faced with massive depression unemployment, federal relief administrators tried to lift the stigma that had customarily been attached to joblessness. Most of the unemployed as they saw it were hardworking people caught up in a widespread economic collapse, not the intemperate or shiftless, as all too many were willing to imply. "They don't drink any more than the rest of us, they don't lie any more, they're no lazier than the rest of us," insisted the relief czar Harry Hopkins.[25] Social workers—and the large majority of relief recipients, according to one poll—strongly preferred work relief over direct relief (money given without the expectation of work) because it presumably avoided the humiliation of accepting charity and allowed the worker to maintain a sense of dignity, ability, and self-worth. The means test requiring proof of absolute poverty before aid was granted was to be avoided, New Dealers argued (as it generally was in new federal programs before 1935); people needed to be given jobs that made use of their training and experience, not all with the same pay but at wages reflecting the work's value. People on relief would thus have predictable incomes that allowed independent choices about expenditures and a feeling of having earned their own way, escaping both the economic and psychological crippling that depression could bring.

Such ambitions for work relief, for all their generosity, contained an element of self-contradiction. They aspired to defend the traditional emphasis on individual responsibility as much as to escape its harsher implications. Relief administrators did not want the jobless to blame themselves for their unemployment or to feel inferior to those in the private workforce, but they accepted as a matter of principle that government projects should not compete with private businesses and that their ultimate goal was to see those on relief find jobs in the private economy once more. Thus, with work manufacturing any products that were being privately produced ruled out, many on work relief—61 percent in a Pennsylvania survey—could not in fact be given jobs that ran parallel to their usual vocations. And although hourly wages on some relief projects compared favorably with those in private industry, the number of hours worked and total income were strictly limited to ensure a clear incentive to seek private employment. Workers on relief were supposed to feel valuable and independent in their roles, yet they were also supposed to remain eager to change their status as soon as possible.[26]

The concern over maintaining individual initiative, responsibility, and dignity that informed New Deal thinking about work relief, and the commitment to upholding the primacy of private employment, illustrated the degree to which New Dealers accepted many of the values of individualism and the essential framework of American capitalism. But they erected beside these assumptions other convictions as well: that suffering was not to be denied or ignored; that human action could be effective in meeting human needs; that government at a national level had to assume a major responsibility for the welfare of its citizens; and that in a modern society individuals had only partial control over their fate. The lines between public and private would be blurred. Individualism as a system, under challenge for many decades, would concede strategic ground. Just as there would emerge in the wake of the New Deal a mixed economy inelegant and inconsistent in theory, there would be, behind national policy and in many American minds, an imperfect amalgam of values. Strains of individualism would remain very important in American culture, but new ideas would entwine themselves with the old.

## A Mosaic of Power and Preference

Tensions over policy and values did not take form only on a national stage in the 1930s. The patterns of authority and belief that made up American political culture were often most evident below the national level, in reactions to the depression and to the sudden importance of federal programs in specific communities. Each of the multiple levels of government characteristic of the United States had something to say about what relief and reform would mean in practice, and strong traditions of states' rights and local autonomy encouraged resistance to uniformity. New Dealers did not create policy in a vacuum, nor did they have the power to work their will on a pliant populace. Conservatives may have charged that the New Deal threatened dictatorship, and radicals that it was doing far too little to bring about fundamental change. Neither acknowledged sufficiently the obstacles placed before any single-minded exercise of power by political structure and tradition; neither calculated correctly the ballast provided by the weight of popular attitudes.

The question of who should make what decisions at what level of government is a longstanding one in American politics, and those seeking change must often choose whether to attempt a rearrangement in the pattern of decision-making or to work through existing channels of power. Even though the New Deal ultimately produced a substantial increase in federal authority, and even though it dealt a better political hand to a greater number of players, the Roosevelt administration did not set out to reorganize American politics. Rather, and with the inevitable exceptions, the New Deal shaped itself around the multilayered patchwork of governments, organizations, and interests that was the American political structure.

The sensitivity to political considerations within the Roosevelt administration was evident in the content of the Social Security Act of 1935. This act established not only the system of old-age insurance for which it is best known but also an unemployment insurance system and several programs to provide aid for dependent children and the disabled. Funds to support unemployment compensation were to be raised mainly through a federal payroll tax. Even so, the system was set up to allow each state to administer its own program. Thus, benefits varied from one area to another, reflecting the disposition and social aims of the several states, not any uniform national standard. A similar disparity developed within programs making direct federal grants to the states to assist them in helping the aging destitute, the crippled, and the blind, in supporting dependent children, and in improving public health services and maternity and infant care. Because these programs required matching funds that some states were willing or able to provide at higher levels than others, they reflected a spectrum of social values and conditions, not a common definition of societal responsibility. The room for variation and the preservation of local authority within the framework of federal-state cooperation left the unemployment and social welfare measures open to various criticisms; the same considerations made them far more acceptable politically than they would otherwise have been.

The system of old-age and survivors' insurance established by the Social Security Act required contributions by workers themselves and by their employers, pulling money out of the depression-ridden economy of the thirties to build up a trust fund from which payments would not be made until 1942. It also left without coverage domestic workers and farm laborers, groups among the least able to save money for their own protection. Both weaknesses grew out of responses to the political circumstances of the period. Powerful agricultural interests did not want to require farmers to pay any tax on behalf of their workers, and southerners in particular opposed the inclusion of domestics, the largest number of whom were African-American. Roosevelt acknowledged that employee taxes might not make the best sense economically, but he had good political reasons for supporting them as the basis for the social security system. He was convinced, as he had said in January 1931 while still governor of New York, that "our American aged do not want charity" but rather the benefits "to which they are rightfully entitled by their own thrift and foresight in the form of insurance."[27] A contributory plan would be in at least partial accord with individualistic values. Moreover, as Roosevelt later explained, the contributions convinced people that they had "a legal, moral, and political right to collect their pensions. . . . With those taxes in there, no damn politician can ever scrap my social security program."[28]

The New Deal acknowledged that American ideas about state and local authority carried both political and cultural weight, and it sometimes built upon them, knowing the result would be uneven policy. Roosevelt was willing to place cultural logic before economic logic to root the social security system in a sense of earned rights consistent with traditional values. This attentiveness to public attitudes did not mean that there was no opposition to the bill. Some conservatives regarded any form of governmentally sponsored insurance as unacceptable interference with individual initiative, and every Republican in the House but one voted to block social security legislation shortly before the measure was passed. They were not wrong to see significant change in the commitment to a national program that recognized, in contrast to most previous assumptions, a public responsibility for the well-being of individual citizens. That the changes came within, on top of, and beside what existed testified both to the assumptions of the New Dealers and to the persistence of entrenched beliefs and practice. Roosevelt and others knew the limitations of the system established in 1935, but they also knew their own political culture.

By the time the Social Security Act was passed, the Roosevelt administration had accumulated a substantial experience with the vagaries of state and local politics. Consider, for example, the federal relationship with cities. Before the 1930s the federal government had taken little direct interest in cities, and cities still battling for greater independence from state controls had no desire for national ties. The rising local relief costs and falling revenue of the early depression, however, had pushed many cities toward the financial brink by 1932, and urban leaders became increasingly convinced that only the federal government could amass resources equal to the economic challenge. Led by such mayors as Frank Murphy of Detroit—who had pushed local relief as far as it would go in a city dominated by the automobile boom in the twenties and the automobile depression in the thirties—urban officials began to lobby Washington for aid in 1932 and in February 1933 formed the U.S. Conference of Mayors to provide regular advocacy. Unable to overcome Hoover's insistence on local responsibility, the activist mayors were heartened by the first streams of New Deal aid. The Civil Works Administration (CWA) in 1933–34, the Public Works Administration (PWA) under the direction of

Harold Ickes, and after 1935 the Works Progress Administration (WPA), led by Harry Hopkins, poured large sums into the cities for the support of major construction projects and work relief. These are the generalizations. Yet they tell only part of the story, for what the New Deal meant in any specific place was strongly shaped by the local environment.

That environment might have included any of a variety of obstacles to unified and consistent policy. State Democratic parties, far from working as parts of any smooth national organization, were often less reform-minded than the New Dealers, were sometimes split into factions, and frequently were interested more in patronage than in issues of governance. State-city relationships reflected not only political conflicts—especially when legislature and city were controlled by opposing parties—but also major cultural tensions. Rural areas were often vastly overrepresented in the legislatures (as they would be until after the one-person/one-vote Supreme Court decisions of the 1960s) and made no secret of their distrust toward cities. Several states put strict limits on the power of cities to tax or borrow money, and when these limits were reached under the pressure of depression, some jurisdictions lost federal grants they desperately needed because they could not raise the funds for a matching share. Ethnic tensions also played a part, as when the Massachusetts legislature used a debt limit to obstruct the Irish machine running Boston. No pleas of emergency were strong enough to overcome existing political and cultural divisions for long.[29]

The conditions in different cities and the attitudes of the people running them also varied widely. Kansas City was exceptional because it handled the depression unusually well on its own. The Democratic boss Tom Pendergast and his city manager initiated a community "Ten-Year Plan" involving some $50 million in public works, and the Pendergast machine (with the aid of the county judge Harry S Truman)[30] orchestrated a campaign that led to the plan's acceptance by a huge margin in a 1931 vote. Kansas City's relief programs, which provided thousands of construction jobs in part by using human power instead of machinery, helped keep suffering and business failure to a minimum.[31] In cities at the other extreme, officials did as little as possible to aid the unemployed, objected to federal aid, or obstructed New Deal programs when they arrived. The Republican mayors of Denver and Syracuse in 1932 resisted seeking help from the national government on the grounds of fiscal conservatism and fear of federal dictatorship. The Democratic mayor of Richmond commented primly that cities should simply live with the revenues they had. And the Pittsburgh mayor, who had won election as a New Deal candidate, nevertheless blocked development of the WPA in that city, vetoed a bond issue to aid the needy, and attacked Roosevelt's relief efforts as "wholesale bribery of the electorate."[32]

Many cities also tried to reshape New Deal programs to fit the biases of existing distributions of power and to protect local habits and prerogatives. Charles Trout in his analysis of Boston and Jo Ann Argersinger in her study

of Baltimore detail the process of what Trout labels the "localization of federal programs." Especially after WPA guidelines returned more control over the
distribution of relief to local authorities in 1935, federally financed jobs in
these cities were more likely to be handed out with an eye to ethnicity, race,
and even class than with a strict adherence to Roosevelt's nondiscrimination
order. In Boston at the end of the decade, Italians from the North End were
receiving at least 40 percent fewer than the number of WPA jobs they should
have had according to their rate of unemployment, and African-Americans 13
percent fewer, while South Boston's Irish received 14 percent more than their
proportionate share. Baltimore's Catholics accounted for 24 percent of relief
recipients but claimed over 50 percent of CWA jobs, while blacks, with 42 percent of those eligible, got only 28 percent of the jobs (and even this proportion
brought complaints from state legislators). Women, meanwhile, who made up
20 percent of the relief load, received only 0.4 percent of CWA jobs. The
*Baltimore Sun* supported city officials who objected to work projects without
clear long-term benefits, and the mayor agreed with the state planning commission that relief for "common laborers" was not in the public interest. In
Boston the political obstacles to the New Deal included "habits of Yankee
thrift ('pay-as-you-go government,' it was called), a swarm of overextended
taxpayers, . . . businessmen accustomed to laissez-faire[,] . . . a conservative
Catholic hierarchy and a number of cautious, parochial trade unions," not to
mention a city council dominated by "worshippers" of Al Smith. In both
Boston and Baltimore, just as the New Deal changed the city, it was in turn
changed by it.[33]

Despite the determined resistance to outside authority in some municipali-
ties, city officials were often of two minds about the New Deal. Many recognized a need for continuing federal involvement in the cities yet did not want
to let go of familiar biases and assumptions. Local groups reacted to specific
New Deal programs in related ways. They, too, harbored divided feelings,
embracing federal programs that benefited their own interests directly while
remaining suspicious of governmental aid to other groups. There was always
a good reason why one's own group had a special claim to attention consistent
with virtuous effort and self-reliance, and why other people should show more
initiative and responsibility. The New Deal pleased enough of the people
enough of the time to win large electoral majorities, even in cities like Baltimore
and Boston. But this support did not indicate that in endorsing new measures
voters felt compelled to give up either particularist or individualist attitudes.

In smaller cities and towns the compromises reached and the contradictions
created were similar in spirit if not always in detail. Robert and Helen Lynd,
who had conducted a detailed sociological study of Muncie, Indiana, in 1925
for their book *Middletown* (1929), returned to Muncie in 1935 to see what had
changed, publishing the results as *Middletown in Transition* (1937). The Lynds
recorded struggles between bankers, the city council, and local grocers over
control of food contracts for relief that mirrored the conflicts over ideas, and

equaled the self-seeking, of any metropolis. They noted the seeming paradox that a Middletown physically stagnant during the prosperous 1920s was improving its facilities markedly in the midst of depression, thanks to federal work projects. And they reflected on the tensions between values that public relief measures brought out in the community. People recognized that immediate needs demanded the expenditure of public funds to meliorate the condition of the jobless, but they were uncomfortable with such aid. They assumed that the process would be dogged by corruption (which was often taken for granted in local politics), and they remained attached to the values of individual responsibility and private charity. Even so, given that large-scale relief measures were necessary, people wanted them managed with efficiency, which implied granting someone central authority, risking loss of local control, and leaving behind the sense of personal responsiveness. New Deal work relief meant living with contradiction.

The Lynds suggested that in Middletown many people had awakened during the depression "from a sense of being at home in a familiar world to the shock of living as an atom in a universe dangerously too big and blindly out of hand." They pointed further to several dislocations and pressures of the period that were "peculiarly conducive to cultural change." Yet the Lynds found in the people of Middletown no tendency to blame their community structure or the national system, and a strong affection for familiar verities. A defensive resentment, among those in the "business class," of increased federal authority, labor activism, and radical ideas, combined with "tenuous and confused new positive values" among workers inspired by New Deal relief and labor policies, seemed to suggest a slight sharpening of ideological lines. But the Lynds found little evidence of class awareness or radical intent.[34]

Scholarly reexamination of two surveys taken in 1939 has provided support for such observations. By far the largest number of respondents to the surveys identified themselves as middle-class, a common result in the United States but significant in a decade of depression. Those who labeled themselves working-class and who believed that labor and management interests were opposed to one another—a group defined in the process of analysis as the "fully class conscious"—amounted only to about 3.4 percent of the white, nonfarm workforce. In all groups the prevalent attitudes toward work seemed to reflect individualistic assumptions. The investigators found, for example, that about 70 percent of the wage workers surveyed would have liked to be self-employed, and despite the frequent association of a preference for security over risk with the depression experience and with the structure of modern corporate industry, two-thirds of the workers put a higher value on advancement opportunities in a job than on job security. A substantial majority of those surveyed also remained optimistic, believing that the future still held out good opportunities for them and for their children.[35]

Perhaps these responses might prompt a reminder that at any given point during the depression a considerable majority of the workforce was employed.

Yet particular fates cannot explain the replies, nor do the surveys suggest that Americans were either unaffected by the depression or unthinking. The attitudes of respondents in all groups toward the issues of government assistance and self-help were more mixed than monolithic. If majorities expressed individualistic work values, majorities also endorsed federal relief and the idea that "the government should see that everyone is above subsistence." A slimmer majority supported government regulation of utilities (which the New Deal had extended), but government ownership of the railroads or the telephone system was solidly rejected, as was redistribution of wealth through taxes or a law limiting excess income. The unemployed and the small group of "fully class conscious" workers were more likely to support radical measures if such steps were necessary to guarantee adequate relief. Yet a majority of the "class conscious" group preferred self-employment (with its capitalist potential) over work for others and valued opportunity for advancement over job security. And the unemployed, though less optimistic about their own prospects, were nearly as hopeful as other groups about opportunities for their children.

These results may be subject to various qualifications. Attitudes can vary somewhat over time, and all polls or surveys have their biases and margins for error. People do not always act in accord with the values or preferences they express. Whatever the majority believes, even a rather small minority of the population can sustain a substantial organization or exert a good deal of political pressure under the right circumstances. Specific national and local issues in the thirties evoked struggle and debate that general attitudinal alignments could not resolve. Nevertheless, allowing for all such considerations, these surveys suggest that a balancing of attitudes pervaded the political culture of the 1930s and established the boundaries for reform. The clear majority seemed to want an expansion of federal responsibility within a framework that would preserve individual opportunity and responsibility—change, that is, that would not interfere too much with the familiar.

Questions of identity, values, and attitudes can be approached in other ways as well. One analysis of working-class political behavior from the late nineteenth century through the 1930s argues that "pockets of class sentiment" had long existed and that during the depression, this sentiment was "translated into political consciousness as the class basis of partisanship became successively more marked from election to election." Workers were mobilized politically as never before, and class differentiation between parties in American voting was on its way toward reaching (for a time) levels equal to those in Europe. Yet the striking fact in the United States was that this worker mobilization came about through the Democratic party, which remained "a cross-class coalition of ideologically contradictory elements." Indeed, the "ideological implications" of workers' cultures, traditions, and priorities were inherently "ambiguous," and the commitments that might flow from political mobilization were highly contingent. The same analysis that points toward a greater consciousness of class and a more acute sharpening of ideological politics during the 1930s than was evident in contemporary surveys tends to reinforce the picture of people and groups juggling competing values within themselves and responsive to varying forms of public expression.[36]

Students of labor activism approach similar conclusions from a different angle. Militance did not equal radicalism. Radical political parties provided labor organizers who were sometimes of considerable importance within specific local circumstances, and groups of workers might at times feel strongly the appeal of the left. Yet radicals did not control the labor movement. In assessing the influence of the Communist party on autoworkers' unions, for example, Roger Keeran has argued that Communists influenced immediate questions of attitude and action, that they provided an early source of trade union experience, and that a few managed to have a disproportionate effect. Yet he concludes that ultimately "Communist influence . . . was superficial and fragile."[37] In evaluating the period as a whole, Robert Zieger offers a striking picture of an assertiveness that found expression primarily within the existing economic and political system rather than against it:

> Throughout the decade workers were uncommonly militant. They resisted further erosion of their standards and struggled to create and sustain organizations to buttress their position and safeguard their working conditions and pay packets. They made clear political choices, voting in heavy numbers and casting their ballots for Franklin D. Roosevelt and politicians closely identified with his policies. They showed little interest in radical parties or unions, and they overwhelmingly avoided extremism.[38]

Commentators on the Roosevelt administration and the New Deal have found no shortage of lapses, inadequacies, and failures. Some have complained that the New Deal did too much, most that it did too little. Although the standards of judgment have changed over time as the concerns of each generation have reshaped perceptions of the past, assertions of what the New Deal failed to achieve have often reflected a belief that it did not go far enough in a particular direction, that it did not commit itself thoroughly to a particular idea or strategy, that it did not build a cohesive reform movement or structure a unified policy of systematic change. Yet many who have undertaken such critiques have also felt compelled to acknowledge that the New Deal, for all its faults, was undeniably a psychological success, generating strong popular support and transforming the mood of the decade. Perhaps it is time to recognize that its weakness may also have been its strength, that the contradictions within the New Deal may have been a source of its appeal. American culture as a whole was filled with "ideologically contradictory elements," and it was no political mistake that the Democratic party embodied such contradictions. People of varying social circumstances were struggling with the tensions between individualist values and public needs, local control and local dependence, personalized responses and institutional efficiencies. In their collective tolerance for inconsistency, in their efforts to balance competing values, claims, and ideas, New Deal programs created channels of political expression for the thought and culture of the decade that earned them their "psychological" success.

*three*

---

# Popular Culture
# and the Dance of Values

Reeling from the depression's onslaught in 1931, the producer Cecil B.
DeMille took up the bold shield of individualistic moralism to declare the
troubles of the film industry a "test of courage." Proclaiming that those who
could stand only "pleasant times and pleasant words" were not of "lasting
value," he proceeded, in the style of Treasury Secretary Andrew Mellon, to
find positive good in the economic collapse and reason for a perverse optimism. "This year will be a splendid year for the industry," DeMille averred,
"for during it we will see much of the purging effect of that greatest of all natural laws: the survival of the fittest."[1] The laxities and inefficiencies encouraged by prosperity were impurities that had to be cleansed; the virtues of
unremitting work, and thrift, and discipline, had occasionally to be tempered
anew in the fires of competition.

In May 1933 Walt Disney's *The Three Little Pigs* first appeared in theaters,
and the popularity of the short cartoon quickly outstripped Disney's ability to
supply copies. Eventually, it became the most widely shown film of the year
and earned Disney his first Academy Award. In the familiar tale it tells, two
sprightly porkers throw together houses of straw and sticks so that they can
"play around all day," only to find themselves in dire straits when they confront the physical and economic peril of the wolf at the door. The third pig—
proclaiming righteously that he has "no chance to sing and dance, for work
and play don't mix"—builds his house laboriously of brick and stone, protecting himself from danger and ultimately providing a haven for the others as
well. It is easy to conclude that there was a transparent moral message in the
film endorsing the traditional virtues of work, discipline, and self-denial, a
message it is tempting to link to Disney's conservative political views.

Even if one accepts DeMille's remarks and Disney's industrious pig at face value, however, a moment's thought will suggest that there is some irony in their preachments. The moral framework centering on productive work and upright character so important to nineteenth-century American culture had come under increasing challenge, especially in the 1910s and 1920s, from rival values that embraced leisure, personal experience, and self-expression. The economic success of the system built up around the older morality had set it to gnawing at its own roots. High levels of production, once achieved, presented an expanding problem of how to market the flood of goods available. Business relied ever more heavily on advertising, reinforced by easy credit and installment buying, to boost consumption—encouraging a quite different behavior than did traditional notions of fiscal integrity, self-denial, and thrift. The trend toward shorter working hours and higher real income gave leisure time new social and economic importance and fostered the marketing of recreation and entertainment. Often the emphasis of the newer forms of selling and of play was on novelty, excitement, personal fulfillment, and self-expression; by the 1910s and 1920s, economic, social, and intellectual changes were loosening traditional restraints for at least some social groups in virtually all areas of life.[2]

The movies were a product of that newer world. When DeMille made his appeal to the stern morality of steady work and purgative competition, he was speaking about an industry dependent on leisure time and the popular consumption of entertainment. Films sold excitement and adventure, the glamour of luxury goods, the titillation of a loosened sexuality, and an extravagance of emotion far more than they dealt in any ethic of self-control or restraint; DeMille himself had gained renown for his exploitation of such patterns. Even if a film seemed to carry a traditional moral message, people could see DeMille's epics or Disney's hardworking pig only if they had spent their money (not saved it) to indulge their hours of leisure. There were inherent tensions between sermons on economic discipline and the nature of the film industry.

In the case of *The Three Little Pigs*, other ambiguities are apparent in the content of the film itself. Where some see an affirmation of traditionalist values, one scholar has found it just as possible to decide that "the most effective pig is the one who does not minimize the fact of crisis and builds with modern materials and tools."[3] Moreover, the pigs who fail in their own protection are not abandoned to the jaws of the wolf, as they are in early versions of the tale and as a strict application of DeMille's "survival of the fittest" might require. Rather, they are welcomed and granted succor by the one who is secure—a version of the story that may have had unpredictable resonances during 1933. In the midst of the New Deal's first Hundred Days, the optimistically defiant theme song "Who's Afraid of the Big Bad Wolf" (with its echoes of Roosevelt's inaugural attack on fear) became a national hit that seemed to reflect the upbeat mood of the new administration—whatever Disney may have intended. Finally, the third pig is ultimately no enemy of play. The products of his dutiful construction include a piano, which he plays not in the manner of the middle-class Victorian parlor but, first, in a melodramatic accompaniment to the wolf's assault that mimics the silent-movie accompaniments of the 1920s, and second, in a honky-tonk rendition of "Who's Afraid of the Big Bad Wolf" that the three pigs sing together at the end. This little piggie has gone not just to work but to market, and having upheld his moral duty, he turns to embrace the popular culture of his day.

DeMille's words and Disney's cartoon provide a caution against deciding too readily what cultural materials mean or hurrying them too quickly into categories. Mixed meanings may offer important messages, and the presence of contradictions is seldom a simple matter of hypocrisy (though Hollywood was hardly immune to that temptation). DeMille may have appealed sincerely to an older complex of work-centered values even as he built his career on visions of indulgence and leisure. The problem is not to choose one or another ethos to represent the 1930s but to discover the ways in which contrasting values interacted through conflict and combination. What may be most interesting about *The Three Little Pigs* in this light is that it allows different value claims. As a result, the cartoon offers at least a tentative reconciliation between its strong dose of traditional moralism and its acceptance of popular leisure. Some expressions of American culture during the 1930s offer no reconciliation at all; others attempt to blend older and newer values in sharply different proportions. We need to ask how popular culture in its various forms coped with the presence of conflicting values during the decade, and how the makers of that culture attempted to resolve or exploit prevailing tensions.

## *Formulas for Success*

The idea of opportunity and the dream of "success" were deeply rooted in American culture. What happened to the idea and its promises during a decade when as many as one-quarter of those seeking work could not find it, and when businesses were collapsing by the dozen? What became of the validation that the success myth offered for thrift, industry, ambition, and character when such virtues, for many, offered no protection from economic failure? Could other values replace a cluster of beliefs that provided both a strategy for gain and a moral compass? Such questions clearly troubled the 1930s. By the end of the following decade, numerous studies of depression images of success and their underlying cultural significance would attest to the importance for contemporaries of the issues at stake.

When economic collapse threatened the American promise, perhaps the strongest response was to reassert the patterns of established myth. One scholar has noted, in popular magazines of the period, an "almost obsessive concern with questions involving success" that tended to pour most easily into familiar molds.[4] Magazine biographies told time and again of a man—for it remained a male myth—who had gone to work as a boy (most likely with only a limited education, preferably with a rural background) and risen through effort, merit, and a touch of good fortune to financial success or public distinction. Articles by the score insisted that America was still the land of opportunity. Magazine writers lauded the prospects in developing fields, such as movies, air-conditioning, and aviation, or encouraged pioneers to explore the dimly perceived frontiers of atomic energy and radiation. Others tried to keep alive the idea of free land and homesteading or boasted of opportunities to make money out of the wreckage of depression. Often in such articles, the key to getting ahead lay in hard work: continuous effort that made anything possible and guaranteed good results; work that occupied the whole of life and left no room for leisure; labor as a form of training that made education a luxury or even an obstacle to success. The near certainty that traditional formulas would leave the aspiring youth ill equipped to make his mark in atomic energy, or the fact that by the 1930s the majority of top business executives had at least some college education, presented no obstacle to those reciting a litany of success that had withstood the force of technological and organizational change for decades.

The traditional formulas for success were for many a bastion of ideological individualism, and by mid-decade they were being pressed into service to reinforce political opposition to the Roosevelt administration. In the election year 1936, one writer recited tales of businessmen who had climbed to success from humble origins and complained that New Deal regulations preventing children under 16 from working were obstructing ambitious young men who might best begin their careers at 13 or 14. The nation's greatest economic problem, from this point of view, was not the depression but federal programs that undermined self-reliance and initiative. The Republican candidate, Alfred Landon, became the embodiment of well-worn myth as a rural boy from the Kansas plains who just might have grown up to become president. The success of "Frugal Alf," one writer declared, came from his practicing "the homely virtues of his country"; he was a man who "counts his change . . . remembers to turn out the lights . . . keeps himself and his state out of debt."[5]

Republicans were not mistaken in believing that appeals to the traditional gospel of work, opportunity, and success continued to have substantial resonance in the 1930s, but the election demonstrated quite handily that their party had no exclusive claim on such themes. And even as its older forms were being harnessed to the political uses of the moment, the idea of success was undergoing internal reformation at the hands of newer disciples. Books of advice had long preached proper rules for climbing the social and economic ladder. Often the trappings of such advice could be kept up-to-date without changing basic patterns, as did many of the success books published in the 1930s: *Through*

*Failure to Success* (1934), for example, struck a note especially suited to the depression context, while *The Super-Science of Success* (1933) tried to claim the modern mantle of "scientific" authority. In a few instances, however, adjusting the precepts of the advice tradition meant restructuring the rules of the game, setting behavior and values within a different cultural frame.

Dale Carnegie's *How to Win Friends and Influence People* (1936), one of the most popular success books of the decade, announces in its title a new set of tactics for getting ahead and a new conception of the process. Carnegie deemphasizes traditional maxims of initiative, industry, thrift, self-control, and dependability to concentrate on ways of making oneself appealing to others and persuasive in dealing with them. Rather than climbing up in the world through superior character, ability, and effort, the ambitious are now urged to cultivate their minds and manners to rise through a kind of interpersonal engineering: they are to train themselves in amiability, celebrate the strengths of others, and avoid friction. References to psychology, quotations from the famous, and a ready assortment of anecdotes are pressed into service to demonstrate that making others feel important is the key to success, a key that can be used only by those who have first retooled their own perspective.

Unlike the older formulas for success that often rested on stern injunctions of considerable moral force, Carnegie's advice places less visible emphasis on right and wrong than on getting along. Its tendency is to push any standards for critical judgment of social institutions or individual behavior into the background through admonitions to accentuate the positive. The gospel of winning friends bore a certain appropriateness for a twentieth-century industrial society increasingly characterized by large organizations and a growing service economy. Concentration on good relations with others could smooth the internal workings of corporate and government bureaucracies, lubricate the direct but largely impersonal contacts of sales and professional services, and varnish nagging anxieties with a coating of affirmation.

Noting this apparent fit, some commentators have ventured to suggest that the emphasis on consciously shaping one's thought and behavior in order to please—on packaging and "selling" oneself—marked the individual's consignment to an expanding domain of marketing and consumption. A related idea holds that the nineteenth-century emphasis on "character" had given way between the early twentieth century and the 1930s to a preoccupation with "personality" as the proper measure of human worth.[6] Intrigued by the evidence of new standards and new behavior, post–World War II social science paid close attention to David Riesman's distinction between the "inner-directed" and the "other-directed" person and to various forms of the idea of the "organization man."[7] Such efforts to categorize and type are perhaps necessary, but they can easily obscure the mix of ideas and values at a given cultural moment from which individual outlooks often take their shape.

Carnegie's advice, like that found in several other success-full books of the 1930s, is actually pulled in several directions at once as it attempts to reconcile different aims, values, and conceptions of individual efficacy. The goal of winning friends broadcast in half of Carnegie's title coexists in tension with the desire announced in the other half to influence people to one's own advantage. Whereas the traditional idea of success had implied the potential loneliness of "setting oneself apart," Carnegie conjoins a promise of distinction and power with a promise of camaraderie and belonging. A combination of ideas that would surface again and again in the culture of the thirties—with relevance for public figures from Roosevelt to Hollywood stars—appears in Carnegie as a "success" model for the self: the individual can be both hero and buddy, exceptional and everyday.

Questions of values are similarly tangled. At times Carnegie seems to urge a computation of the cash value of every smile and to assume that getting ahead is justification enough for the tactics he prescribes. Yet after providing his calculating lessons on making others feel important, Carnegie takes pains to distinguish between "appreciation" and "flattery," adding the rather too vigorous protestation, "No! No! No! I am not suggesting flattery!" Flattery is "shallow," "counterfeit," and "insincere"; appreciation offers praise that is "sincere," "from the heart," "unselfish." Those who cannot offer smiles and appreciation without expecting something in return are "contemptibly selfish" and deserve to fail. This declaration seems to attack the very idea of self-interested action and with it the program for success that Carnegie is teaching, but the teacher admits no contradiction.[8]

Carnegie papers over the difficulties with a revised standard version of the relationship between success and morality. His program assures readers that getting ahead in a world of large organizations and salesmanship is not just compatible with but dependent upon a moral stance that abjures social frictions and downplays the competitive pursuit of wealth. Those who do not adopt the strategies of good feeling for the right reasons—reasons that give a substantial place to nonmaterialistic ends and to family and community harmony—will "meet with the failure [they] so richly deserve" through the operation of a Carnegie equivalent of natural law. Conversely, those who begin to "appreciate" others in the right spirit will earn not only satisfaction and love but also a just and deserved profit. Like the products of streamlined design, Carnegie's model of success promises both stability and a frictionless advance.

A stockbroker who had put a part of Carnegie's advice into operation reported with elation that "smiles are bringing me dollars, many dollars every day," and went on a few sentences later to declare, as if with complete consistency, that he was "a richer man, richer in friendships and happiness—the only things that matter much after all." Money and a sentimental morality that denied its importance were closely linked. The new world of "techniques in handling people" and "dramatization" and "showmanship" ("The movies do it. Radio does it. Why don't you do it?") was presumed to be in harmony with the values of an idealized village life.[9] Perhaps Carnegie and his more astute readers sensed at some level that the emphasis on fitting oneself to others, on being positive and upbeat, on public relations, could lead all too readily to false representation, to personality as performance, to cynicism behind the public fronts. If so, Carnegie's ethical protestations provided the necessary assuagement: getting ahead could be "unselfish"; moralisms could purify manipulation.

Carnegie, finally, offers a mixed response to the question of just how effective individuals can be in shaping their lives and their world. The whole framework and purpose of his book was tied up with a program for self-reconstruction that, like the entire success tradition, asserted the power of will and desire to mold each person anew. Within this tradition, individuals were asked to hold themselves responsible for their own fates, as many did who took joblessness in the depths of depression as a personal failing. Yet at certain points, Carnegie ventures quite different claims. If a person possessed the inherited traits and had lived with the "environment and experiences" of Al Capone, Carnegie declares, then that person would be "precisely what he is—and where he is. . . . You deserve very little credit for being what you are." Although Carnegie does not pursue the implications of such remarks, they seem to leave little room for personal responsibility or individual will.

Between the promise that anyone can be self-made and the warnings of an inevitable fate lay a message that imputed to individuals the power to attain success but limited their prospects for doing so. Even as Carnegie pledges that his program can "achieve magic" for the reader, he acknowledges that it is "difficult to apply these suggestions all the time" and warns that the "natural thing" to do is "usually wrong." Indeed, the listings of six ways and twelve ways and nine ways and seven rules to accomplish one thing or another guaranteed both that strivers would always have something to work on, and that they could never do enough. The more elaborate the program for success, the more it carried the subtle message that readers must be prepared for failure.[10]

Carnegie's preachments on how to succeed thus carried no brief for intellectual consistency; nor did they convey any simple cultural intent. Although the major lines of argument seem evident enough, *How to Win Friends and Influence People* combines advice on standing out with advice on fitting in; lessons in hardheaded management with sentimental moralisms on the superiority of love over money; claims of efficacy and responsibility with a biological and cultural determinism that denies both; the promise of success with the likelihood of failure. The presence of such mixed messages, far from diminishing the book's attractiveness, may well have been an important source of its appeal.

Through its ambiguities and seeming contradictions, Carnegie's advice offered tentative reconciliations between competing outlooks and values (more consciously so than in either DeMille or Disney). What appeared to be specific instruction allowed wide flexibility of response. Readers who embraced Carnegie's formulas, or something like them, could rest first on one foot and then on the other as circumstances warranted, relying most heavily on values and explanations that served the needs of the moment. There was no need to make binding choices or exclusive commitments. Carnegie presented ready-made the kind of mosaic that people often construct for themselves from varied sources, even as his advice left room for individuals to balance competing values in their own ways and to function as makers of their own culture. In cushioning the tensions inherent in changing economic and social conditions, and in easing the more specific pressures of depression, a degree of eclecticism could be a decided strength.

## *Advertising: The Assurance Industry*

Cultural advice of a different sort flowed unbidden to most Americans in the form of advertising. The main purpose of advertising, of course, is to sell particular products, yet with growing frequency during the decade or two before 1930, that function had become purposefully knotted with others as advertisers aspired to shape ideas, manners, behavior, and values. As early as 1908, American Telephone and Telegraph had attempted to guide public opinion on the issue of regulated monopolies through advertising. During World War I, George Creel's Committee on Public Information mounted a full-fledged campaign of patriotic propaganda that, before the CPI's reputation soured, gave advertisers a chance to claim that their industry had performed a great national service in a moral cause. On a more practical level, advertisements offered instruction: in telephone manners, in the use of modern products, in the proper way to shop. And if advice of this sort provided partial orientation to a world of expanding consumer goods, such literal guidance had a more flamboyant twin. During the 1920s it became apparent that although advertisements had once emphasized quality or reasoned choice by describing their products in straightforward detail, many were no longer doing so. They now appealed to consumers by associating merchandise with the experience of luxury or adventure, by identifying products with the up-to-date and the stylish, or by presenting goods as solutions to emotional problems and personal dilemmas. What the newer kind of ads increasingly sold was fantasy, status, and therapy.

In the early 1930s appeals of this kind remained an advertising staple, striking in their adaptability. Some uses were predictable: Studebaker added to an accumulating list of ads linking automobiles to excitement and adventure by combining in one layout an "Indianapolis Speed Classic" picture that promises buyers "speedway stamina" and a drawing of a car in front of a ship that is winning admiration from stylish couples, including dashing ship's officers.[11] Other appeals required a greater stretch: a young woman standing ecstatically with hands upraised in "sun-drenched fields" turns out to be selling the "tonic" available from a Dualator heating and cooling system; under the carefully scripted words "Beautifully Modern," a sleek woman in a shimmering pink evening gown yearns toward a "satin-smooth" product of "dynamic, modern, arresting" design—a "steel!" General Electric refrigerator; from a roadster stopped on a wooden bridge, a relaxed man leans out to talk with a boy fishing, reinforcing the promise that "You too, can be as carefree as Huckleberry Finn!" thanks to an Aetna automobile insurance policy.[12] If such ads frequently seemed about to stumble over their internal incongruities, greater inconsistencies pushed to the fore as the depression clamped its economic vise on the advertising industry. The appeal to consumers through luxury and leisure stood in sharp tension with the business outlook of advertisers themselves, and the nature of the conflict mirrored the separation between words and works evident in DeMille.

When hard times came, the well-worn language of discipline and character stood ready-to-hand. Predictably, some advertising executives asserted that the economic collapse brought a deserved punishment to an industry grown lax, that people and products would be better for having been tested, even (in the 1932 ads of one watch company) that parents should be thankful to have their children graduating in tough times that would discipline them for the future. In trade publications, advertising agencies tried to assure each other and potential clients that they still had an economic future through repeated images of light at the end of a tunnel, or light breaking through the clouds, or light bathing the countryside after a storm.[13] To get to that brighter tomorrow, businessmen must not be quitters or weaklings or cowards but must demonstrate their courage and meet the toughest challenge (a rhetorical appeal to masculine virility that appeared during the depression in wildly different arenas of American culture). This display of character had to be accompanied by unremitting hard work on the battlefield of sales and a determination often symbolized in ads by a clenched fist.

Roland Marchand has tied the recurring symbol of the fist to "harangues" that "fiercely reasserted the validity of the success creed": in 1932, E. R. Squibb and Sons called for "intestinal stamina, hard work, long hours," because "the day of the survival of the fittest is here"; Metropolitan Life Insurance trumpeted the individualist theme that each agent was responsible for his own economic fate and asserted that "the year ahead can be as good a year as the individual agent wills it to be." The clenched fist thus provided a shorthand for the doctrines of work and discipline. Yet the symbol was not without its ambiguities. Marchand himself has suggested that many clenched-fist ads connote anxiety as well as determination, an effort to induce tough-minded fortitude as much as to honor it.[14]

Further probing suggests additional complexities. The economic struggle associated with the symbol of the clenched fist implied a need to eliminate waste, to set aside leisure and luxury, to be hard-headed and hard-boiled. In this spirit, an ad for Powers Accounting machines shows a fist squeezing the juice from an orange under the heading, "The Last Drop May Be Profit."[15] Meanwhile, a full-page layout from the Young and Rubicam advertising agency pictures a large hand clenched around several dollar bills and declares in bold type, "America Has Closed Its Fist." The same Americans who once spent money "like a drunken sailor" had become by 1931 "a people who think twice" about spending at all. Advertising's challenge was to "overcome the reluctance to part with that money."[16] Logical in their own terms, the two ads taken together disclose messages in conflict. Discipline, work, and hard-headed thrift were appropriate values for business it seemed, but not for the buying public. Consumers had to be urged to live by a contrary standard: they had to be lured toward looser spending—toward indulgence, therapy, and fulfillment—and away from thinking twice. Business leaders thus clenched their fists in order to unclench the fists of consumers. Two quite different sets of values found a curious resonance in the same visual image.

Such tensions within advertising were kept at least partly under control through the cultural practices of the advertising industry and its dominant assumptions about audience. Industry analysts did not assume their audience was everyone. Making ability to buy the basis for market citizenship, advertisers generally excluded from one-third to one-half of the population from the "mass" that advertising attempted to sway. Like many success fables and the advice of Dale Carnegie, advertisements made little direct appeal to African-Americans, the rural poor, nonacculturated ethnics, or others on the lower economic rungs of American life.[17] With the problem of audience simplified through these exclusions, advertising could more easily contain and express limited conflicts over values, and it found a ready vehicle in assumptions based on gender. The clenched-fist calls for toughness and discipline that reflected older, work-centered values appeared primarily in ads aimed at advertising firms and their corporate clients: the expected audience was dominated by men. In the wider market, however, women were believed to account for more than three-quarters of consumer purchases, and advertisers shaped their messages around cultural stereotypes of women. Women were presumed to be emotional, full of longings for romance and fulfillment, subject to personal appeals more than reason, weak before the blandishments of fashion. Yet they were also taken to be the guardians and transmitters of culture and beauty, appreciators of genuine "style," and potentially (with the right goods) embodiments of it. The Americans pictured in advertisements reflected these assumptions about different roles and, implicitly, different values: the men are dressed primarily in work-related middle- to upper-class business suits; women often appear as aesthetic or decorative presences celebrating the modern possibilities of style and consumption. Through a partial separation of competing values by gender, advertisers tentatively balanced the elements of a divided outlook within which an ethos of hard-headed competition spurred the production of fantasy and promise.

A mixing of values lay implicit in the newly distinctive style of 1930s advertising as well. In the 1920s some advertisers had maintained that their industry could serve as a major educational force to raise the cultural level of the population. Touched by such claims, New York Governor Franklin

Roosevelt commented that if he were starting life over, he might well go into the advertising business, because "it is essentially a form of education; and the progress of civilization depends on education."[18] With the arrival of the depression, however, pressures for aggressive marketing undercut any serious pretension to public service and weakened nearly all aspirations to high standards: "Depression advertising was 'loud,' cluttered, undignified, and direct." To advertising journals, this was the style of "shirt-sleeve advertising" or "Advertising in Overalls"—fitting images for the reassertion of work-centered values.[19] But a different message resided in the forms and materials that ads now borrowed.

Advertising craved the attention of potential consumers. Ready to attach itself with chameleon intent to whatever seemed effective in getting people's attention, advertising became a mimic and mixer of other forms of mass communication and entertainment. When a study by the opinion researcher George Gallup (soon to be employed by the Rubicam Agency) showed in 1931 that comic strips had a wide social appeal, and when a Hearst experiment demonstrated that newspaper readers cared far more about their Sunday comics than about any other section of the paper, comic sections became rather suddenly a bustling frontier for advertising. Food, soap, pens, and razors were newly marketed with sequential storytelling squares and speech balloons.[20] Movies, confession magazines, and tabloids provided other formats to be copied. On radio, already pervious lines between advertising and entertainment were further breached when radio stars began to glide from the show itself into promotions for their sponsor's product. Print ads, meanwhile, identified products with the appropriate radio "personality" or perhaps with a sports "celebrity." Gillette razor blades managed to combine in one print ad a tabloid style, a sponsored radio show, a popular contest, and a heavyweight boxer as it challenged readers to "Name Max Baer's Dog."[21] New merchandise was created to tie in with the sales potential inherent in radio and movies: in the midst of the recession of 1937–38, a factory working overtime after the release of Disney's *Snow White* would still fail to keep up with the market for rubber dwarfs. As advertising put on its overalls of hard work and competitive discipline, its tools as well as its purposes reflected the appeal of indulgence and leisure.

The principles and practices of advertisers thus contained inherent tensions, yet the central ambition of the industry was clear. Advertising sought to build upon and to manipulate public tastes for the sake of greater sales. In considering this industry effort to shape individual and cultural perceptions, it is important to maintain a sense of perspective. Advertising strategies were often successful, but their influence was neither complete nor automatic. Some efforts to market fashion and behavior simply failed, and many consumers seemed to preserve a happy consciousness of the bombast and blarney in advertising's flamboyant courtings. In 1931 the magazine *Ballyhoo* fed upon this skepticism to win instant popularity by devoting itself to mocking well-known ads.

A more sober resistance to advertising found expression through a burgeoning consumer movement. Having appeared in response to the critique of American selling in Stuart Chase and Frederick J. Schlink's *Your Money's Worth* (1927), the organization Consumers Research grew from 1,200 members in 1929 to 25,000 in 1931 and 45,000 by 1933. Schlink and a new partner added the book *100,000,000 Guinea Pigs* in 1933 and sold 250,000 copies in six years.[22] It would be folly to believe that advertising's efforts at manipulation were unperceived or its versions of the world uncontested.

Yet advertising was an undeniable force in American culture during the 1930s. Whatever the industry's targeted audiences, its wider presence leaps out from photographs of the period: migrants and breadlines appear under billboards that identify buying with security and happiness; sharecropper dwellings and Hooverville shacks are decorated (or constructed) with advertising signs that evoke images of leisure and fulfillment. Advertising's promises were perhaps only partly silenced by incongruities. To reach those it did intend to target, the advertising industry spent millions testing responses to its messages, and it had every incentive to follow public attitudes closely enough to evoke positive reactions. Increasingly pervasive, advertising repeated itself again and again, introducing into the culture phrases and images and ideas that helped establish a common language of national scope. Without being entirely persuasive in its huckstering claims, advertising both reflected and molded certain broad public attitudes, apprehensions, and hopes during the 1930s, providing reason enough to attend to its subdued messages.

Over the anxieties of social change, advertising tended to lay a blanket of assurance. Indeed, it was in the counterpoise between anxiety and assurance that advertisements often found their characteristic tone, with implications that reached well beyond the merits of particular commodities. The advertising industry itself, like most of the products it sold, belonged to a world of increasingly centralized and standardized production characterized by large organizations and bureaucratic administration. The ads, and the products, were aimed at a mass audience and tied to a marketplace of such scope that it could only be called impersonal. Yet what many advertisements tried to achieve was a personal touch, a sense that they were speaking specifically and even intimately to each person. Like the commercially discovered dangers of "Halitosis" (Listerine) and "Body Odor" (Lifebuoy), many of the problems dramatized in advertising threatened individuals one by one. Ads in a single magazine issue of the midthirties offered the drama of a mother's embarrassment by "tattle-tale gray" and the satisfaction achieved with Fels-Naptha soap; urgings to "play safe" by trusting a family doctor's recommendation on laxatives (Ex-Lax); promises that the proper shaving cream could protect men from aging (Barbasol); and reminders that "good-looking hair is a social asset" (Vitalis).[23] Whether manipulating social fears or lending guidance to vanity and aspiration, advertising served a function that seemed to defy its own nature: in a society of large institutions and contacts with strangers, messages addressed to millions were providing personal counsel.

With their talent for blending crassness and caring, advertisers were quick to recognize that the depression provided opportunities to exploit familiar themes with new emotional impact. Advertising was alert to the pressures that economic collapse exerted on the mythology of success, for example, and ads were as quick as advice books to offer guidance for the ambitious. Consumers were warned about the importance of the first impression, on which their fate might rest. Whiter teeth, modern furniture, a "fresh, firm, fit" face, men's garters, or house paint, might lead to the positive judgment that would ensure individual success; dated clothes, a bad shave, even an "old-fashioned wood toilet seat" could destroy one's chances. Like Dale Carnegie, these ads assumed an urban world of mobility and of interaction between relative strangers in which "others" were very important. Yet where Carnegie counseled the individual to take control of the situation through behavior, the ads left each person subject to the constant scrutiny of "critical eyes" and able to gain an advantage only through the use of appropriate products. In one sense, buying was an ironic and even a harsh answer to the problem of success for those strapped by depression. From another perspective, the ads offered a curious promise that there was still room for aspiration. Both the anxieties being manipulated and the assurances at hand suggested significant cultural concerns.

Some of those concerns focused on children. Surveys taken in the later thirties indicated an enduring faith in American progress and the promise of success: a majority of parents continued to believe that their children might be better off than they were. Advertisers played upon these hopes, and the potential for parental anxiety and guilt that went with them, by expanding dramatically in the early years of the depression a child-centered "success" ad of a kind little used before. A boy or girl lacks energy or fidgets in school or has poor grades because parents have failed to purchase the correct cereal or toilet paper or pencils. The ads took for granted a context of competitiveness and looming frustration but offered assurances that the doors of opportunity could be held open for families who were wise consumers. They both recognized social anxieties and provided the salve of a ready solution.[24]

If buying could help affirm the persistence of opportunity, it could address related concerns as well by attesting to a democratic equality between those at the top and common folk below. In a decade of fitful worries about social class and political stability, this was no mean assurance. Regardless of wealth, the ads proclaimed, no one could have a better coffee, skin cream, mattress, vacuum cleaner, or tire than was available to all at an affordable price. The "diseases" that menaced the rich along with the average, from bad breath to athlete's foot, could be cured for people in all stations with the same convenient product. Ads on a slightly different tack reminded consumers, in a new recitation of a much-rehearsed justification for industrial capitalism, that comforts once beyond the reach of kings were now everyday delights. Using the measure of goods, advertising could endorse established American attachments to notions of social unity, the democracy of possibility, and progress. Like "success" heroes with roots in the common clay, the wealthy had to be both different, to provide a standard of aspiration, and the same as everyone else. Tensions and anxieties met with reconciling myth.

In depicting the products they were selling as guarantors of opportunity and democracy, advertisers argued implicitly that the changing world of modernity was easily compatible with the rooted concerns of American life. Through its visual imagery, advertising offered even clearer assurances that the traditional and the new, the past and the future, could exist in harmony. The security of the home was repeatedly upheld in representations of families together. Advertisements showing a husband, wife, and at least one child comfortably gathered in a living room after dinner often favored a fuzzy soft-focus technique that stood in sharp and sentimental contrast to the clean hard lines used to depict the world of work. Such scenes carefully blurred not just their edges but the tensions between traditional assumptions of the father's dominance and more "modern" ideas of family democracy and women's and children's rights. Sometimes a particular product—a radio or phonograph perhaps—has been introduced into the scene, suggesting the compatibility between advancing technology, with all it implied, and the sanctity of the traditional family. Another wide-ranging set of ads included in a single image iconographic versions of pioneers or New England villages and skyscraper cities of the present or future. The values of the past, including the individualism of the pioneer and the neighborliness of the village, were presumed to be congruous with the vastness and complexity of modern or futuristic urban landscapes. Advertising's standard visual imagery was not meant to be thought about, simply accepted. As with the admixtures of traditional and modern, the images were often comforting ones that seemed able to ease tensions without even granting them recognition.[25]

The advertising of the 1930s, then, not only gave expression to competing sets of values but also recognized personal, family, and community concerns over balancing the familiar and the new. For each contradiction, anxiety, or ill, the industry offered a palliative, not a cure. Different values could be made only partly or superficially compatible by associating them with separate spheres or opposite sexes. Cultural concerns could be dimmed but seldom erased by selling impersonal products personally, by merging images of traditional families and modern goods, or by linking pioneers and skyscrapers. Yet the larger point may be that the tensions did not need to be fully resolved. Many Americans targeted by the ads were no doubt torn themselves between the values of individualism, character, and work and those of personality, self-expression, and consumption. Many who had experienced firsthand the limitations of cultural myth nevertheless welcomed firm affirmations that opportunity remained open, that democracy prevailed, and that change was consistent with tradition. The ads might slant their pitch toward one set of standards or another, combine images in the search for universal appeal, or provide ample grounds for more than one interpretation without necessarily losing touch with major strains of public feeling.

The range of impulses or ideas that found expression in advertisements did, of course, have important limits. Because advertising as popular culture existed to serve an evolving industrial economy, it had little interest in espousing values that challenged that economic system from either the right or the left. Its business was not critique but promotion. When advertising held out images of lives more glamorous or powerful or secure or fulfilled, they were accompanied by the promise that at least partial satisfactions were readily available. When advertising played the delicate game of stirring up ambitions and fears, it did so to direct the energies released into a system-affirming purchase of commercial products. If depression affected the style and the themes of some advertising, it did not change its purpose. A staggering economy meant that advertising must concentrate intensely on its work, indirectly reinforcing its role as an industry of assurance. Whether anxieties were rooted in the immediate crisis or in long-term social and cultural transformations, the central message of advertising was that, with the help of modern goods, things were ultimately going to be okay.

## Sounding out the Movies

The descent into depression overtook a movie industry in the midst of major transition and explosive growth. At the turn of the decade the revolution driving silent pictures into oblivion through the triumph of the "talkies" was just striking with full force. Careers were ending or taking off based on an ability to accommodate new forms as the whole industry explored how sound might serve both art and commerce. Many of the films of the early thirties that were still making the adjustment seem technically crude by later standards, and the actors frequently clung to the exaggerated gestures and expressions typical of the silent era. Yet even as the depression lurked at the industry's door, sound was being fully assimilated to give many of the movies produced after mid-decade an integrated quality that continues to satisfy.

This conjunction of internal transformation and external pressure only begins to suggest the range of forces that shaped the movie business during the 1930s. Claims of commerce and culture, politics and art—individually and in combination—tugged on, molded, and burnished the images and values that gave life to the films of the period. Like advertising, the movie industry tried both to read public tastes and to alter them, to respect the strength of existing attitudes and to stretch their limits. But films were tied to a less constrictive purpose than advertisements, and they were freer to respond more emphatically and more disparately to varying impulses and shifting concerns.

Moviemaking in the thirties was formed and reformed by audience reactions, by discoveries about the power of the movies, by moral-cultural pressure groups, by political developments inside and later outside the United States, by the ambitions and calculations of those who controlled the industry, by the individual vision of particular directors, by idealism, and by humbug. Early films of the thirties demonstrated the sense of liberation as well as the degradation and the bleakness that could accompany an experience of social collapse; in the later thirties movies rallied far more around traditional themes and positive ideals, especially as Americans weighed the nature of democracy and contrasted it with fascism and communism. This larger pattern and the dynamics that swirled within it told a multifaceted story about the culture of the period.

Between 1928 and 1930, thanks in part to the arrival of sound, average weekly movie attendance leapt upward from 65 million to 90 million, and the industry fairly glistened with confidence. One-third of this audience disappeared as the economy sank into the trough of 1933. When the general upturn began in 1934, the movies, like other industries that attracted discretionary consumer spending, tended to recover more quickly than older basic industries like steel and lumber. In the second half of the thirties, weekly attendance stabilized between 80 and 90 million in a population of between 30 and 35 million households. Moreover, throughout the decade the movies consistently attracted about 20 percent of all that Americans spent on recreation (as opposed to less than 3 percent a half-century later).[26] In retrospect, the film industry suffered less than many others during the depression, but no such comfort was available to the major studio and theater conglomerates during the skid from 1930 to 1933. At the worst point, almost one-third of all theaters had closed; admission prices had been forced down from 30¢ to 20¢ on average; and four of the eight large movie companies were in a state of collapse. Moviemakers, like advertisers, reacted to hard times with an intensified competitiveness seldom restrained by the boundaries of taste, and they delivered products with a tone and content provocative to established sensibilities.

A surge of interest in social issues during the early 1930s carried with it a certain eagerness to confront conspicuous problems in their sordid detail. In the case of the movies, this tide merged inextricably with a topical exploitation of crime, sex, and political corruption motivated, as one historian has put it, by the "crassest expediency." Movie companies shaken by declining receipts were alert to "whatever forms of shock or titillation would lure audiences into theaters," and they looked for "settings that provided the fullest opportunity to raise the pitch of excitement on the screen, to amaze, frighten and even sexually arouse."[27] Leading actresses, including Greta Garbo, Tallulah Bankhead, Marlene Dietrich, Jean Harlow, and Irenne Dunne, were, or became, prostitutes or mistresses in a striking number of early 1930s movies that tended both to exploit sexuality and to confine women to a dependent identity. The frightening or bizarre found ample expression during 1931 and 1932 in *Dracula*,

*Frankenstein*, *The Mummy*, *Murders in the Rue Morgue*, and *Freaks*. Some of the famous images from the films of these years brought together sex and violence (and sometimes horror), as in the case of Fay Wray in the arms of *King Kong* (1933), or James Cagney assaulting Mae Clarke's face with a grapefruit in *The Public Enemy*.

Sound in films became a method of seeking stronger effects through its ability to shape a whole environment, to build suspense or shock, and to make telling use of colloquialism or innuendo in spoken language. (Anyone who has listened to a horror or suspense movie with the volume turned down will understand the difference sound can make.) Moviemakers quickly learned to use music to intensify mood and reaction, and song or dance situations provided new possibilities for conveying romantic or sexual suggestion. The sheer number of films being produced—some 500 each year meant that the range of topics was wide and that the quest for "shock or titillation" was a trend rather than a dominant mode. Yet that trend, combined with the lust for new material that a high level of production required, created an openness to new themes and a mixing of values and styles that was emblematic of the early thirties.

Changes in mood and outlook, combined with the quest for sensation, had more than enough power to reconfigure cultural stories like those the movies told. A tale that began with the experience of Robert E. Burns can stand as an example. Burns had been implicated in a robbery attempt, convicted, and subjected to the brutal rigors of a southern chain gang; having escaped to build a new life, he was betrayed by a lover back into chains once more, only to flee again. With dramatic and sometimes formulaic elaborations, Burns's story, *I Am a Fugitive from a Georgia Chain Gang!*, was serialized over seven months in *True Detective Mysteries* in 1931 and was then published as a book. The real Burns ended up as a tax consultant in New Jersey, but this was hardly the stuff of popular drama.

*True Detective Mysteries* belonged to a type of "confession" magazine (*True Story*, *True Romance*, *True Confessions*) that gained a major following in the 1920s and built to a peak of popularity in the 1930s by publishing what appeared to be first-person accounts of the extremes of experience and emotion. Bernarr Mcfadden, who owned several such magazines, employed a staff of writers to shape the "confessions" and a clergyman to ensure that all stories had a moral ending to redeem their content. In the hands of the Mcfadden team, Burns became not simply a standard victim but something of a success hero for his rise by initiative and hard work after his first escape. Moreover, when it became clear that the strongest reactions to the story centered on its exposure of chain gang conditions, Mcfadden's writers simply turned their hero at the last minute into a committed social reformer who declared, "It's now my life's ambition to destroy the chain gang system." With this twist, the narrative adapted smoothly to the growing concern with social issues and evils.[28]

The story took another turn in 1932 when it was made into a film, *I Am a Fugitive from a Chain Gang*, directed by Mervyn Leroy. Building in part on a

Edward G. Robinson as Rico in *Little Caesar* cuts down those who stand in his way along the path of upward mobility, only to die alone as the ultimate consequence of his criminal ascendance. Tensions between the values of success and of morality, between violations and affirmations of social order, enlivened many of the gangster movies of the early 1930s. Iconographic scenes of confrontation such as this one would appear by mid-decade in G-man films and Westerns, where the protagonist stood clearly on the side of justice in vanquishing evil. *Museum of Modern Art/Film Stills Archive*

host of early depression prison movies filled with themes of stifling confinement and innocence punished, *I Am a Fugitive* not only attacked the arbitrary torments of the chain gang but also suggested a society in which creativity and industry were frustrated, in which the law was estranged from justice, and in which the individual had little control. At the end of the film the protagonist is neither tax consultant nor crusading reformer but a desperate, hunted man. When asked by his wife on a last furtive visit, "How do you live, Jim?" he responds before disappearing into the darkness, "I steal." One scholar has found this moment "the absolute nadir of hopes and possibilities as depicted in the movies."[29]

The film's ending took its cue from the bleak outlook of the depression at its worst. Yet even in 1932 hopelessness and despair did not typify any common national feeling, and some theater owners complained that the ending of

*I Am a Fugitive* spoiled the picture or "left a bad taste." Bleakness honestly rooted in its cultural setting was not necessarily more meaningful or more legitimate for its audience than the formulas of *True Detective Mysteries*. The same basic story could be packaged and repackaged to create variations on themes of morality, success, reform, and despair, with each version playing out the possibilities for emotion and sensation, whatever its thematic intent.

A flamboyant pairing of social issues and lurid effects, pliant to a range of potential meanings, also characterized the cycle of gangster movies in the early thirties. Leading examples of the genre, including *Little Caesar* (1930), *The Public Enemy* (1931), *Smart Money* (1931), and *Scarface* (1932), concentrated their attention on individual gangsters who were generally of lower-class immigrant background and who were always driven by a passion for power and wealth. To fit what became the standard pattern, the individual at the center of the story had to achieve substantial success in his "business" only to face ruin or death at the end. The mixture of criminality, aspiration, and ultimate failure at the core of these films made for disparate and sometimes confused reactions from the start.

An early outcry in some quarters condemned the seeming glorification of gangsters: in cities like New York and Chicago censors made significant portions of their cuts from gangster movies; liberal magazines as well as conservative attacked the lawlessness of the type; and there were the requisite congressional hearings. Yet people flocked to the theaters to see gangster films, which economically hard-pressed film studios could not take lightly. Will Hays, president of the Motion Picture Producers and Distributors of America (MPPDA), suggested that too heavy an emphasis on gangsters was undesirable, but he claimed in his 1932 annual report that the films successfully taught that "crime does not pay."[30] Warner Brothers sent a major gangster picture to theaters with instructions that publicity campaigns should not emphasize the gangsters so much as the law. Some of the films attached prologues reminding viewers that the all too successful and exciting characters they were about to see were evil. Such efforts were roughly equivalent to Mcfadden's clergyman attaching moral maxims to confession stories. The assertion of respectable values struggled against a clear public attraction to vitality and violence that threatened to counter their effective force.

Later readings of the gangster films have reached conclusions no less divided than the claims of contemporaries. One interpretation holds that though the attraction to social outlaws during the worst of the depression is an important reflection of the period, the standard gangster movie was primarily an assertion of faith in older formulas for achieving success. The young hoodlum fights his way upward through ambition, drive, talent, hard work, and, within his peculiar context, self-discipline and good character (Rico in *Little Caesar* avoids both alcohol and women). Yet because the only believable path to success in those years stood outside the law, and because such success could not be affirmed directly, the hero has to meet finally with destruction or death.

The central fact remained, as this reading would have it, that familiar values were being reasserted in an unfamiliar context.[31]   Another interpretation explicitly rejects claims of the success myth at work.  Rather, the gangster movies were films of "social pathos" reflecting in the lives of their main characters the "social conflicts and disorders" of the period.  The films indicated that the gangsters' "chaotic lives were more than matched by the chaos in society around them," for "their friends, their rivals, the police, all seemed capable of greater dishonesty and disloyalty than they."[32]   There was no reaffirmation in the face of depression in this view, but only the anxieties of a world out of joint.

Writing in 1948, the critic Robert Warshow suggested that gangster movies conveyed a more complex network of implications within American culture. The gangster to Warshow represented the city of the American imagination— the antithesis of the romanticized countryside—and he was thus identified with the direction in which the modern industrial world was traveling. Possessed of the "city's language and knowledge, . . . its queer and dishonest skills and its terrible daring," the gangster-hero raises himself over others with a brutal assertion that betokens an "unlimited possibility of aggression," representing for modern Americans "what we want to be and what we are afraid we may become."  A deep dilemma of American culture and the success myth thus emerges: all efforts to succeed involve aggression; every drive to stand out from the crowd leads to loneliness; and as the conventions of gangster movies insist emphatically, there is danger in being alone.  The gangster asserts himself as an individual and must die because of the separateness this entails. Success "is evil and dangerous, is—ultimately—impossible," in the imaginative world of the gangster film.  The gangster's death provides a temporary resolution for what is really a wider cultural dilemma.  Tensions between country and city, past and future, communal identity and individual achievement, become, in Warshow, tragic contradictions.[33]

Elements of culture are nearly always open to some range of manipulation. Nevertheless, the variant readings of the gangster films, like the differing themes and endings attached to the chain gang story, point toward an unusual fluidity of value commitments in the early thirties, a willingness in American culture to entertain different ideas or forms, an openness linked nervously to the insecurities of the moment.  Robert Sklar has found the Disney cartoons of these years "magical," "free from the burdens of time and responsibility," part of a world "plastic to imagination and will"—in all, a reflection of the "exhilarating, initially liberating, then finally frightening disorder of the early depression years."[34]   Mickey Mouse was a creature of fantasy and occasional lust in the escapades of his youth.  During these same years, Mae West's sharp tongue and suggestive presence affronted limitations on sexuality and women's roles: Robert Forsythe (the Communist party pseudonym of Kyle Crichton) declared in *New Masses* that West "epitomizes so completely the middle-class matron in her hour of license," "so obviously represents bourgeois culture at its apex," that she would "enter history as a complete treatise on decay," while "such children as Katherine Hepburn" would be rapidly forgotten.[35] The Marx Brothers comedies of the early thirties, meanwhile, subjected respectability and predictability to a verbal and physical dismantling. As one student has put it, "Absurdity has never had it so good in American film" as between 1930 and 1934.[36]

This mood was not to last. By the release of the Marx Brothers' *Duck Soup* in late 1933—a film that held up to ridicule patriotism, leaders, and government itself—audience attitudes had shifted and the film did not do well. Mickey Mouse, at about the same time, was turning "respectable, bland, gentle, responsible, moral."[37] Mae West met with restriction and began to fade. And actors who had played leading gangsters were reappearing on the screen as defenders of the law.

Several developments came together in 1933–34 to change the tone of the film industry. Perhaps most important, the arrival of Franklin Roosevelt and the New Deal altered the country's mood, with the evidence of the shift sometimes strikingly explicit in the movies themselves. Three of the most successful film musicals of the decade appeared in 1933—*42nd Street*, *Gold Diggers of 1933*, and *Footlight Parade*—all of them offering plenty of singing, dancing, and glittering escapism but also telling stories of people who got a break or had an idea that opened the door to success. This renewed optimism seems to be tied to a tangible source when in the last number of *Footlight Parade*, the dancers hold up flash cards of the NRA Blue Eagle and a smiling Franklin Roosevelt. The musicals came from Warner Brothers, where a degree of enthusiasm for the New Deal ran contrary to the heavily Republican preferences of film industry leaders during the thirties. So did *Wild Boys of the Road* (also 1933), a social issues film in which a battle between homeless youths and police gives way to resolution by a compassionate judge (looking a bit like Roosevelt) who presides under the sign of the Blue Eagle. The *Motion Picture Herald* suggested that the conditions portrayed were already passing and that theater owners might promote *Wild Boys* by acknowledging the remedy of the New Deal's Civilian Conservation Corps (CCC).[38]

Other forces pressing for change in the tone and direction of the movie industry during 1933–34 drew on persistent anxieties over the capacity of films to shape cultural values. Both private organizations and public boards had long worked to control what they regarded as the immoral or socially dangerous possibilities of the movies and, preferably, to turn them into bastions of acceptable middle-class standards.[39] The MPPDA had appeared in 1922 to promise industry self-regulation in the wake of scandals, and in 1927 and 1930 the organization had issued specific lists of rules and exclusions covering movie content. These regulations proved a permeable barrier for the entrepreneurial, aggressive, and often flamboyant leaders of the film industry. Meanwhile, conscientious concern over the influence of the movies, especially on children, led to an extensive investigation by psychologists, sociologists, and educators under the auspices of the Payne Fund, resulting in 12 volumes of evidence and conclusions that began to appear in 1933. Although most of the studies were cautious in their claims and tended to emphasize the variability of individual responses, they did hold that movies could have a strong influence on the young, rivaling schools and homes in shaping ideas and attitudes (whether for good or bad), and that movies had encouraged antisocial behavior in at least a fraction of young delinquents. Popularized and misrepresented, particularly through the book *Our Movie Made Children* (1933), the Payne Fund studies provoked a considerable response and a hurried MPPDA promise to promote high moral and artistic standards by beginning work at once on films of improved quality.

Shortly thereafter, a burst of interest and organizing by the Catholic church brought a centralized national thrust to the reform campaign that older Protestant efforts had lacked. After six months of agitation and preparation, Catholics were asked in April 1934 to sign pledges of support to the Legion of Decency, which condemned "vile and unwholesome moving pictures." The legion found a receptive audience not just among Catholics but among many Protestants and Jews, claiming 11 million members within ten weeks. More as a result of the implicit threat than any evidence of reduced movie attendance, the MPPDA established the "Production Code," which held, among other things, that "law, natural or human, shall not be ridiculed"; that "correct standards of life . . . shall be presented"; and that the "sympathy of the audience shall never be thrown to the side of crime, wrong-doing, evil or sin." The producers and distributors named one of the Catholic activists, Joseph Breen, to administer the code. For the rest of the 1930s, Breen would have a sometimes extraordinary power to review movies and scripts and to block the making or release of films containing material to which he objected.[40]

The shift in public mood and the pressure on films to become more responsible and respectable marked a distinct turning away from negativism and disorder. Positive images of authority and social unity now came to the fore. This by no means erased the reliance on sensationalism, for the Production Code left ample room to exploit the exciting malevolence of crime and corruption so long as it was ultimately countered on the screen. Moviemakers quickly found ways to modify tested formulas to suit new demands.

By 1935 the film industry was bending over backward to reverse its gangster-movie treatment of officers of the law (and by implication, of government itself) as invisible or ineffective. This inversion of cultural messages was no simple matter controlled by the industry alone. In the early thirties a set of real gangsters, including Al Capone, Dutch Schultz, Legs Diamond, Mad Dog Coll, and John Dillinger, had become symbols of both criminality and the weaknesses of law enforcement. With his emphasis on local authority, Herbert Hoover had downplayed any national responsibility for dealing with crime. Roosevelt's attorney general, Homer Cummings, by contrast, along with the director of the Federal Bureau of Investigation (FBI), J. Edgar

Hoover, set out not just to run the gangsters to ground through a series of con-victions and shoot-outs but to publicize the federal anticrime campaign and make the FBI a heroic model of modern law enforcement that less effective local police might eventually copy. Representatives of the federal government were made heroes by conscious design.

The publicity for the new films starring federal agents gave them explicit political significance. *Public Hero Number One* (1935), according to its adver-tisements, was a "public service" that allowed people to "see Uncle Sam draw his guns to halt the march of crime." In publicizing *G-Men* (1935), Warner Brothers claimed that "the last hold of the criminal mobs on the imagination of the public will be broken by this picture which shows criminals as they really are—and how helpless they are when the government really starts after them."[41] Perhaps because it was the first of the federal agent films in 1935, *G-Men* carefully justifies the decision of its leading character, played by the for-mer gangster star James Cagney, to join the FBI. Cagney and Edward G. Robinson (who played the good guy in *Bullets or Ballots* (1936), a "mirror reverse of *Little Caesar*"[42]) could still be tough, but they now delivered their sensationalist quota of toughness and violence in the name of law and order. Cowboy heroes could perform a similar function as part of a pseudohistorical process of bringing civilization to the West. Having lost much of their popu-larity during the early thirties, westerns came storming back into town by mid-decade with their affirmative tales of evil and corruption giving way before the forces of progress and prosperity. Celebrating law-bringers and— in two different senses—the building of nationhood, the classic G-man and cowboy films were "almost national pageants"; in an America still struggling against depression, they were "metaphors for the country's unity."[43]

Another kind of film characteristic of the later thirties delivered an affir-mation of social unity in quite a different way. The "screwball comedies," like many major box-office successes after 1934, relied little on explicit violence or blatant sexuality. Rather, they prospered by cultivating a spirit of wackiness that made the rich seem appealingly idiosyncratic, that poked fun at social pre-tension, and that pushed acceptable standards (and plots) toward their break-ing point, only to pull up at the end in rousing reaffirmation of basic social arrangements. Given charm by talented stars, including Cary Grant (in sev-eral roles), Douglas Fairbanks, Jr., Katherine Hepburn, Carole Lombard, Irene Dunne, and Jean Arthur, the screwball comedies developed enormous appeal through films like *My Man Godfrey*, *Nothing Sacred*, *Easy Living*, *The Awful Truth*, *Holiday*, *Joy of Living*, and *Bringing up Baby* (all 1936–39). Social tensions were not ignored in these comedies; indeed, they were often their direct or indirect subject. But apparent divisions of class, conflicts between rural and urban, and frictions between men and women were explored only to be ultimately overcome.

Depending on how strictly and by what elements one attempts to define the boundaries of the genre, Frank Capra can either be considered the most

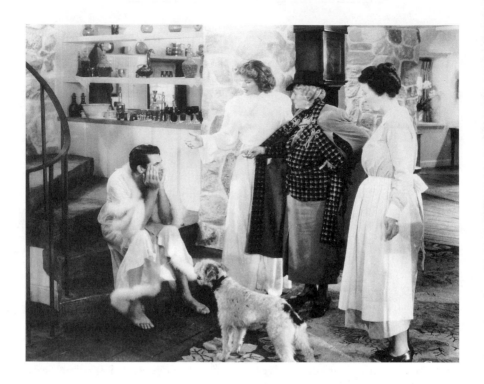

In *Bringing up Baby*, Katharine Hepburn (Susan) and Cary Grant (David) race through a series of incongrous episodes that affront decorum and stodginess while ultimately affirming the existing order, a pattern characteristic of the immensely appealing "screwball comedies." The quick-talking, rambunctious, leopard-capturing Susan is a strong heroine who controls the action of the film. David acknowledges the obvious when he declares, "You can think much faster than I can." Yet where Susan maneuvers the plot is toward a predictable romantic ending, offering little threat to traditional gender roles. *Museum of Modern Art/Film Stills Archive*

important of the screwball comedy directors or not in the genre at all. His tremendously successful film of 1934, *It Happened One Night*, plays on a developing romance between a sharp-talking, shallow-pocketed urban reporter (Clark Gable) and a spoiled rich girl rebelling against parental control (Claudette Colbert). The two are ultimately married after the intervention of the fundamentally wise and caring father, who welcomes the personal strength and integrity of the reporter compared with the weakness and fortune-hunting of the playboy to whom his daughter had been engaged. The values of self-reliance, ingenuity, and integrity could cut across class lines and link the businessman-father with the aspiring young man, and they could attract the daughter away from more flighty beaus, affirming both social unity and social strength. In *Mr. Deeds Goes to Town* (1936), starring Gary Cooper, Capra's trademark emphasis of the late thirties on the virtues of traditional small-town America, on neighborliness and common sense, on genuine responsibility and social feeling, reached full-blown expression.  Having inherited a fortune out of the blue, the village-minded Longfellow Deeds travels to the city, shows up the scheming lawyers and the pretensions of high society, and wins the heart of the initially cynical woman reporter, who has replaced the millionaire daughter as heroine.  When Deeds, who plans to distribute his unearned wealth democratically by buying small farms for the dispossessed, is called insane by the lawyers, he triumphs in a final courtroom scene that brings city and country together in the embrace between him and the reporter and in the celebration of the common people around them.

Capra's emphasis on unity took another turn toward the end of the 1930s as a consciousness of world politics, and especially the Nazi threat, produced a fervent interest in reasserting the basic principles of democracy.  In *Mr. Smith Goes to Washington* (1939) and *Meet John Doe* (1941), Capra told tales of an American political system threatened by the powerful and corrupt, with clear references in each film to the present dangers of fascism.  Two simple, idealistic heroes, played by James Stewart and Gary Cooper, combat political machines and conniving villains whom they can counter only with massive popular support from the plain and decent folks of the land.  Common values and an everyday hero demonstrated the power of democracy and the combined ability of the American people to stand up against political evil.  Perhaps only Walt Disney made films that pleased as wide an audience as Frank Capra's in the 1930s.  In Capra's reconciliations of social differences, in his visions of small-town values triumphant, in his celebrations of the people, there were unquestionably strong elements of fantasy; but it was, or became, a collective fantasy that large numbers of Americans clearly wanted to endorse.

The themes consciously developed in the movies, of course, represented only one layer of the meanings they conveyed.  Whether films offered visions of order restored, affirmations of work-centered values, or celebrations of a culture rooted in the mythic American village, they also held out images of competing worlds that might be entered through mimicry or consumption.  The impact became apparent in the stream of women at beauty parlors wanting hair like Jean Harlow's and in the enduring life of the "platinum blonde."  When Clark Gable undressed in *It Happened One Night* and revealed that he wore no undershirt, sales of men's underwear went into a steep decline.  Strategy replaced happenstance through conscious advertising tie-ins, and no one outdid Disney's merchandising division, which reported 147 contracts to produce 2,183 different items based on the cartoon figures in *Snow White* alone.  The development of an economy relying more heavily on consumer goods went hand in hand with a culture more cosmopolitan in its contacts and tastes.  Films could provide models of how to live in a world of goods, of how to look or travel or order in a fancy restaurant, even as they seemed to promote a social allegiance to small-town verities.

A climactic scene in *Mr. Deeds Goes to Town* brings together distinctive elements of Frank Capra's unifying vision. Longfellow Deeds, played by Gary Cooper, is a small-town, folksy, community-oriented soul whose mental competence is challenged by established power and wealth when he tries to use his recently inherited millions to purchase land for small farmers. Jean Arthur plays a workingwoman, a city newspaper reporter, whose layer of cynicism is melted away by Deeds's sincerity and whose urban sophistication is brought to the aid of village values. When good deeds (providing land deeds) are upheld by a wise judge and the authority of law, justice and romance triumph as the two lead characters are raised together on the shoulders of the crowd and acclaimed by the common people, with George Washington looking on. *Museum of Modern Art/Film Stills Archive*

In addition, relationships with more than a surface complexity existed sometimes between nicely wrapped up endings and the spirit of the characters portrayed. If independence and career nearly always gave way at last to love and marriage for the heroines of screwball comedies and other films, many women characters nevertheless conveyed images of competence and spunk. The "battle of the sexes" at the heart of many screwball comedies, one critic has claimed, was "a battle of equals" that limited male authority for the sake of a "larger equilibrium." The fondness for "smart, crackling dialogue" in the thirties allowed women to show intelligence and self-possession: "The more a heroine could talk, . . . the more she seemed to define herself by her own lights."[44] Strong heroines carried the possibility of challenging gendered social conventions even as they seemed, in the end, to be reconciled to them. In a similar vein, Capra's Longfellow Deeds, Jefferson Smith, and John Doe have been interpreted by one scholar as characters whose "comic disengagement" from society represented "a form of radical criticism," whose "somewhat childlike" idealism had teeth.[45] Capra's celebrations of the significance of the individual and his insistence on the importance of moral choice can strike viewers as a powerful social critique, as sentimental melodrama, or as one wrapped within the other. On matters of both behavior and character, implicit cultural messages often stood in tension with explicit themes, and the contradictions and balances within the movies helped define the experience they offered.

Off-the-screen models sometimes provided important support for the representations that appeared in film. In stretching dominant notions about the capabilities of women, for example, Amelia Earhart helped lead the way. In 1928, she became the first woman to fly the Atlantic, and in 1932 she became the first to do so alone. The first pilot, male or female, to solo from Hawaii to the mainland (in 1935), she was also a lecturer, editor, and airline vice-president before her disappearance over the Pacific in 1937. Popular culture sounded echoes of Earhart. When the magazine *Pictorial Review* promoted itself in 1931 by celebrating "the change that has come to woman," it emphasized the point with a picture of a stylish modern woman looking upward toward a helicopter knowing that "even the skies are hers."[46] And before *Bringing up Baby* and *Holiday*, Katherine Hepburn played a record-setting pilot in *Christopher Strong* (1933). Yet if real models of accomplishment and heroism contributed to images in the movies, the hoopla surrounding the movies more often tended to obscure real achievement and to devalue its worth.

Entertainment and fantasy made a bid to overwhelm reality for those drawn most strongly to the manufactured flamboyance that was Hollywood's trademark. The business of promoting films and stars was an exercise in exaggeration, in gaseous inflation, in emotional overkill. Movie publicists made the exclamation point their most common form of punctuation and seemed to pride themselves on overreaching: one film was "Packed with power! Racing with romance! Teeming with thrills!" while another blurb proclaimed "Sock! At the heart, at the funny bone, at the tear ducts, at the purse strings." To heighten the impact of horror movies, theaters were advised to hire a nurse and a person to faint at each performance so that the stricken viewer could be carried to an ambulance past those waiting in line. The difference between what was real and what was staged became increasingly blurred even for the illusion-makers themselves, as the contemporary observer Margaret Farrand Thorp recognized in referring to "the searchlights and spots, without which Hollywood would not believe in the opening of even a filling station." Events sometimes took their very eventfulness from self-conscious fabrication.

The careers of the stars depended heavily on image and reputation shaped by constant attention. The cultivation and consumption of celebrity kept the press agent actively employed, supported the Hollywood gossip industry (dominated in the thirties by Louella Parsons), and provided an audience for the breathless reporting in fan magazines. The most important requirement for a star in the magazines was "personality," which, as Thorp recognized in 1939, suggested some of the tensions or competing desires in American culture. "Personality" in this context suggested less a way of getting along than a denial of modern standardization, a consumer's version of individualism. To gain personality and individual distinctiveness, avid fans copied fashions and behavior with a seemingly contradictory awareness that many others were doing the same thing. The stars were pictured as glamorous, wealthy, and exciting, yet also as commonplace or, as one editor put it, "very much like you and me." They were held up as examples of the traditional virtues of hard work, energy, and perseverance yet often seemed to have been finally successful only when struck by the lightning bolt of being "discovered." They belonged to both the world of work and the world of play. No single set of values, no unitary notion of success, came out of the Hollywood magazines, but a blending and blurring of competing values that fed similar composites in the minds of many readers and reflected something of the menu available in the culture as a whole.[47]

Social and cultural tensions of a different kind sprang from the nature of the filmmaking industry and the characteristics of its leading figures. Hollywood was a boom town in the still-developing West, with plenty of raw edges and showers of money for the successful, the clever, and the lucky. Many of its studio moguls, most of them Jewish, were immigrants (or the children of immigrants) who had tended during the growth of the industry to be at once extravagant in their ambitions, pretensions, and appetites and sensitive about their reputations and social status. One current that arose from this milieu affected the content of several major films in the later thirties. The "better" movies after 1934 reflected not only public preferences and pressures but also the ambitions of a younger generation of producers who identified Western culture as their own and pictured themselves as gentlemen and natural leaders. Big-budget films with historical settings, based on classics or best-sellers, provided both profit and claims to respectability. Led by three of the younger producers, Irving Thalberg, David O. Selznick, and Darryl F. Zanuck, Hollywood turned out between 1934 and 1939 *David Copperfield*, *Anna Karenina*, *Les Miserables*, *Mutiny on the Bounty*, *The Good Earth*, *Romeo and Juliet*, *Marie Antoinette*, *A Tale of Two Cities*, *Gone with the Wind*, *Rebecca*, and biographies of Louis Pasteur and Emile Zola.[48]

However well these films served to demonstrate cultural seriousness and belonging, they could not erase suspicion of Hollywood in traditional bastions of cultural power. The "movie colony" on the far fringe of the country was envied, resented, wondered at, and looked down upon in the intellectual centers of the East. Literary people in particular chafed and gaped at a spectacle that both drew them in and threatened to supplant their authority. Hollywood could and did pay talented writers inflated salaries, attracting people like F. Scott Fitzgerald and William Faulkner as well as hosts of others, yet the producers often treated writers as hired hands or technicians, and the credit for good films went elsewhere. By the later thirties, moreover, intellectuals were acutely conscious of the idea of cultural myths and of the role of social communication and propaganda. In the past, the cultural functions of describing and interpreting the world had generally fallen to people who "had come from similar ethnic and class backgrounds and had utilized the same means— the written and spoken word."[49] Now a new group, of different background, exercising authority over a different medium, seemed to possess a culture-shaping force of indeterminate potential. The commercialism of the movies, their extravagant promises of vicarious experience, and (with the example of fascism at hand) their possible influence over the mass of people, all provided cause for apprehension. Critics struggled to balance cultural anxiety and fears of displacement against fascination with the creativity and power of films.

One unsettling vision of what Hollywood might mean in American culture incorporated a number of these reactions into a tale of fantasies accepted, frustrated, and unleashed: Nathanael West's 1939 novel *The Day of the Locust*. West's Hollywood is a land in which the artificiality, illusion, and false promise of the movie screen intersect with reality and enter into the lives that people are actually trying to lead. A field of discarded movie sets constitutes "a dream dump" presenting its own history of civilization, for there is no dream that will not eventually turn up there, "having first been made photographic by plaster, canvas, lath and paint." To West, this exploitation of dreams and the wider cultural pattern of sensationalism and exaggerated promise to which it contributed were far from benign. California was filled with people from across the country who had been drawn there by fantasies of luxury, excitement, and fulfillment only to meet with frustration and boredom—and in the mass, their repressed bitterness was dangerous.

At the end of his book, West describes a crowd waiting at a movie premiere for a glimpse of arriving stars. Individuals and families, unassuming on their own, turn "arrogant and pugnacious" as they merge with the crowd. A radio announcer stands amid the massed bodies proclaiming, "A veritable bedlam! What excitement!" and so on, all in a "rapid, hysterical voice . . . like that of a revivalist preacher whipping his congregation toward the ecstasy of fits." And the crowd rises to the stimulus. West saw a people made "savage and bitter" by an existence that fell short of expectations. A life of dull striving and the promises of leisure had led them to the land of sunshine and oranges, but once there, "nothing happens. They don't know what to do with their time. Their boredom becomes more and more terrible. They realize they've been tricked and burn with resentment." West's premiere turns to riot, flame, and apocalypse. What Hollywood portended for modern society was a pervasive disappointment that threatened to destroy all concepts of meaning.[50]

West's vision, concerned as it was with the relation between the imagined and the real, derived in part from actual incidents. The Persian Pleasure

"Dodge City, Kansas . . . A general view of the tremendous crowd that turned out in Dodge City to welcome the cast of Warner Brothers movie story of the wild and woolly days of that city. A trainload of glamour came from Hollywood to attend the premiere of the movie [3 April 1939]." The power of the newer media of communication and entertainment to stir mass audiences aroused both hope and anxiety in the 1930s. Early movie premieres, stirring up the emotions and expectations of a crowd, had sometimes threatened to get out of control and escalate into riots. The process of spreading out the premieres, staging them to take advantage of the local and historical appeal of new films, and framing them with dignitaries and pageantry had by the end of the thirties made this form of mass gathering seem celebratory, democratic, and safe. *UPI/Bettmann*

Palace in *The Day of the Locust* seemed to mimic the exotic appeal of Sidney Grauman's Egyptian and Chinese Theaters—scenes of some of the more elaborate movie premieres of the late 1920s and early 1930s. The opening of the Chinese Theater in 1927 with the premiere of *King of Kings* attracted 25,000 people, and the newspapers reported the story under the headline, "Hundreds of Police Battle to Keep Crowds in Check." The throng at the premiere of *Grand Hotel* at the Chinese Theater in 1932 broke through police lines and nearly flooded into the theater itself; at the gala for *Strange Interlude* a woman's leg was broken in the crush of the crowd; and the 1933 premiere of *I'm No Angel* came "very close to a dangerous street riot." The premieres represented a particularly volatile situation when the worlds of on-screen fantasy and off-screen actuality were suddenly blended in the street, when screen idols were paraded in front of an agitated and expectant crowd that was itself denied admittance to the show inside. They clearly suggested that the movies and popular culture could arouse audiences in ways that escaped social and cultural controls. West saw this explosive possibility in the premieres of the early thirties, but he did not see what had happened to such events by the time he wrote.

The movie premiere by the end of the decade, according to its closest student, had exchanged the pursuit of "carnival splendor" for a "spirit of civic festival," with the energies generated flowing into an affirmation of public, and often patriotic, values.[51] It became the fashion during the thirties to "take Hollywood to the nation" by staging premieres in cities and towns around the country, usually involving large segments of the area's population and building upon local pride. *The Buccaneer* (1938) was first shown in New Orleans, *The Texans* (1938) in San Antonio, and *Brigham Young—Frontiersman* (1940) in Salt Lake City. *Dodge City* (1939) opened in its namesake after a train carrying not only the requisite stars but also the equally essential film crews, news commentators, and a broadcasting studio arrived from Hollywood to be greeted by three governors and local dignitaries dressed in costume for the occasion. Omaha went further for *Union Pacific* (1939) with weeks of costume-wearing, false fronts on stores, a Sioux encampment, and celebrations upon the arrival of the appropriate train. While West had allowed his imagination to play darkly in the gap between dreams and reality, the premieres had been democratized to build bridges from Hollywood to Omaha and link glitz with community traditions.[52]

The impact of the movies did not remain confined to the screen in the 1930s but reached outward to blur the lines between entertainment and news, fantasy and reality, public relations and public values. Unquestionably the movies were driven by commercialism, and often they were dominated more by crassness than by craft. Perhaps it was also true, as Daniel Boorstin would later argue, that the ready-made dreams of movies and the media interfered with citizens having real social dreams.[53] Yet we may want to reflect a bit further. The movies traced and exaggerated broad swings in public mood during the 1930s; they also explored more particular tensions and aspirations. Neither the films themselves nor the publicity mechanisms of the industry offered a unified message about American society. What they did was to give expression to competing values, to seek tentative resolutions, and to leave audiences with room for choice. Such contributions may not be insignificant to the process of adjusting meanings within a culture. After mid-decade, one attitude did become relatively fixed—a positive and increasingly emotional support for the idea of effective government and of democracy. From a viewpoint skeptical toward existing social institutions and practices, this was a retreat from a much-needed stance of questioning and challenge. From another perspective, it was a demonstration that a culture undergoing modernizing transformations of economy and values, when threatened by depression and international crisis, retained enough vigor and cohesiveness to channel the force of popular culture toward holding the society together rather than ripping it apart.

## *The World on the Radio Dial*

Radio had entered American life after World War I and developed rapidly in the 1920s. During the thirties it claimed a central place in what was, thanks in part to its influence, an increasingly *national* culture. As technological advances made radios smaller and less expensive, ownership spread rapidly despite hard times. By 1935 twice as many American homes had radios as telephones; the number of households with at least one receiver—12 million in 1930—had risen to 28 million by 1939 (covering about 86 percent of the population).[54] Social workers reported during the depression that families would give up furniture or bedding or most anything rather than their radio—whether because it offered entertainment, something to fill the time, or a sustaining emotional link with a larger community. Even more strongly than the movies, radio brought a certain commonality of experience to much of the country through its most popular programs, and for better or worse, it worked a kind of erosion on local and regional distinctions of language and custom. Still a relatively new phenomenon, radio stood ready to serve those who could exert their control or discover its cultural uses.[55]

In 1927 Congress had tried to bring order to the growing industry by creating the Federal Radio Commission (FRC) to license stations and regulate the frequency and power of transmitters. Over the next few years a system of national networks emerged led by the National Broadcasting Company (NBC), with its blue and red networks, and by the smaller but dynamic Columbia Broadcasting System (CBS). Arguments over the control of radio continued to be waged vigorously during the early thirties by commercial interests, proponents of educational use, and advocates of tighter government control or ownership. Whatever the merits of the various cases, those seeking changes in the way the industry was developing found it difficult to overcome the advantage of broadcasters and sponsors associated with national shows that had a strong popular following. The establishment of the Federal Communications Commission (FCC) in 1934 brought no dramatic changes. The FCC proved more interested in preventing broadcasting offenses than in establishing positive requirements for the type and quality of radio fare, an attitude that allowed neither constructive guidance nor threatening control. Radio would remain primarily a commercial medium.[56]

The open debate over control sometimes masked a quieter evolution in values: a shifting understanding of the boundaries between public and private. At the beginning of the decade, commerce was still restrained by assumptions about integrity, privacy, and good taste. Whereas the movies had climbed upward from lower-class origins, radio had at first been associated with the upper classes because of receiver costs. This association reinforced the tendency to emphasize the special nature of the radio-listener relationship. Unlike the movies, radio did not pull together a mixed audience of people in a public place; it entered the private arena of the home and spoke to the intimate family circle. Only gradually did it come to seem acceptable to admit advertising to the parlor. The brief mentions of sponsorship permitted before the late 1920s first gave way to commercials interspersed throughout the program and then, in 1931, as the depression took hold, to direct statements of price, which networks had earlier prohibited. Standards were indeed changing when a manufacturer could combine the declaration that its cigars cost 5¢ with the elegant hygienic assurance, "There is no spit in Cremo!"

As sponsored radio programming searched for its largest possible audiences, the depression provided a context for other shifts in the content of home entertainment as well. (To measure the popularity of specific programs, Archibald Crossley organized the first national ratings system for the Association of National Advertisers in 1930.) Declines in other communication and entertainment industries sent a flood of performers into radio early in the decade, perhaps most notably from the collapsing world of vaudeville. At the beginning of 1933, the most popular show in the country, according to the Crossley ratings, featured Eddie Cantor (sponsored by Chase and Sanborn coffee). Other comedy and variety shows with vaudeville ties were legion, including those starring Ed Wynn (Texaco), Al Jolson (Chevrolet), Rudy Vallee (Fleischman's yeast), the Marx Brothers (Esso), Jack Benny (Canada Dry), Fred Allen (Linit), and George Burns and Gracie Allen (Robert Burns cigars). As some noted appreciatively at the time, such upbeat comedic shows were most popular when the depression was at its worst.

Advice shows also seemed to evoke a special response as conditions worsened, generating programs based on various systems, from astrology and numerology to palmistry and success charts. A man known on the air only as "The Voice of Experience" claimed by 1933 that some two million people had sought his counsel, and Haley's M-O was reported to have increased its sales severalfold as a result of sponsoring the show. Advertisers promoted special mail-in offers to encourage ties between the audience and their products, and radio stars were regularly identified with particular brands in print advertising as well. With the distinctions between them rapidly eroding, commerce and entertainment marched together into private homes, and the listeners who reached outward to offer their personal problems to the purveyors of public advice collaborated eagerly in blurring the lines between public and private.

A similar blurring, in a different form, was implicit in the spread of a relaxed, mellow, smooth-voiced style that in singers was identified as "crooning." Part of what crooning seemed to involve was an effort to convey to listeners the sense of a friendly, personal relationship with the public per-former or announcer, a relationship that denied the scale and distancing implicit in mass communication. Some crooners also displayed the "person-ality" touted by Dale Carnegie and the movie magazines, contributing to an intensifying interest in personalities during the thirties—or, as Reuel Denney has put it, in "the consumption of other people's personalities."[57] Easing the anxieties of impersonal scale, the presumed intimacy of crooning and the per-sonal element in personality signaled a cross-migration of values that helped fit the public institutions of mass media to private expectations, and vice versa.

Radio's relationship to social and political events presented a different set of issues and evolved through a different pattern of developments. Companies sponsoring radio programs craved large audiences to maximize their advertis-ing exposure and generally tried to offend no one; this priority often led to programming caution and a wariness about social issues. By the midthirties the assumption was clearly established that sponsors paying for a show could determine its content—a kind of corporate censorship over prime broadcast-ing periods. Sponsors tended to keep their distance from news programs and to shiver at the prospect of controversy. In 1935, when Alexander Wolcott criticized Adolf Hitler on "The Town Crier," for example, Cream of Wheat canceled the program after Wolcott refused to promise he would make no such remarks in the future. One significant exception to the sponsors' know-noth-ing attitude toward current events was "The March of Time" on CBS, sup-ported by *Time* magazine. This was hardly a news show in the later meaning of that term, but a weekly dramatization of current news events by actors with the support of sound effects, music, and scripting. Sometimes a product more of imagination than reporting, the program nevertheless suggested promising possibilities for radio that would require developments in technology, an evo-lution of principles, and the demonstration of popular appeal.

Ample room remained for the evolution of radio's public information role because sponsors by no means laid claim to all broadcast time. In 1931 about 65 percent of the scheduled programming on NBC and 75 percent of that on CBS was not sponsored. The demand for material to fill this time was most often met by playing music, yet the available hours also provided room for experiment and, increasingly, for new kinds of shows. Various staged demon-strations had shown that sound could now be sent around the world. In 1930 the networks had broadcast speeches and news reports from a naval confer-ence in London. This experience led to a series of talks over CBS by promi-nent British politicians and authors, and these in turn helped frame questions about the intellectual principles and responsibilities appropriate to public broadcasting. When George Bernard Shaw ruffled a good many feathers by speaking favorably of the Soviet Union, a Catholic priest from Georgetown University was given time for a critical reply—an important moment for radio's slowly developing notions on the free exchange of ideas. In June 1933 the political columnist Walter Lippmann and the economist John Maynard

Keynes in London took part in what was billed as the first broadcast of a conversation between people on different sides of the ocean. Although limited in their immediate impact, such programs held out the prospect that radio could engage rather than evade public issues.

The importance of broadcasting to politics changed with the arrival of Franklin Roosevelt. The Republican and Democratic parties had earlier purchased airtime during presidential campaigns to broadcast set speeches, and huge audiences had been able to tune in to a major event like Hoover's inauguration (some 65 million). But Roosevelt as a politician was made for radio: he created a relaxed, "personal" contact as successfully as any announcer or performer, and he drew enough mail to make any advertiser jealous. Other politicians, and those seeking to influence politics, took to the airwaves as well. Father Coughlin, the "Radio Priest," built his reputation and following almost exclusively through broadcasting. Huey Long fattened his reputation on a rich diet of media attention and made skilled use of the radio and of sound trucks in his campaigning. Critics of agricultural policy could reach a scattered farm population through radio, as Milo Reno did between 1934 and 1936 in talks over station WHO in Des Moines. And Liberty League radio addresses were an important part of that organization's effort to unseat Roosevelt. The pattern, as it came to fullest definition in the year or two before the 1936 elections, seemed to suggest the power of the mass media to give a wider hearing and national exposure to legitimate but volatile voices, with an impact on national politics that was then hard to predict.

In other instances, the only clear impact was to demonstrate that radio's power was completely undiscriminating: whether hollowness, geniality, or substance predominated, almost any radio presentation could strike a responsive chord in at least some substantial part of the radio audience. W. Lee O'Daniel used a radio show jingle to sing his way to the governor's seat in Texas. Mayor Fiorello La Guardia endeared himself to New Yorkers when he read the comics over the radio during a 1937 newspaper strike. The Supreme Court nominee Hugo Black, accused of earlier membership in the Ku Klux Klan, helped defuse the issue by explaining himself in a radio talk, keeping the door open to a distinguished judicial career. In each instance, radio provided an opportunity to reach large numbers of people directly. The blending of the serious and the farcical reflected an absence of broadcasting controls, as well as wariness before the thought that any single standard might actually become controlling.

Discoveries about the power and possibilities of radio were meantime accumulating in other spheres through a combination of aspiration, experimentation, and accident. After 1935 William Paley led CBS in introducing new programming ideas, most of which made use of unsponsored network time. NBC's John F. Royal reacted to CBS gains in the "vaudeville tradition . . . of competing marquees": "He watched the marquee across the street. Any strong move called for a similar but more spectacular countermove."[58] When

93

CBS announced a Shakespeare series with distinguished actors for Monday evenings in the summer of 1937, NBC responded with a John Barrymore Shakespeare series scheduled at the same time. Because CBS was winning a positive response by airing the New York Philharmonic, NBC formed its own orchestra, directed by Arturo Toscanini. The CBS show "American School of the Air" prompted NBC's "University of the Air," and two poetry series squared off in like fashion.

Perhaps the most irksome CBS program to John Royal was "The Columbia Workshop," which had been established in 1936 specifically to provide a context for experimentation. Early shows were often built around the discovery of specific sound effects that led to ideas about how to use them—as spaceships, ghosts, echoes, or whatever. The major landmark for the program, however, was an abstract commentary on international politics contained in Archibald MacLeish's verse play, *The Fall of the City* (1937). The play encouraged experiments with both verse and narration, especially after it made a major performer out of a young actor named Orson Welles. The closest parallel at NBC to "The Columbia Workshop" came through the work of Arch Oboler, whose creativity and technical abilities allowed midnight listeners to prepare for sleep by listening to the beating of a chicken heart as it grew to engulf the earth or to sound effects suggesting a man being turned inside out. The plays presented on both networks used unsponsored time to stir the imagination through radio in ways that movies (and later, television) could not easily match.

On occasion, the qualities of the medium and the circumstances of the moment meshed with extraordinary power, leaving a permanent mark on radio history. One such moment struck without warning on 6 May 1937, as the announcer Herbert Morrison was reporting on the arrival from Germany of the zeppelin *Hindenberg*. Morrison had a breathless, excited speaking style—the kind that some announcers used to manufacture enthusiasm for predictable or staged events. When the *Hindenberg* as it was being moored burst into flames before Morrison's eyes, and as people leaped from it to their deaths, real drama overtook the artificial style, and Morrison became virtually hysterical. Listeners were pulled into the middle of the tragedy, and what they heard was almost overwhelming. Both CBS and NBC to this point had observed strictly a rule that all material except sound effects had to be produced live; shows heard nationally were regularly performed twice by the actors to suit different time zones. So powerful was Morrison's broadcast that NBC suspended this sacred rule to allow replay, and large numbers of people were immersed in an experience of unprecedented intensity.

Real dramas began to unfold with rising frequency as events in Europe and innovative commentators pushed radio news toward the center of listener consciousness. The realm of unsponsored time now played a part in the struggle to define the nation's values in foreign affairs. In 1936 H. V. Kaltenborn, a 58-year-old journalist, traveler, and radio broadcaster, set out to cover the

Spanish Civil War, paying his own way at a cost greater than the $100 per week he was receiving to do two broadcasts for CBS. In one of his most notable ventures, Kaltenborn established himself, with an engineer, on a finger of French territory reaching into Spain that was in the middle of a battle; with a microphone planted in a haystack to pick up the sound of live fire, he then transmitted to the United States a report that was audibly from the front lines of war. In Spain, Francisco Franco led fascist forces that were attempting to overthrow an elected socialist government. Franco was soon receiving direct support from Germany and Italy; the government and its supporters (the Loyalists) gathered some aid from the Soviet Union and from politically motivated volunteers from many countries. The United States, along with Britain and France, maintained a posture of nonintervention. In his several broadcasts on Spain and in the talks he gave upon returning home, Kaltenborn's mix of reporting, interpretation, and opinion criticized nonintervention and suggested the likelihood of a wider war in Europe. The Hearst newspapers and others, by contrast, tended to refer to the Spanish government as the "reds" and to the fascists as "insurgents" or as the "Franco regime." The power of local and regional newspapers was under challenge. Americans were being offered two different versions of the conflict from two different sources of "news." Radio was helping to mount a communications revolution that was altering the cultural world just as the transportation revolution had altered the physical world in the century before—shrinking distance and expanding the range of contacts.

If newspapers remained confident that theirs was the greater influence, that attitude would change in 1938. CBS had shipped a new program manager to Europe the year before—28-year-old Edward R. Murrow. Expected to act as a supervisor not a broadcaster, Murrow broke his mold in March 1938 during the *Anschluss*, Hitler's anticipated occupation of Austria. Informed by William L. Shirer, a veteran reporter on Germany then in Vienna, that German troops had crossed the border, Murrow flew into Austria to cover the story while Shirer hastened to London, where he could transmit an eyewitness report. On 13 March, CBS accomplished a major feat of radio technology and reportage by coordinating from New York a sequence of on-the-spot accounts from London, Paris, Berlin, Rome, and Vienna (the last being Murrow's first major broadcast). News reporting from Europe had reached a new level, and Murrow, Shirer, and an expanding staff kept up their reports as Hitler began to turn his attention toward Czechoslovakia.

When the Czech crisis came to a head in September—with threats, war preparations, appeals, and concessions leading up to the legendary appeasement at Munich—CBS offered extensive coverage that was reinforced by an only slightly less thorough NBC. For 18 days, from 12 to 29 September, radio listeners could follow the tense European situation through regular reports from major capitals and hear the voices of the leaders of Germany, Italy, Britain, France, and Czechoslovakia. Kaltenborn held the news together for

CBS with at least 85 separate reports during this period, reading European bulletins and commenting, translating from German and French, explaining when necessary, sometimes staying on the air for two hours at a time. The news now took priority over sponsored shows, which were canceled right and left.

This change in broadcasting style and technology was a sign of where news reporting was heading. Leading commentators were actually beginning to attract sponsors themselves, and some became celebrities whose incomes shot skyward. CBS received some 50,000 fan letters on its Munich coverage. That coverage had brought prestige to news operations, which were now expanded in preparation for the war that seemed certain to come. During the crisis, Murrow had opened a report with, "This . . . is London," a phrase that would become famous through his landmark broadcasts during the German bombing in 1940; it added to the growing emphasis on trademark expressions and identifiable personality in news reporting. In the winter of 1937–38, a study had found that more than half the people surveyed preferred to get their news reports from newspapers rather than radio; by the month after the Munich crisis, better than two-thirds declared they favored radio. Radio news no longer stood on the fringes of broadcasting or of American culture.[59]

The Munich coverage and the events it described also helped set the stage for one of the most extraordinary episodes in radio history. On 30 October 1938, CBS presented as part of its "Mercury Theater on the Air," led by Orson Welles and John Houseman, a rewritten theatrical version of H. G. Wells's story, "The War of the Worlds." In preparing the script for the show, Houseman and others had worried that it was too unreal to hold much of an audience, and the network had required script changes to make it seem even less authentic. The story described a Martian landing and assault on the New Jersey countryside—not a tale that would seem to demand immediate credence. The method of telling, however, once the initial announcement of the show was past, mimicked the news techniques so recently established in people's consciousness: a presumptive regular program was interrupted for a "special bulletin"; the musical show returned only to be interrupted again with updates and eyewitness reports of creatures emerging from spaceships; reports seemed to come in from various locations as the story developed. Significant numbers of listeners throughout the country took what they heard on the radio at face value. Calls flooded in to newspapers and police stations; people in the New York to Philadelphia area tried to flee in their cars; panic struck individuals and groups in several locations; and an electrical failure convinced a town in Washington State that a final calamity was indeed at hand.

The relationships that could develop between creative work and the tensions of a period was never more clearly in evidence, and the credibility that radio could achieve was never demonstrated in more startling fashion. One commentator after another pondered the nature of the panic, the presence of preexisting fears, and the implications for mass movements thus implied. Interruptions for news broadcasts in fictional works were banned from radio. Was the "Mercury Theater on the Air" destroyed? On the contrary, the evidence of its impact drew the attention of sponsors, including a soup company, and it soon became "The Campbell Playhouse." Radio, like the movie premieres, obviously could stir popular passions; the inescapably pertinent question for the thirties was how and by whom such mass energies might be controlled. In the case of radio, the fate of the "Mercury Theater" suggested an answer from practice. Just as premieres were democratized into docility, radio's potentially explosive power to communicate and convince came under regulation in part through the very eagerness of advertisers to harness that power to the cause of profit.

Although radio plays and news coverage had flourished in the freer realm of unsponsored time, radio in the United States remained a business eager for the income advertising provided. When successful innovative ventures found sponsors, they gained regular support but often faced limitations as well. Campbell Soup did not want another panic. Likewise, with an eye to avoiding controversy, networks during the late 1930s and early 1940s tried to restrict commentators with a clear point of view from shaping broadcast news, preferring the presumably more objective notion of "news analysts." Because radio was a business, and because the networks reached a huge and diverse audience in a nation of competing values, standards emerged that tended to soft-pedal the conflicts between those values and to dampen the medium's potential to stir up fundamental controversy or destabilizing passions.

The main diet of sponsored programming, meanwhile, concentrated on a few successful formats. The evenings still belonged to comedy and variety and to a new efflorescence of quiz shows. Sports broadcasts, especially of singular events, could attract even larger numbers; the listening audience for the Joe Louis–Max Schmeling boxing match in June 1938 set the record for the 1930s. An increasing number of daytime radio hours were being sold to soap operas, which took their name from the advertising that accompanied them. Originating in 1931, these never-ending formulaic dramas had multiplied to 12 by 1933, 19 by 1935, 31 by 1937, and 60 by 1940.[60] Daytime programming also included shows based on conversation and interviews, for which Mary Margaret McBride was perhaps the leader, and advice programs hosted by sponsor-invented "personalities," like "Beatrice Fairfax" on romance, "Betty Crocker" on cooking, and "Betty Moore" on decorating.

The listeners were not all the same. Studies indicated a split between the audiences for soap operas and for "reality-oriented" shows of interviews and advice; neither group generally listened to programs of the other kind. Yet interestingly, both groups seemed to seek information and guidance from the radio in their contrasting ways. In the case of soap operas, this quest was less obvious, but interviews with listeners demonstrated that many valued the stories because they seemed "real" and that people looked to the radio serials for examples of how to be attractive or relate to a spouse or handle children. The characters in soap operas were generally either helpers or in need of help, and some listeners joined the process by writing to characters to offer suggestions or guidelines of their own. In brokering specific ideas about how to deal with others, how to appear, or how to behave, the soaps and the direct advice-giving shows provided their audiences in different ways with opportunities to test their own values, to give and to receive advice on how to live in a changing world.

Radio during the 1930s evolved not just around issues concerning its own emerging practices or the problems posed by the depression but around questions arising out of an ongoing cultural transition. Like *The Three Little Pigs* and the literature of success, radio programming juggled tensions between work and leisure, discipline and indulgence, character and personality. Like the advertising that helped support it, radio offered guidance on the proper treatment of modern ills and paid a homage to the family sphere, even as it helped to undermine the private nature of that sphere and absorb some of its functions. Like the movies, radio provided models of speech, style, and behavior and offered experiences of wider worlds both real and imagined, often suggesting potential tensions with localism or the habits of the past. Although sometimes an agent of change, the radio industry seldom set out to sharpen or define the conflicts of values that were a part of its necessary business. Rather, it sought to balance or combine, to blur exact distinctions, to present, within limits, a variety show of behaviors and values. The effect was almost certainly to help ease and contain the tensions of culture and politics; individuals and audiences of varying commitments were left with the space for (and the burdens of) interpretation and choice.

There was one important exception to the pattern of mixed representations: the coalescence around a central idea of American political-cultural identity. Radio brought European politics into American homes and tracked the advance of fascism with growing concern. In the process, its reports and commentaries helped sharpen a definition-by-contrast of the United States as a country pledged to democratic liberties and resistant to any monolithic appeal. From this perspective, the presence of different groups and values in American culture became evidence of a unifying national commitment, and by extension, a meliorative treatment of conflicts among the parts verified the presence of an enlightened understanding of the whole. Although this idea would be developed more directly elsewhere, its sometimes piecemeal emergence in the realms of popular culture gave evidence of its potent appeal and usefulness. The economic pressures and cultural tensions of the 1930s were powerful and real, yet they were frequently overmatched by a revivified American belief that multiplicity was not just consistent with, but the very heartbeat of, a cohesive democratic nation. Wherever it appeared, this message asserted its stabilizing claim.

## Studying the Media

In the sweeping survey *Recent Social Trends in the United States* published in 1933, the authors of the section on "The Agencies of Communication" noted that the new machinery had the capacity to create "mass impression," that these impressions necessarily affected individual "attitudes and behavior," and that the direction of modification depended "entirely on those who control the agencies." The simple existence of mass media posed questions of power and values. "Greater possibilities for social manipulation, for ends that are selfish or socially desirable, have never existed," the authors went on. "The major problem is to protect the interests and welfare of the individual citizen."[61]

These remarks conveyed an acute awareness that mass communication technology might work for good or ill depending on the wielding. They also implied a belief that "the interests and welfare" of citizens might easily be recognized, and that the "socially desirable" could be readily distinguished from the "selfish." Yet who would control such a winnowing was just as important a question as who would control the media. In a 1935 promotional brochure for advertisers entitled "You Do What You're Told," CBS publicists claimed that seven or eight or nine times out of ten, people obeyed instructions from voices representing authority or caring, and that radio, not other advertising media, could provide such voices.[62] Whether these claims represented threat or promise, cynical manipulation or good marketing, the selfish or the socially desirable, depended on one's point of view.

The contemporary social scientists who examined the newer forms of popular culture, and particularly radio, often found themselves caught up in their own dilemmas of competing outlooks and unyielding assumptions. In *Radio and the Printed Page* (1940), Paul F. Lazarsfeld (who directed the Office of Radio Research at Columbia University) explored the impact of broadcasting on reading, reporting in an "optimistic" vein that "radio has not impaired the reading habits of the population" and that "if properly used radio offers a rich opportunity for the promotion of reading." The question, the conclusion, and the notion of "proper" use all implied a traditional mainstream belief in information and education as engines of progress. Yet Lazarsfeld suggested potentially serious limitations on this capacity for progress in arguing that the consequence of radio depended on "the social forces prevailing at a certain time"; the medium reflected its context, and in that sense, it could be understood as "a stupendous technical advance with a strongly conservative tendency in all social matters." In the United States this tendency shaped the industry so as to serve the ends of capitalism and commerce; in another social context (German or Russian, perhaps) it might work to conserve quite different arrangements. Whether the bias in favor of prevailing social forces was consistent with an "optimistic" view of radio's educational potential, Lazarsfeld did not say.[63]

Hadley Cantril and Gordon W. Allport presented *The Psychology of Radio* (1941) as the first attempt to describe "the new mental world" created by the medium, and they emphasized, in keeping with a common posture in the social sciences, the need for a "strictly objective and dispassionate attitude." Their language hardly seemed dispassionate, however, when they spoke of radio as an "altogether novel" medium, "epochal in its influence" and "preeminent as a means of social control"; a medium that "thrilled" romantic souls while evoking in "reflective souls" a feeling of "helplessness and dismay." More than a hint of trepidation lay behind their declaration that soon "men in every country of the globe will be able to listen at one time to the persuasions or commands of some wizard seated in a central place of broadcasting, possessed of a power more fantastic than that of Aladdin." And their reminder that radio development took its shape from the society's "framework of political and economic philosophy" seemed grounds for concern when it introduced an analysis of advertising as propaganda.

Yet at other points Cantril and Allport sang a hymn to radio as "by nature a powerful agent of democracy": "Distinctions between rural and urban communities, men and women, age and youth, social classes, creeds, states, and nations are abolished. As if by magic the barriers of social stratification disappear and in their place comes a consciousness of equality and of a community of interest." Radio brought an almost unlimited expansion of experience, overcoming poverty, parochialism, and loneliness, and it served the "middle classes and the underprivileged" as "a gigantic and invisible net which each listener may cast thousands of miles into the sea of human affairs and draw in teeming with palpable delights from which he may select according to his fancy." Such lyrical celebration had a tenuous connection with the image of a broadcasting industry shaped by propaganda or with the pose of dispassionate objectivity, yet here all were intertwined. The reactions of social scientists to the new medium, like those of many in the general population, constituted an intellectual and attitudinal balancing act that blended hopes and fears about the modern into an evolving effort to grapple with contemporary life.[64]

Not all responses tried to bring off a feat of balance. Many assessments of popular culture entered into an old debate about the uses of leisure and the desirability of popular entertainments. Montaigne in the sixteenth century welcomed diversion, variety, and escape as healthy antidotes for isolation and the pressures of life, as Leo Lowenthal once noted, while Pascal in the seventeenth condemned constant activity and distraction as a source of great unhappiness.[65] More recent commentators of the nineteenth and twentieth centuries, assuming aristocratic or elite traditions as a background, tended to split between those who praised the spread and democratization of leisure entertainments in popular culture and those who complained of qualitative deterioration and the loss of the true character of art. If some, including those involved in industries like radio and film, were quick to indulge in inflated celebrations of the newer media in the 1930s, others were just as quick to condemn everything associated with popular culture as a mess of pottage.

Lowenthal, whatever his consciousness of contrasting traditions of argument, aligned himself squarely behind a harsh critique of the mass media and their output. Associated with the Frankfurt School, a group of German intellectuals who shared a general social theory strongly influenced by Hegel and Marx, Lowenthal had fled Hitler's rule and, along with several of his colleagues, arrived by 1934 in the United States. In the late 1930s and early 1940s, the radical outlook of these émigré social philosophers influenced a number of American intellectuals and joined with native complaints against commercialization to help produce a general critique of popular culture that Lowenthal sought both to advance and to summarize. Whereas art consisted of "genuine experience," popular culture amounted only to "spurious gratification." The decay of true individuality in modern "mechanized" society made for an "unbearable reality" from which the media offered escape through "a false fulfillment of wish dreams, like wealth, adventure, passionate love, power, and sensationalism in general." Lacking any of the attributes of "genuine art," popular culture offered a diet of "standardization, stereotypy, conservatism, mendacity, manipulated consumer goods," all following the model of advertising. In Lowenthal's argument, with its greater concern for theoretical analysis and political commitment than for attention to specific cases, even the presumably "objective" exploration of the mass media by the social sciences became little more than an agency of control: social research was really "nothing but market research, an instrument of expedient manipulation." Popular culture in this description was simply a blunt tool that economic and social elites could use to control the masses and to resist fundamental change.[66]

Elements of this characterization must be given their just weight. Much of popular culture makes little direct effort to raise the level of human insight, to intensify cultural meaning, to express the aspirations of either intellect or beauty, or to expand the limits of expressive forms—even if particular examples may stand to the contrary. Mass entertainment exhibits high levels of repetition, the formulaic copying of familiar patterns and plots, and the simplistic exploitation of emotions and desires. A commercial framework with profit as an end and advertising as a means encourages such tendencies and often fences in popular culture behind boundaries of manner and content. It is hardly surprising that in a capitalist society commercial products do not develop any acute critique of capitalism. Yet it is important to acknowledge the truth in the claim that popular culture often works to strengthen and justify existing social and economic relationships, just as it is important to recognize the legitimacy of opposite fears, such as those expressed by the Legion of Decency and other morally cautious groups, that popular culture can undermine traditional standards and values. This double nature both encourages and mollifies evolving tensions within a culture.

In looking to only one side of the picture, Lowenthal provided an argument that was narrowing and occasionally dogmatic. By insisting that the media could offer "nothing but entertainment and distraction," his analysis denied the value that entertainment may have, left itself helpless to explain the best products of popular culture, and failed to grapple with the power and appeal of the materials in question. Writing at the same time, the critic Robert Warshow took a less traveled path in trying to comprehend the real attractions of popular culture without dismissing the idea of aesthetic standards. He had seen a "great many very bad movies," Warshow reported, but he had "rarely been bored" by them; when he had been bored, it was usually "at a 'good' movie" with artistic pretensions. What was needed was "a criticism of 'popular culture' which can acknowledge its pervasive and disturbing power without ceasing to be aware of the superior claims of the higher arts."[67] The critic had to begin with perception, not with an outlook that predetermined response and restricted scope.

The emphasis on the false and manipulative nature of popular culture in the Lowenthal argument took for granted the power of elites to control tightly the content and the impact of the media. Lowenthal's argument not only assumed a greater unity of authority over the production of popular culture than ever existed, it also assumed a ready receptivity and a complete absence of discrimination in mass audiences. Such a position largely denied the presence of significant variety of content or quality in the materials of popular culture; it downplayed the possibilities of multiple responses and different understandings of media creations that might stand apart from any structured intent; and it ignored the capacity of individuals and groups to give meanings of their own to elements of popular culture. According to Lowenthal, the "prevailing view" of the people's taste was that "only the bad and the vulgar are the yardsticks of their aesthetic pleasure." There was little room left, once such blinders were put on, for seeing popular culture with any complexity or for finding in it anything but degradation.

The question of what to make of the media and of mass audiences attracted increasing attention from intellectuals at the end of the 1930s and beyond. Although the issues involved were not entirely unprecedented, they were substantially reshaped by the emergence of new means of mass communication between the world wars, and they were shadowed by the looming presence of fascist and communist movements and regimes. Those trying to read the import of the newer media looked to an experience that was short and often contradictory; every effort at description quickly became tangled with conclusions. The radio audience could be understood as a scattered body of individuals and families making independent choices, or as an aggregated mass controlled by a distant voice. Popular culture could be hailed as democratizing and as a solvent of class inequities, or castigated as a tool of elite domination and a threat to the very basis of democracy. The media could be described as breaking down parochialism and allowing all to have "cosmopolitan interests" (Cantril and Allport), or as demeaning to everything that deserved the name of culture. And more specifically, radio could be praised for bringing Americans closer to events, or maligned along with other forms of popular culture for providing artificial experience that separated them from reality. The issues were difficult ones, and assessments of the popular media often implied judgments on all of modern culture. Perhaps it is no wonder, then, that the work of intellectuals reflected tensions between ideas, and an ongoing dance of values, fully as much as the media they evaluated.

*four*

# American Culture
# and American Cultures

The structure of beliefs and assumptions supporting expectations of white Protestant dominance in the United States had many parts. Among its central tenets was the conviction that industrial society was superior to all others past and present: modern Western society belonged where many social thinkers had placed it, at the highest level yet attained in a sequence of stages marking human progress from savagery to civilization. Because northern Europeans, and particularly Anglo-Saxons, had presumably created the most advanced societies (including that of the United States), the conclusion seemed obvious that white and predominantly Protestant peoples had a particular aptitude for the material progress and democratic self-government that marked their ascendancy. By extension, people of other "races"—within a loose use of the term that frequently extended to distinctions of religion or nationality—had to have a lesser aptitude, with the degree of their inferiority proportionate to their distance from the economic behaviors, political institutions, social and religious practices, and educational forms of the prevailing model. Physical appearance, even among groups of Europeans, was often assumed to reflect these varying capacities. The "culture" that accompanied advanced civilization consisted of those works of intellect and art adjudged the best products of historic tradition, primarily the tradition of western Europe traced back to Greece and Rome. The United States was an outpost of this tradition but had as yet contributed little of its own to higher culture. It was in any case clear that culture, whether inherited or borrowed, belonged primarily to the affluent and the educated.

In the first decades of the twentieth century, at least four overlapping but distinct patterns of intellectual development began to challenge these conceptions of society and culture. First, the emerging field of anthropology was gradually taking the lead in a fundamental intellectual transformation of the meaning of *culture*. Second, in seeking to demonstrate that America was not without resources of its own, some writers were helping to alter assumptions about where culture came from and who had it. Third, modernist sensibilities in literature and the arts were calling into question dominant social and cultural forms and offering new frameworks of value. And fourth, a cosmopolitan ideal was gaining strength among liberal intellectuals by providing a new model for personal and cultural relationships. During the 1930s ideas associated with each of these patterns reached beyond the limited circles that gave them birth or expanded in new directions to push toward more generous conceptions of cultural worth.

The anthropological challenge to belief in hierarchical stages of societal development took its direction primarily from the work of Franz Boas and his students. Beginning as early as the 1880s, when the German-born Boas spent many months living among the Eskimos and among the Kwakiutls on the Pacific Northwest coast, his writings raised basic questions about evolutionary assumptions. His critique took more general form in *The Mind of Primitive Man* (1911). Boas pointed out that the belief in a necessary progression from simpler to more complex as the only route to higher civilization made technological change, at which Europeans and Americans had excelled, the measure of all societies and peoples. Not only were actual patterns in the acquisition of technology less regular than the theory presumed, but there was also evidence from other spheres, including language, that primitive societies might demonstrate more complex structures than modern ones. Each society, Boas argued, involves a series of responses to particular experiences and conditions and cannot be judged according to standards reflecting an altogether different history. Because meanings and aptitudes are relative to a specific context, systems of ideas presuming to measure "advance" or establish superiority across a range of societies are of no use. From this viewpoint, the "culture" of Western art and ideas has no special claims. Indeed, *culture* should be understood as a broadly inclusive term recognizing the structures of meaning associated with every part and every product of human life.

Although Boas's ideas were not widely influential before World War I, cultural relativism gained supporters in the 1920s both among social scientists and among others for whom the war had only strengthened a skeptical attitude toward modern verities. Near the end of that decade and into the 1930s, a string of works by students of Boas preached the newer anthropological outlook and moved its version of culture into common parlance. In Margaret Mead's descriptions of *Coming of Age in Samoa* (1928) and *Growing up in New Guinea* (1930), less "advanced" societies are presented as dealing successfully with the process of maturation from child to adult; industrial cultures, by contrast, had confessed their difficulties by bemoaning a troubled period of adolescence. The nation of "flaming youth" had to question who might learn from whom. Ruth Benedict's *Patterns of Culture* (1934) emphasizes the "relativity of cultural habits" and the variability of human frameworks for interpreting experience. Benedict contrasts cultures based on competition with those based on cooperation, and she places great significance on the shift away from a single template for "primitive culture" toward the study of "primitive cultures." Because every culture tends to be "integrated" and to embody a "more or less consistent pattern of thought and action," Benedict insists on the need to see each culture in its entirety and to assess the meaning of every ritual, idea, or object in relation to the "whole configuration."[1]

*Patterns of Culture* reached a substantial audience in the 1930s and became, along with Mead's work, a staple of college curricula into at least the 1960s. The newer anthropological ideas opened rich possibilities for research and interpretation that popularizers and scholars were not slow to apprehend. Although some assumed that relativism allowed a neutral stance and attempted to assess cultures, including that of the United States, dispassionately, there was a clear tendency to turn the relativist approach toward a critique of modern (and American) culture for not fulfilling the full range of individual and community needs. Rooted at times in a romanticization of indigenous or peasant societies, such applications—for all their aptness and bite—relied on implicit models of what a culture should achieve, reintroducing a system of judgments that made some cultures "better" than others. Combined with the susceptibility of relativism itself to a relativist analysis, these tendencies left ample room for dispute and for multiple reconfigurations of the protean concept of culture. Yet by the middle of the 1930s, the impact of cultural relativism was undeniable. Belief in fixed stages of civilization within a single model of societal development had fallen into serious decline. Assumptions about cultural superiority and "racial" aptitudes faced a serious intellectual challenge, though they persisted in varying forms. The idea of culture as something comprehensive and inclusive was rapidly taking hold. Indeed, Warren Susman has argued that it was in the 1930s that Americans, discovering this concept, "began thinking in terms of patterns of behavior and belief, values and life-styles, symbols and meanings," producing a spate of popular references to the "American Way of Life" and "The American Dream."[2]

The newer anthropological concepts found a contemporary fit with the mood of self-examination stimulated by the depression. Interest in a more broadly elaborated American culture was compatible as well with an intellectual current just freshening into a stream as the 1930s began: the study of American folk culture. Perhaps no one was more important in providing a rationale for such study and a demonstration of its potential than Constance Rourke. Rourke found in folk materials a response to the charges of inadequacy that Van Wyck Brooks had leveled against American culture in *America's Coming-of-Age* (1915). Brooks had described an aesthetic tradition divided throughout its history between intellect and experience, between a highbrow world of attenuated ideals and a lowbrow world of "catchpenny realities." To create great works of literature that would raise American culture to European levels, American writers needed a grounds for synthesis that had been lacking, a "secure and unobtrusive element of national character" that might provide a "certain underlying coherence and background of mutual understanding."[3] In *American Humor* (1931), Rourke disputed Brooks's analysis at its foundations. With her subtitle pointedly announcing "A Study of the National Character," she presented evidence that the foundations of American literature rested on a culture already unified. Highbrow and lowbrow alike looked to folk humor—to the overlapping comic traditions of Yankee, backwoodsman, and minstrel—for resources of myth and language. Writers on both sides of Brooks's divide shared with popular storytellers a "homogeneous world of the imagination." Within this argument was another assertion: if the roots of literature and art lay among the people, then the folk were both the originators and the possessors of culture.[4]

Rourke's case for a cohesive American tradition shared certain assumptions with the outlook being developed by Benedict (with whom Rourke was privately acquainted), but it was markedly different in attitude and emphasis. Rourke welcomed the anthropological argument for variable forms of cultural development, finding in it a confirmation that Americans had constructed a legitimate culture of their own. Where Benedict saw in cultural relativism a deflation of industrial society's superiority claims and an impetus to social change, however, Rourke discerned a release from the American sense of cultural inferiority to Europe and an incentive to discover the unity and value of American tradition. If American culture deserved to be measured in its own terms and not according to borrowed standards, there was no need to look toward European models in a quest for great works, as Brooks had been inclined to do. Rather, attention should be paid to what made America American, and that meant the culture of the folk in all its legend-creating fertility and in all its practical and decorative inventiveness.[5]

During the 1930s Rourke published three more books: *Davy Crockett* (1934), *Audubon* (1936), and *Charles Sheeler* (1938). She was at work on a broader ranging study at her death in 1941, parts of which were published as *The Roots of American Culture* (1942). Having helped organize a national folk festival in St. Louis in 1934, she became two years later the first editor of the *Index of American Design*. Made possible by the inventiveness of New Deal relief efforts, the *Index* put artists to work across the country seeking out and preparing careful drawings of American textiles, silverwork, furniture, pottery, and the like. Ultimately, some 20,000 examples chosen from the drawings became part of the *Index*, demonstrating a widespread American creativity in the practical arts and crafts that had been little noted or valued as an evidence of culture. Other projects both governmental and private greatly expanded the awareness of folk materials during the 1930s, and a radical interest in asserting that culture came from the "people" provided reinforcement on the left flank. Most of this work carried a nationalistic claim, an assertion of democratic identity sometimes combined, as in Rourke's case, with the belief that folk materials offered a demonstration of cultural unity. Yet such versions of nationalism more often opened up than restricted the possibilities for being "American." An emphasis on culture as an inclusive idea, a concern with common people, an attraction to multiple forms of imagination and creativity, all encouraged attention to a wider range of social groups. As scattered works on particular ethnic and racial traditions were beginning to show, an emphasis on folk culture provided good reason to take the variety of American patterns more seriously.

By the time Rourke was making her case for the worthiness of a national tradition based on folk sources, modernist works in literature and the arts had built a substantial record of using folk, "primitive," and mythological materials to override inherited assumptions and to question the fundamental direction of Western cultures. Modernism challenged the established structures of industrially advanced societies that the nineteenth century had invested with moral meaning. It protested large-scale institutions and their devaluation of individual experience. Modernists both assailed the excessive rationalism of modern life that denied basic human instincts and needs, and questioned whether modern societies were indeed rational. And in variant ways, modernists looked for new forms of expression to probe notions of human fulfillment whose roots were very old indeed. Important intellectual sources for modernism frequently drew attention to the prerational or the irrational. Sir James Frazer's *The Golden Bough* (1890–1915) provided a great compendium of myth, especially the recurring myth of death and rebirth. Friedrich Nietzsche's *The Birth of Tragedy* (1872) stressed the importance of the Dionysiac rapture of emotion and impulse that warred against the Apollonian constraints of ethics and reason. The work of Sigmund Freud spoke of the repression of human instincts and desires in the process of becoming civilized, a theme summarized in *Civilization and Its Discontents* (1930). Among the array of tendencies and experiments that made modernism resistant to precise definition appeared paintings using African masks, novels and poems built around patterns of myth (including that favorite poem of young modernists, "The Waste Land," by the American-bred T. S. Eliot), and music seeking to evoke the primitive, like Stravinsky's *The Rite of Spring*, subtitled "Pictures of Pagan Russia." All became part of the modernist rebellion within, and the modernist continuation of, Western aesthetic traditions.

The modernist use of materials from outside industrial societies was not necessarily compatible with the arguments of cultural relativism. Rather than insisting on the need to see each culture in its totality, modernists borrowed piecemeal and adapted freely. Working primarily from the concerns of the present, most valued the "primitive" not for its equality with but for its distance from the "civilized." Reveling in the problematic and the difficult, modernists created works that could find an audience only among an educated elite; in their politics, especially among writers, modernists were as likely to identify with the right as with the left. Yet the impact of modernism was no servant to the power of intent. Because modernism by critique and example challenged a whole system of social and cultural assumptions, it helped open the way for new attitudes and ideas and provided through its restless experimentalism a stream of postures and techniques that could be turned to quite variable application. The idea of psychological repression became faddish during the 1920s as justification for a looser morality, and notions of self-fulfillment were welcomed into channels of advertising and commerce many modernists claimed to despise. An interest in customs and behaviors regarded as freer, more natural, or more instinctive brought samplings of ethnic and minority cultures into vogue. There was condescension involved in escaping the burdens of civilization by visiting the nightclubs of Harlem, by communing with Indian culture in bohemian Taos, and by romanticizing things Mexican, but there was also, for some, an awakening respect.[6] Meanwhile, the techniques and concerns of literary modernism were shaping the perspective of American writers who would, in the 1930s, produce novels on the Irish of Chicago, the Jews of New York, and a changing South. Modernism was helping to readjust the framework of what might be valued.

A different current of intellectual development that sometimes ran confluently with each of these streams had also gained considerable force by the 1930s. Always a multiethnic society, the United States had added new layers to its evolving complexity with the massive immigration, between the 1880s and World War I, that brought millions of people from southern and eastern Europe to America. This "new" immigration increased the religious diversity of the nation by expanding dramatically the number of Catholic and Jewish Americans and, according to the categories of the day, extended the "racial" spectrum as well. From the 1910s onward, the question of how varying groups might live together in one society presented a problem of major import not only for the world of policy but for the realm of ideas. Among those who searched for paths to coexistence, three significant positions emerged. The first, and the most powerful in the early twentieth century, generally accepted white Protestant civilization as the American standard and looked for an eventual assimilation of other ethnic groups through their conformity to that model. With the training provided by "Americanization" programs and the passage of time, assimilationists believed that ethnic differences and identities should disappear. A second and contrary position, associated particularly with Horace Kallen's "cultural pluralism," rejected any notion of a melting pot and gave primacy to the preservation of ethnic identities. In seeking to maintain and even cultivate feelings of difference as a positive good, ethnic particularism had little to say about what might hold a society of sharply distinguished groups together.

The third position, which can be called cosmopolitanism, stood between the more single-minded alternatives of assimilationism and cultural pluralism, suggesting that differences might strengthen a culture that Americans would hold in common. The national identity of the future would be based not on "Anglo-Saxon tradition" alone but on an inclusive American culture continually enriched by the differences between individuals and groups, practices and beliefs, within the country as a whole. Ethnic traditions would be valued for what they could bring to this larger culture more than for their separateness. A cosmopolitan outlook encouraged ideas that promoted openness and breadth and opposed those deemed close-minded, narrowing, or parochial. Randolph Bourne provided an early statement of such a position in his 1916 essay celebrating a "Trans-National America," and a fledgling model of cosmopolitan cooperation appeared in the mix of Protestants and German Jews who founded the *New Republic*. As the children of East European Jewish immigrants began entering American professional and intellectual circles in large numbers during the 1930s, cosmopolitan assumptions took on added importance, shaping and contributing to some of the more heated arguments of the decade. In part because of the results of those debates and the conclusions drawn from experience with fascism and Stalinism in the 1930s, cosmopolitan assumptions about ethnic interaction became a commonplace of liberal intellectual life in midcentury.[7]

The four patterns of ideas described did not drive opposing values from the field or produce any sudden transformation of American custom and behavior. Those who constructed or adopted the newer ideas were often seeking answers to different questions, and the solutions they found did not point toward a single conception of American culture. They had in common, however, a recognition of cultural multiplicity—of traditions, resources, instincts, needs, and possibilities that made existing frameworks of social hierarchy and aesthetic value seem limited and inadequate. And with gradually accumulating strength from the 1910s onward, they brought to American discourse new angles of vision on the perennial problem of American identity. In the 1930s ideas would combine with politics and policy to begin to reshape some of the most persistent questions of American group relationships, particularly those involving the social and cultural status of Native Americans and African-Americans.

## Attitudes and Indians Reorganized

National policy toward Native Americans changed in 1934 with the passage of the Indian Reorganization Act. In explaining the significance of the new law, Secretary of the Interior Harold Ickes was also shaping attitudes toward American identity and variations on the idea of culture. "Fundamentally," Ickes contended, "the Reorganization Act is a declaration by the Government that the Indian as a race shall have the opportunity to live on; that the Indian civilization, as an element of human culture, shall live on. It means also that the life of the Indian shall not be a segregated or artificially protected existence, but shall be part and parcel of those cultures and interests which, in their aggregate, constitute the United States."[8]

Manifesting the influence of the newer anthropology, these remarks indicated that Native American culture was distinctive and valuable in its own terms. More strongly than cultural relativism, however, they also asserted the larger unity of "human culture," of which any particular society could be only a variation and a part. Where older ideas took "civilization" to imply a desirable modern superiority and newer ideas tried to distinguish the harmonies of "culture" from the unnatural burdens of "civilization," Ickes happily referred to "Indian civilization," avoiding the implicit disparagements of either comparison. Ickes rejected both the sharply separate existence for Native Americans that a strict cultural pluralism might have implied and the melting pot of assimilation. America must be an "aggregate." If the reference to the "interests" that were part of this aggregate had more to do with economic and political conceptions, the use of "cultures" suggested an outlook akin to cosmopolitanism, requiring constant balancing within the national framework between group distinctiveness and an American whole. Ickes's comments were indicative, perhaps, of the way ideas often pass into the public arena. They mirrored no single strain of thought but reflected an understanding constructed through a combination of ideas, and an argument shaped by experience, imagery, and intent. In its effort to envision a multifaceted American identity, Ickes's statement became one of many acts of reorganization in the culture of the 1930s.

The road to the Indian Reorganization Act was neither smooth nor direct. The reigning national policy toward Native Americans had been spelled out in the Dawes Severalty Act of 1887, which removed any legal recognition for tribes as organizational bodies and provided for individual allotments of land, 160 acres to each family head and 80 acres to each single adult. Although the Dawes Act was intended as a reform that would bring Native Americans into American society, the model of the small independent farm that stood behind the allotment plan took little account of Indian culture, the arid nature of much of the land involved, or the development of the national economy. "Surplus" Native American lands not assigned to individuals, and often the allotments themselves, passed over time into the hands of non-Indians, leaving little basis for Indian self-support. When a 1922 proposal in Congress threatened to seize still more Indian lands from the Pueblos, reformers of varying stripe joined with Native Americans and other sympathizers to block the bill, launching a decade of renewed dispute over Indian policy. Assimilationists continued to level their sights on whatever helped maintain or define Native American distinctiveness. In 1923, for example, they supported recommendations to limit severely Indian dancing—branding it "obscene," "superstitious," and "immoral"—as a way of undermining Indian religion. Those mounting opposing arguments drew upon several lines of ideas that had risen in objection to a single model of civilization: the social work magazine *Survey* argued for the centrality of religion in Native American culture, relying on an anthropological approach; D. H. Lawrence expressed a modernist urge to take "an old dark thread from their vision"; Mary Austin praised Indian arts and crafts and called for them to be seen as a "National Asset," a part of the American cultural identity.[9]

The continuing clamor over Indian policy led Secretary of the Interior Hubert Wouk to seek in 1926 an independent report assessing conditions among Native Americans and offering recommendations for change. Prepared by the Institute for Government Research under the direction of Lewis Merriam, *The Problem of Indian Administration* appeared in 1928. Although balanced and sometimes conciliatory in tone, it demonstrated in more than 800 pages the widespread failure of the allotment policy and the evils of Indian boarding school attempts to wipe out Native American culture. Where the report was most original, however, was in its argument that policymakers needed to pay greater heed to the "Indian point of view" and in its suggestion that Native Americans help determine for themselves an appropriate balance of modernity and tradition, assimilation and separateness. Elected in the year the Merriam report was issued, President Herbert Hoover seemed to endorse change in appointing a new head of the Bureau of Indian Affairs, Charles J. Rhoads, and a secretary of the interior, Ray Lyman Wilbur, who genuinely desired to improve the conditions of Native Americans. The policy they enunciated spoke of making Indians self-supporting, whether as individuals or through the incorporation of tribes as entities similar to business corporations. Yet Rhoads and Wilbur still looked primarily toward assimilation. Especially with the coming of the depression, the pace of change crept along far too slowly for veteran advocates. Shortly after his own election in 1932, Franklin Roosevelt received a plea, over more than 600 signatures, that described the condition of Native Americans as "extreme, even tragic," and looked to his administration as "almost a last chance for the Indians."[10]

To whom, then, was Roosevelt to turn for leadership on Indian policy? Knowing that some were calling for the reappointment of Hoover's officials, Franz Boas wrote to oppose such a course, arguing that the two men continued to make the "fundamental error" of the 1880s in assuming that "by administrative measures the Indian can be changed immediately into a white citizen."[11] Boas did not have long to worry. Roosevelt's choice for commissioner of Indian affairs, John Collier, reflected as much venturesomeness as any appointment the new president made. Collier had been hired in the early 1920s as a "research agent" on behalf of the General Federation of Women's Clubs, which was centrally involved in the movement to defend Pueblo lands. Moralistic by nature and a skilled publicist, Collier gained prominence during the decade as a critic of federal policies and of assimilationist assumptions.

Roosevelt turned the controversial critic into an administrator, placing him in the front line of responsibility for defining what the relationship between Native Americans, the federal government, and American society should be.

Collier's ambitions for what came to be known as the "Indian New Deal" began with the goal of "economic rehabilitation." In August 1933 he moved to protect remaining Native American holdings by blocking all sale or transfer of Indian lands. Other steps were taken under the umbrella of the Civilian Conservation Corps. Within four months of Collier taking office, more than 12,000 Native Americans had been put to work on their own lands, with the tribes making decisions on the projects to be done. (Here, the reliance on local authority that sometimes produced conservative and discriminatory results in cities or states carried near-radical implications.) Much of the work did not fit normal patterns for an agency devoted to the reclamation and improvement of public lands. Operating by different rules than the rest of the program, the Indian Division of the CCC demonstrated considerable flexibility and signs of a long-absent cultural sensitivity. Although some Native Americans were housed in typical camps of single men, others lived in family camps found nowhere else in the CCC program, or workers were provided with transportation from their homes. Approved projects helped preserve sites important to Native American culture. And especially after 1938, the Indian CCC taught industrial skills to widen the possibilities for employment. By the demise of the CCC in 1942, the Indian Division had employed 85,000 people, largely on projects connected with their own well-being.

Collier made it a second objective to provide "civil and cultural freedom and opportunity for the Indians." Grounded intellectually in the changing calculus of relative cultural worth, this goal marked an emphatic shift in the assumptions guiding federal policy. An executive statement issued as Circular 2970 on 3 January 1934 made explicit Collier's insistence that Native Americans should have "the fullest constitutional liberty, in all matters affecting religion, conscience, and culture": "No interference with Indian religious life or ceremonial expression will hereafter be tolerated. The cultural liberty of Indians is in all respects to be considered equal to that of any non-Indian group."[12] The right to a distinctive culture was further affirmed in a second Collier order a few days later that gave Native American religious leaders equal status with Christian missionaries at Indian schools—a step disturbing to many Americans for whom the moral and cultural primacy of Christianity was a central tenet. Having declared as well that Indian arts and crafts were to be "prized, nourished, and honored," Collier worked hard for a 1935 law establishing the Indian Arts and Crafts Board to promote craft production as a source of economic self-support and to acknowledge and preserve an aesthetic heritage. These activities edged beyond the provision of cultural liberty to an active cultivation of distinctiveness. Balancing such purposeful direction in federally sponsored reform with Native American freedom of choice would not always be easy.

Collier uncovered some of the possible frictions in his pursuit of a third goal, the "organization of the Indian tribes for managing their own affairs." Working from a skepticism toward modern industrial society that was fairly standard intellectual fare by the 1920s, Collier sought to promote cooperation over competition, the community before the individual, artistic values in preference to material standards. This outlook suggested strongly that federal Indian policy should promote a reattachment to traditional cultures and a commitment to collective ownership and control. Like other visions of community that came from both radicals and conservatives in the 1930s, Collier's hopes grew out of serious social critique and high-minded ambitions without being able to escape elements of paternalism. His first draft of a new Indian rights law emphasized tribal autonomy and authority so strongly that it brought a wave of negative reaction from those Native American leaders who did not want an aggressive assimilationism replaced with a forced particularism. Some saw no reason to reestablish tribal organizations at all—Congressman William Wirt Hastings from Oklahoma, a Cherokee himself, declared that the self-government provisions would turn "the hands of Indian civilization back for a century"[13]—and Indians who had succeeded best as individual property owners did not want to lose their rights. The leader of the New York Senecas decried the bill as a proposal for "mass legislation, which is not applicable to all tribes," and feared that it pointed toward "increased and continued Bureau control." A group from the Five Civilized Tribes detected an unwelcome segregation in the "vicious policy of separating our interests from those of our friends and neighbors."[14] The reactions demonstrated yet again that Native Americans were not, and had never been, of one culture and of one mind. For reformers to make their own judgments or their own dissatisfactions with modernity a reason to decide once again what was "best" for all Indians would have reversed federal policy without improving it.

A redrafting of Collier's bill satisfied some critics and temporarily stole the thunder from others. And in this case, the kind of compromise frequently criticized in New Deal legislation proved a positive good. The Indian Reorganization Act that passed in June 1934 with Roosevelt's timely support combined an endorsement of tribal organization with provisions for choice. The act provided for a considerable degree of tribal self-determination and the right to incorporate for the ownership and management of property. Unsold lands that were part of the "surplus" under the defunct allotment system were returned to the tribes, and $10 million was set aside for development loans to Native American corporations. Yet tribal government and incorporation could only occur if a majority of tribal members themselves voted for such collective organization. Along with a stipulation encouraging the hiring of Native Americans in the Bureau of Indian Affairs, this mechanism of choice provided an important opening to an "Indian point of view" in federal policy, as the Merriam report had recommended. Between 1934 and 1936, 181 tribes representing nearly 130,000 people voted to accept organization under the act, while 77 tribes representing just over 86,000 people voted to reject it.[15] Although these results suggested solid support for the new law, Collier chafed at the rejections, especially the negative vote by the Navajos, who made up the largest single tribe of some 40,000 people. Collier had launched a stock reduction program to prevent overgrazing by Navajo sheep and goats that would lead to soil erosion. Like many other Americans before and since, the Navajos proved less responsive to the environmental danger than to the threat to their immediate interests, and the vote on organization reflected this reaction. Within their own variations of circumstance, the large majority of tribes chose to see reorganization as a positive opportunity.

Swept in by a new broom in Washington, the Indian Reorganization Act brought reform yet made continuing controversy over Indian policy the norm during the late 1930s. Opposition flourished in areas where tribal autonomy, the reversion of surplus lands, and efforts to expand the Native American economic base competed with patterns of dominant local authority and private ambition. A broader critique came from those who remained committed to assimilation, including the members of a small Native American organization, the American Indian Federation, which charged Collier with atheism, communism, and interference with the Indian's opportunity "to enter American life as a citizen."[16] Some saw in the act an effort to push Native Americans back into the past or to force them into a static cultural position. This was not necessarily a criticism to be easily dismissed; Randolph Bourne, in welcoming the refusal of ethnic groups to be melted, had also cautioned against the trap of "arrested development." Yet the better spirit of the Indian New Deal was clearly not an effort to lock Native American culture into a single mold. In 1935 the federal official in charge of Indian education, W. Carson Ryan, argued that "native life itself has values that urgently need to be maintained," but he also went on to say that Native Americans had "an unusual opportunity to combine such advantages as there are in modern civilization with the special advantages of their own culture." This outlook, too, opened the door to choice.[17]

Because Native Americans stand in a unique constitutional relationship with the federal government, changes in Indian policy must come as acts of the nation. More often than not, they reflect shifting attitudes toward cultural difference, changing notions of federal responsibility, and evolving arguments over the meaning of "American." The assimilationist conjunction of political nationhood with a single cultural identity retained a powerful appeal at the end of the thirties. Making clear its hostility to difference and its quest for nationalistic unity, a House committee led by the South Dakota Republican Karl Mundt would complain in 1945 that Indian education was too concerned with Indian culture and too little devoted to turning out real "Americans."[18] The contest over Indian policy would continue because it was a contest over visions of the nation.

For those who welcomed distinct Native American cultures and supported tribal authority, inherent dilemmas remained in the notion that the federal government must be at once responsible for the conditions of Native Americans and committed to their independence and autonomy. Yet the good news from their point of view was that the terrain of debate had changed. With a fresh grounding in ideas and in law, Indian cultures had begun to claim within the larger society an intellectual respect and a cultural recognition that was of fundamental importance. At the same time, Native American communities were themselves compelled to wrestle with questions of organization, economics, and identity. For all the problems that remained, the shift in Indian policy in the 1930s represented an important step toward a more complex and more open American culture.

## *African-Americans: Shifting the Balances*

Whereas Native Americans in 1887 had become objects of an assimilationist policy designed to force them into the mold of the dominant society, African-Americans at roughly the same point had faced a gradual elaboration of systems for their legal and social segregation. These different histories shaped and limited the ways that reformers thought about structures of discrimination during the 1930s or undertook to change them. Ideas that challenged notions of racial or cultural superiority were being used by Indian activists like Collier to uphold the distinctiveness of Native American cultures and provide a legal basis for their separateness. The same ideas served an opposite purpose for many white advocates of African-American civil rights. The liberal New Dealer Will Alexander rejected traditional religious and anthropological claims about racial inferiority as "entirely unscientific." There was simply no sound reason to "give a racial explanation to everything distinctive in the Negro community in America."[19] The battle to be won, in the context of segregation, was not over the right of African-Americans to be separate and distinct but over their right to be integrated and equivalent.

The economic circumstances of the early 1930s also pushed black leaders toward commitment to an integrationist ideal. In the 1920s Marcus Garvey had stirred aspirations toward a separate economy of black businesses and a black nationalist identity, but it was hard to maintain such hopes against the force of a depression that wiped out better than half of all African-American retail stores and savings institutions. Unemployment made worse by discrimination created a bleak picture in most urban communities. And the greater number of black people depended (as they had through the agriculturally depressed 1920s) on the declining productivity of tired fields. Of some 12 million African-Americans in the United States in 1930, over 9 million lived in the South, two-thirds of them in rural areas, where they normally found little margin for survival.[20]  Where was the prospect for sustaining an independent black economy?  An ideal of separatist self-sufficiency could not thrive on economic decay.  The central theme of African-American thought in the 1930s became the quest for economic and social integration.

Between this attitudinal turn and the impact of the depression, radical political parties had a remarkable opportunity to seek black political support during the early 1930s.  Both the Communist and the Socialist parties preached an integrationist and assimilationist message welcoming blacks as members of the working class and identifying their interests with the struggle for a classless society.  A carefully crafted image of the Soviet Union as a place where particularist identities were dissolved in a sea of brotherhood and unity became an element in the Communist appeal and an influence on Party policy.  In its efforts to recruit the oppressed to its revolutionary cause, the Communist party repeatedly took assertive positions on behalf of black rights or black equality: Communists faced physical assaults in the South; they demonstrated against public and private discrimination from the local to the national level; and they chose blacks for leadership positions and nominated an African-American, James Ford, for the vice-presidency.  The Party was nevertheless inhibited by its own rigidities of organization and doctrine: radical blacks in Harlem, as Mark Naison has pointed out, voiced "discontent with the inner workings of the Party—its pattern of decision making, its language and ideology, and above all its interracialism."  The Party's insistence in 1930 that northern blacks were "working for assimilation" and that there should be no "special Negro organization" went beyond equal treatment and equivalent opportunities to oppose specific expressions of black social and cultural identity.  Like Native Americans who balked at the prospect of an enforced separatism, some African-Americans on the left resented Communist denial of the room to "*choose* between interracial and ethnic forms."[21]

As black leaders and intellectuals recognized at the time, militant Communist involvement in civil rights causes was frequently double-edged.  Party propaganda and support did much to make a national issue out of the Scottsboro case, in which several young black men were dubiously accused of rape.  But the Party seemed at times to have more interest in the creation of martyrs than in the fate of the men.  Communists brought support and publicity to battles against segregation or specific injustices.  But they also made all African-Americans a "ready target for anti-Communist venom" (as one black editor remarked) and provided an excuse for conservative opposition to civil rights laws as radical and un-American.[22]  Moreover, as Harvard Sitkoff has noted, "the disruption, deceit, and duplicity often practiced by the Communist party, and the use of the race issue for its own sectarian ends complicated the work of established civil rights organizations."  Sitkoff nevertheless concludes that left activism probably helped black causes more than it hurt them in the 1930s.[23]

Yet the Communists were relatively few and their impact was spotty.  Gains were clearest when circumstances gave African-Americans a chance to move toward equality through their own actions and numbers. Labor unions had long discriminated against African-Americans, and many segregated their southern locals or excluded blacks altogether throughout the thirties. Yet especially with the rise of industrial unions and the emergence of the Congress of Industrial Organizations during the later 1930s, black workers became a significant labor constituency and gained an important future ally in the battle for civil rights. Although radicals were sometimes at the center of CIO organizing drives, it was not political activism but necessity that proved primary: where blacks made up a large portion of the workforce, an industry could not be successfully organized without them, and the CIO became a defender of civil rights. The depression opened the way for the exercise of at least this form of black economic power.

Although the Communist party had "seriously proselyted" among blacks, Ralph Bunche observed in 1935, it had achieved only "indifferent success." What had become far more important to African-Americans by that time was the behavior of the Roosevelt administration and the New Deal. The assumptions of New Deal liberals sympathetic to the needs and desires of black citizens proved similar in some respects to those of radicals, an overlap that itself limited the distinctiveness of the radical appeal. Liberals, too, wanted African-Americans to become, as Will Alexander put it, "more class conscious and less race conscious."[24] The frequent use of "class" in such contexts did not imply a Marxist analysis but an assumption that there was a commonality of interests among less-privileged blacks and whites that could serve as the basis for new forms of interracial cooperation. The term also drew attention to economic issues and to the belief that programs improving the circumstances of both poorer blacks and poorer whites were the key to greater opportunity and even to national recovery. Thus, although some New Dealers argued for special attention to the needs of African-Americans as a distinctive group in the South, the central theme in their approach was "harmony of interests." Harold Ickes, at the Atlanta dedication of the first housing project for blacks in 1934, declared that the interests of the "whole country" rested with the condition of each group, because "discrimination against a section, a race, a religion or an occupation is harmful to the people as a whole and disturbing to any attempts to work out a balanced economy."[25]

From such a viewpoint, the needs of African-Americans could only be weighed along with other considerations in seeking a wider set of political, social, and economic adjustments. To advocates of forceful and consistent measures to assert black equality, this outlook fell short in its unwillingness to give that cause primacy, which might have upset the New Deal's political scales. Yet there was a striking contrast between the federal hostility or indifference to African-American concerns under most previous administrations and the introduction of racial and ethnic fairness to the realm of legitimate policy considerations under Roosevelt. As in Indian affairs, the New Deal brought into government people whose ideas about ethnic relations had been peripheral in the 1920s, especially white liberals like Edwin Embree, Clark Foreman, Alexander, and Ickes who identified the interests of African-Americans with Roosevelt's success. These "race liberals" (including a number of southerners) appointed black officials or advisers in their own domains and encouraged other federal departments and agencies to do the same. The black economist Robert C. Weaver, for example, became Foreman's assistant in advising Ickes on economic conditions among African-Americans. Robert L. Vann served in the Justice Department, Eugene Kinckle Jones in Commerce. Efforts in 1934 to press black interests through an interdepartmental committee advocated by Ickes did not get very far, however, against the resistence of people like Agriculture Secretary Henry Wallace (who, somewhat ironically, would run for president in 1948 as a progressive, with Communist support). Expressing attitudes shared by many, Wallace warned the committee to move slowly and insisted that showing a particular concern for African-Americans would weaken support for the New Deal and damage other groups.

For the first two years of the Roosevelt presidency, a combination of inherited attitudes, political assumptions, and powerful opponents suggested little possibility that the New Deal would ever move quickly on issues of black concern. African-American intellectuals and leaders at a 1935 conference repeatedly condemned the New Deal's failure to provide adequate relief for black Americans or a substantive lessening of discrimination. Yet countercurrents were already under way. Although African-Americans were not receiving proportionate benefits under early New Deal programs, the jobs and payments that were coming their way made a substantial impact on those affected and on their communities. Moreover, in northern cities where blacks represented a potentially significant group of voters, the local control that often sustained discrimination provided occasional advantage as some Democratic machines began to court the black community. In the 1934 elections, for the first time, a majority of black voters cast their ballots for the Democrats. Although the preponderance of African-Americans in the South remained disenfranchised, the potential significance of the black vote in industrial states with high electoral counts made both major parties newly attentive in 1936. Despite a Republican civil rights plank and efforts to revive loyalties to the party of Lincoln, Roosevelt gained the support of more than three-quarters of black voters, who were turning out in substantially greater numbers. The New Deal thus prompted a shift central to the history of African-American political affiliation. And combined with the surge in ethnic voting that had occurred in 1928 and 1932, the increasing black vote of the 1930s marked a diversification of political participation that carried important cultural implications.

Shifting black voting patterns no doubt added momentum to changes occurring within administrative circles after 1935. No person was more important in drawing increased attention to African-American concerns by this point than Eleanor Roosevelt. Having entered the White House with no particular awareness of civil rights issues, Mrs. Roosevelt allowed herself to be educated through her friendships until she had become a forceful opponent of segregation and discrimination. She had a unique influence on her husband, who began to offer declarations on the principle of equality and to grant attention to black leaders and organizations. She pressured program administrators to end discriminatory practices and by example made it easier for them to do so. She took a highly public stance against prejudice and in favor of specific measures of protection for African-Americans as citizens. The friends who did the most to educate Mrs. Roosevelt were Walter White of the National Association for the Advancement of Colored People (NAACP) and Mary McLeod Bethune, the founder of the National Council of Negro Women who came to head the Office of Minority Affairs in the National Youth Administration (NYA). These two black leaders exemplified the dominant African-American political strategy of the 1930s: to gain representation within the government while generating pressure for civil rights measures from outside it. The remarkable Bethune became the leader of a group of black administrative officials and civil rights spokespersons (including White and A. Philip Randolph) who met almost weekly to exchange information and plan strategies. The combination of Eleanor Roosevelt and this "Black Cabinet," or the "Black Brain Trust," as it came to be known, meant at least that the concerns of African-Americans could not easily be overlooked.

In May 1935 the president issued an order banning discrimination of any form in the massive relief programs of the Works Projects Administration, and Harry Hopkins did his best to enforce that order, though not with complete success. The NYA, the CCC, the Farm Security Administration, and even the benefits paid under the Social Security Act all demonstrated conscientious efforts to achieve equity after 1935. Meanwhile, the expansion of federal employment was opening jobs to thousands of black professionals, and the total number of black government workers reached 150,000, or about 10 percent of the total federal workforce, by 1941. Even so, a system of legally supported segregation remained fully in place in the South, and discrimination remained the national norm. Liberal New Dealers still seeking their own bearings on issues of ethnicity and civil rights often found the path to new legislation blocked after 1937 by a conservative coalition of Republicans and southern Democrats. The southerners, generally wary of New Deal threats to local authority, made race increasingly central to their rhetoric of opposition. And to the degree that Roosevelt still needed the support of southern Democrats in some spheres—including, toward the end of the 1930s, the ever more insistent realms of foreign policy and defense—the interests of African-Americans were compromised.

The New Deal, then, developed into an arena of complex relationships and difficult choices for African-Americans. The new prominence of the federal government complicated older issues of authority, self-reliance, and dependence in black thought. Immediate gains sometimes came at the expense of fundamental principles and goals. An administration that was better than any preceding it remained unable to keep up with invigorated hopes and expectations. Reflecting this complexity, members of the Black Cabinet helped orchestrate organized demonstrations and protests to pressure the very government some of them served. Direct action boycotts, rent strikes, hunger marches, sit-downs, and the like surged to a peak in the 1930s that would not be equaled until the late 1950s and early 1960s. These protests gave black leaders much of their effectiveness but could not overcome some of the more difficult dilemmas. To gain much-needed federal aid for the majority of blacks in the South, for example, Bethune found it necessary to accept segregated programs. Torn as they sometimes were, Bethune, White, Robert Weaver, and others from the Black Cabinet represented something of a center of gravity in black thought during the 1930s. They identified integration as the ultimate goal, pressed for greater involvement of African-Americans themselves in shaping their own future, and looked to federal economic and political power as a key to widening opportunity. Along with the NAACP and the National Urban League, they would praise the New Deal for its positive achievements and criticize sharply its failings and hesitations.

This stance of simultaneously urging on and chastising liberal reformism represented a balancing act that could never subsume the full spectrum of black opinion. Not all African-Americans who served under the New Deal remained convinced that the patterns being established were predominantly beneficial. Robert Vann and Forrester Washington recognized the importance of federal programs aiding blacks during the depression, but both feared that African-Americans might come to rely too heavily on a government and a political party that would not take a bold stand against segregation or allow blacks a strong political role. Each chose to leave his government position. W. E. B. Du Bois, meanwhile, placed himself on the periphery of black thought in the 1930s by opposing integration and, thus, all programs of interracialism. Du Bois argued for African-American distinctiveness and unity, segregation without discrimination, and a program based on "the race conscious black man cooperating together in his own institutions and movements."[26] A controversy within the NAACP over these views led in 1934 to his departure from the organization he had helped found.

A. Philip Randolph worked out his own combination of ideas. Like Du Bois, Randolph hoped to build up group strength and self-reliance among African-Americans, and like Vann and Washington, he worried about the psychological and political costs of depending too much on others. Thus, although a veteran Socialist and head of the Brotherhood of Sleeping Car Porters, Randolph ultimately found black dependence on Communist or CIO allies no better than an overreliance on the New Deal. Direct protest seemed the path to political efficacy, and Randolph would organize at the beginning of the 1940s the "March on Washington Movement," which ensured black leadership and control by excluding whites. Nevertheless, black political independence remained for Randolph a step toward ultimate equity and integration.

Well aware of the differing strains in black thought, Ralph Bunche paused more than once during the 1930s to analyze the ideas, ideologies, and tactics of African-American leaders. In mid-decade he found none of the existing programs satisfactory. Liberal reform did not adequately address the economic and social circumstances of most blacks, and the outlook of the NAACP and the Urban League was irredeemably middle-class. Garvey's black nationalism, a "defeatist" philosophy on equal rights, offered African-Americans "an emotional escape" but few real prospects. Organizations that encouraged such tactics as black boycotts under the "don't-buy-where-you-can't-work" banner suffered from a "narrowly racial" outlook, creating no new jobs while seeking black jobs at the expense of whites. This tactic would necessarily increase tensions with white workers and threaten an actual reduction of jobs for blacks to the lesser number the black community could support. The separatism proposed by Du Bois rested on an "absurd" belief that the deprived African-American could thrive "by setting himself up in a black political and economic outhouse." Like other African-American social scientists, including E. Franklin Frazier and Charles Johnson, Bunche did not believe that there was a separate and distinctive black culture; hence, he found race an inadequate basis either for analysis or for politics. Consistent with radical political views, Bunche looked in the mid-1930s toward a transformation of the economic and political system, arguing that the "basic interests" of the "masses" in every American group were "identical." Yet by 1938 to 1940, when he extended his analysis while serving as chief research assistant for Gunnar Myrdal's investigation into the "Negro Problem and American Democracy," Bunche acknowledged substantive gains under the New Deal and emphasized the importance for blacks of defending democracy against fascism. His critical faculties and his concern with economic issues remained in place, but as alternative outlooks proved disappointing, he was approaching an outlook similar to that of the Black Cabinet.[27]

Bunche's repeated surveys of ideas and strategies underscored the difficulties black intellectuals faced in the continuing search for effective "tactics and programs." Like Roosevelt and the New Deal, leaders or organizations seeking to represent African-Americans had multiple constituencies and faced a mixture of ideological positions. Ministers, labor leaders, politicians, and academics had roots in different black communities and approached civil rights issues with varying ideas about benefits and needs. Separatist and assimilationist arguments challenged in opposite ways the push for integration. Controversies were endemic over the primacy of race or class, over the effectiveness of economic or cultural strategies, over conceptions of the "elite" or the "masses." What emerged from African-American politics and thought during the 1930s was no unified and cohesive program secure in its clarity of purpose and achievement, but a record of efforts shaped by contingency and limited by circumstance, of substantive but irregular gains, and of forced accommodations in the present that left an ample agenda for the future.

To one side of the direct struggle over governmental policies and civil rights, meanwhile, developments in intellectual and cultural life were chipping away at the edifice of discrimination. Scores on IQ tests administered during World War I had provided a presumably "scientific" basis for claims of black inferiority. Influenced in part by Boas, Otto Klineberg offered a closer analysis of the test results in 1935, demonstrating that African-Americans who had migrated north scored better than either southern blacks or southern whites. Combined with arguments about the cultural bias of the tests, this evidence did much to undermine ethnically based claims of differences in innate ability.[28] The work of Kurt Lewin in social psychology argued that racism reflected a personality disorder in those carrying the prejudice. Hence, those who were the objects of racism had no responsibility for causing it.[29] Others offered evidence that social contact between groups decreased prejudice and argued that contemporary racism derived primarily from inherited attitudes and customs, not from any direct experience. Scholars in many fields began to give close attention to black-white relations and the effects of prejudice on both groups, with school desegregation emerging as a major goal. Four times as many African-Americans (nearly 200) earned Ph.D.s in the 1930s as had done so from 1900 to 1930, and a significant number of black intellectuals began to gain prominence with research and writing that belied any challenge to their ability.[30] By the end of the 1930s (with Nazism in the wings), the predominant scholarly opinion had done a striking turnaround from a 1920s belief that racial characteristics were innate and racial antipathies "instinctive," to a newer conviction that differences and prejudices were primarily products of society and, therefore, subject to change.

African-American culture and history also attracted a higher level of attention in the 1930s. New Deal work relief programs that set out to gather information about the American experience interviewed elderly former slaves, providing an important resource for future scholarship. In Virginia, an all-black unit of WPA employees led by Roscoe E. Lewis worked through countless archival sources and conducted interviews over several years to produce *The Negro in Virginia* (1940), a landmark study praised for its thoroughness, balance, and vibrancy. Zora Neale Hurston launched a more individual effort that combined an anthropological outlook influenced by Franz Boas (with whom she had studied), a passion for folklore that would have pleased Constance Rourke, and her own special skills as a storyteller. Traveling and stopping in Florida, Alabama, Louisiana, and the West Indies, Hurston recorded the black folktales, songs, and hoodoo rituals that became *Mules and Men* (1935), a book that concentrated not on what blacks said to whites but on the culture they shared with one another. Her autobiographical novel *Jonah's Gourd Vine* (1934) had helped win publication of *Mules and Men*; Hurston moved on rapidly to produce her best fiction, *Their Eyes Were Watching God* (1937), a story, employing modernist techniques, of a woman's struggle toward love and eventual independence.

Hurston was criticized by some black writers for looking too much toward a white audience and leaving out the anger and bitterness among African-Americans, a charge that reflected contemporary struggles over black ideology and perhaps resistance to the literary success of a black woman. Richard Wright was at least as conscious of a white readership as Hurston, yet his *Native Son* (1940) was nearly all anger and bitterness. Having won attention and a WPA award for the novellas in *Uncle Tom's Children* (1938), Wright echoed social science arguments in making the negative effects of a racist environment responsible for the brutality of *Native Son*'s Bigger Thomas. Adding to the continuing impact of the Harlem Renaissance writers, Hurston and Wright staked out a wider place for African-Americans within both older and newer conceptions of "culture."

In theater, music, radio, film, and dance, specific productions began to pay respectful attention to African-Americans. Although roles reflecting stereotypes of black inferiority remained commonplace, greater consciousness of prejudice was leading toward new characterizations. Perhaps most of what was accomplished through steady struggle within the arts and the media represented incremental gains. Yet a few events reached a wide popular audience and achieved special resonance. Symbolic in circumstance and result, these events gave impetus to the emerging idea that discrimination was contradictory to "American" principles.

Adolph Hitler's attempt to make the 1936 Berlin Olympics a showcase of Aryan superiority drew attention to Nazi racism. When the track star Jesse Owens won four gold medals in the heart of the Reich and was snubbed by Hitler, the incident provoked a sharpening hostility toward Nazism and even some minimal self-examination of American practices. Albeit tentatively, perhaps, a black man stood as a representative of the nation. That same year, the German Max Schmeling defeated Joe Louis in a heavyweight title fight and compounded Hitler's insult to Owens by declaiming Louis's racial inferiority to the press. Their rematch two years later was burdened with international ideological implications. When the "Brown Bomber" knocked out the "Aryan Knight" in the first round, he did so as an American delivering a blow against Nazism.

In 1939 the Daughters of the American Revolution (DAR) refused to permit a concert by Marian Anderson, or any other black performer, in Constitution Hall in Washington, D.C. Anderson was a well-known and highly respected operatic talent, and the negative reaction from organizations and newspapers, orchestra conductors and public officials, was overwhelming. Eleanor Roosevelt resigned from the DAR, winning the approval in doing so of two-thirds of those polled. The NAACP and the Interior Department arranged for Anderson to give her concert in another location. Already the *New York Times* had questioned editorially whether the DAR could be thought of as a "patriotic" organization, and when Anderson stood at the Lincoln Memorial and began singing "America" to a crowd of 75,000, the moment

When the DAR refused to allow a performance by Marian Anderson at its Washington concert hall in 1939, Eleanor Roosevelt resigned from the organization and the concert was rescheduled to take place at the base of the Lincoln Memorial. The negative public reaction to the DAR's stance marked an important moment in the gradual turn against open racial and ethnic discrimination. The bank of radio microphones testifies to the wide interest aroused by the concert, which had grown into a major public event. *Thomas McAvoy,* Life *Magazine,* © *Time Warner*

powerfully affirmed that the challenge to open racism had found new strength in the 1930s not against but within the framework of national ideals.[31]

The political context of the New Deal, the strategies of black organizations, shifting ideas in the social sciences, the achievements of individual African-Americans, and the threat of fascism all contributed in greater or lesser degree to a discernible shift in the fate of civil rights issues in the American legal system. Civil rights law as a field of study or practice hardly existed at the beginning of the thirties. Charles Houston began to change that when, as the new dean of Howard University's law school, he brought in gifted black faculty like William Hastie, obtained accreditation, and started producing young lawyers like Thurgood Marshall and Oliver W. Hill. When the NAACP's planned campaign of legal challenges to segregation ran aground over deficiencies in funding and leadership, Houston stepped in as its head in 1935, with Hastie and Marshall at his side, and a case-by-case attack began to unfold. Roosevelt's appointments in the second half of the decade made their own statement. Hastie became the first African-American federal judge, and William Houston (father of Charles) became an assistant attorney general. To the Supreme Court, Roosevelt nominated the decidedly liberal William O. Douglas; Felix Frankfurter, who had been a teacher of Hastie and Charles Houston at Harvard Law School and an NAACP official; and Frank Murphy, a former director of the NAACP and the man who as attorney general had created a Justice Department division of civil rights. Increasingly after 1937, though the sphere of equal protections expanded slowly, Court decisions insisted on due process (in the words of another Roosevelt appointee, Justice Hugo Black) for citizens "of whatever race, creed, or persuasion." As one historian has remarked, "What would culminate in the Warren Court clearly began in the Roosevelt Court."[32]

The African-American struggle for recognition and rights recorded significant gains during the second half of the 1930s, but newer patterns could not quickly overcome the persistence of prejudice. Perhaps the campaign against lynching demonstrated both change and lack of change as sharply as any other issue. The lynching of black men in the South involved assertions of racial hierarchy, questions of community order and control, the maintenance of economic domination, and complex issues of sexuality and gender. Calls for federal action against lynching threatened to speed the process of national intervention in the South's regional culture that was leading many southern politicians into increasing opposition to the New Deal. The campaign for a federal antilynching law thus seemed by the later 1930s a central test of the strength of the civil rights cause and of segregationist abilities to resist change. The number of lynchings in the early thirties provided ample grounds for the campaign, and the moral clarity of the issue gave it a strong interracial appeal. In 1934 and subsequent years, congressional committees held hearings on antilynching bills; radio networks broadcast testimony and provided free time for special antilynching programs; authors and artists supported an exhibition for the cause in New York; and dozens of organizations joined the campaign. With the accumulation of allies and the increasing sophistication of their public relations tactics, civil rights organizations forged around the lynching issue a new political force.

Yet the campaign also provoked its opposite: a resistence to any antilynching bill through a virulent and explicit appeal to racism led by southern Democrats in the Senate and House. A 1935 Senate filibuster against such a bill was relatively tame since neither supporters nor opponents were ready to endanger support for the New Deal over the issue. By 1938, when the bill again came to the floor, many southern conservatives were already entrenched against further reforms and Democratic liberals were prepared for a fight. For almost seven weeks, while northern Democrats failed twice to win cloture, southerners like "Cotton Ed" Smith of South Carolina, Theodore Bilbo of Mississippi, and Martin Dies of Texas tied up the Senate with an outpouring of sectional appeals and racial venom. Smith won reelection in 1938 by identifying himself as the candidate of white supremacy; Bilbo then and later ranted about protecting southern white women, praised Hitler for appreciating "the importance of race values," and proposed deporting all blacks to Africa; Dies mixed anti-Semitism and anticommunism with his racism and tried to brand all he opposed as "alien" and "un-American."[33] The 1938 filibuster did its work: the antilynching bill never reached a vote. Sustained attention applied enough pressure to reduce the number of lynchings from between fifteen and twenty each year in the early 1930s to eight, six, and two in 1937, 1938, and 1939.[34] Yet even in opposition to the practice of murder by mob, civil rights forces at the end of the decade were still unable to overcome the politics of white dominance.

Nevertheless, the tide was turning, as the sharp defensiveness in the southern conservative position itself attested. Since the late nineteenth century, assumptions of black inferiority had met little public challenge, and support for civil rights was seldom an important part of any elected official's political stance. By the end of the 1930s, arguments for innate equality had generally triumphed in intellectual and artistic circles outside the South, and support at some level for African-American equality as an idea and a goal was entering the basic definition of a liberal in American politics. If the lives of ordinary black people were seldom fundamentally changed and few barriers crumbled completely in the 1930s, the near-monopoly of cultural beliefs and stereotypes tied to the ideological justifications of segregation had been broken. Ideas and organizations were now in place that could sustain an ongoing struggle for civil rights. As the rapid appearance of the label "un-American" suggested, that struggle would be in part a contest over the meaning of the nation, and it would thrust new complexities into the definition of American identity.

*five*

---

# Writing Wrongs and Asserting Rights: From "Social Evangelism" to the Defense of Modernism

Writing as the 1930s edged to a close, the journalist Frederick Lewis Allen offered reinforcement to a common belief that the intellectual and artistic concerns of the decade just past stood in sharp contrast to those of the 1920s. Imagine a New York cocktail party of around 1925 attended by "writers, critics, artists, musicians, and professional men and women" interested in the arts, he suggested. The opinions likely to be expressed would include the following: that the country needed expanded personal freedoms and fewer reformers and laws; that most of the population was slow-witted and painfully conventional; that American culture was afflicted with Victorianism, Puritanism, and a layering of inflated myths and heroes that needed to be "debunked"; that "Babbitts, Rotarians, and boosters" promulgated a business ethos that was "hopelessly crass"; and that an increasingly standardized and mechanistic United States continued to lack the freedom and sophistication of Europe.

Now look into a similar gathering in the mid-1930s. Economic reforms, new laws, even calls for revolution have become grist for the conversational mill. Major segments of social opinion now claim that ordinary citizens are the best subjects for artistic and political attention; the "people" have become for some an object of boundless sympathy and a source of ultimate justification. American culture and its history are taken to be inherently interesting and worthy of close study, whether as part of an effort to raise and celebrate or an impulse to confront and remedy. Between the gatherings of the twenties and the thirties, in Allen's version of the change, intellectuals and artists acquired the "secular religion of social consciousness," sparking a "social evangelism" characteristic of cultural life during the depression.[1]

In part this picture of socially committed intellectuals, like the notion of a "lost generation" in the 1920s, was an image consciously cultivated by the people it purported to describe. Just as it had seemed a mark of sophistication to stand aloof from, to mock, or to flee American society in the previous decade, so in the 1930s it became an accepted indication of advanced thinking to want to engage that society and to change it. Writers and artists commonly looked back on the twenties as a period of indulgence and irresponsibility, and the very idea of an immersion in art for its own sake struck many as inappropriate when depression was asserting so strongly the claims of the world. In *Exile's Return* (1934) Malcolm Cowley both chronicled his generation's "literary odyssey of the 1920s" and affirmed the newer attitudes. The shift in views contained much that reflected a rational response to economic collapse, a search for means of protest, and an aspiration toward positive change. Some were no doubt hurried along the path through personal exposure to unemployment and shrunken opportunity. All could bask in the easy assumption of a higher morality that tended to accompany the idea of social commitment.

The image of the 1930s as a decade when writers and artists turned toward politics and the people draws attention to a number of important strains in the cultural life of the period. There was a heightened interest in radicalism—which has often been taken as the defining intellectual thrust of the era—that changed in character as the decade progressed. Rooted in part in the radical or reformist urge, there was also a compulsion to record or document American life, concentrating at first on the impact of the depression and on continuing social deprivation. A similar interest flowing in a different channel, sometimes with an antiradical emphasis, led to celebrations of American traditions (or efforts to create traditions) that could easily take on the tones of militant nationalism. Especially during the second half of the thirties, strains of radicalism, documentary recording, and nationalistic feeling became intertwined in sometimes improbable ways, helping both to mold and to confuse lingering impressions of the decade.

An emphasis on socially engaged intellectuals alone, however, would provide a misleadingly narrow impression of American culture during the depression. Allen noted at least some of the limitations of his own cocktail party representations when he remarked that the "new mood was most widespread in New York" and among the "young and rising." It was not a concern shared by all intellectuals or university scholars; indeed, "academic" was often a term of contempt among artists and radicals in the thirties. It was not a shift embraced by most of those middle- and upper-class citizens with a traditional interest in "culture." And it was not a mood that ever became dominant in popular choices of books, music, art, or plays. The best-seller lists showed the occasional breakthrough of novels with contemporary social themes, like Sinclair Lewis's *It Can't Happen Here* in 1935 and John Steinbeck's *The Grapes of Wrath* in 1939, just as similar exceptions occurred in other fields. But more commonly, popular favor streamed toward historical novels, books of advice, and, in the later thirties, works on Europe, Asia, and foreign affairs. Efforts to focus attention on economic and social issues had to share the cultural stage.

The passage of half a century has introduced further qualifications. Individual artists and writers deemed in retrospective versions of American cultural development to be among the most important of the period—William Faulkner, for example—sometimes had little to do with the social enthusiasms of the thirties or were scantly appreciated at the time. From a middle distance, moreover, the glare of contemporary headlines begins to fade, allowing increasing visibility for efforts to situate experience within a broader historical flow. Both those writers who sought immediate social engagement and those who stood apart shared in conscious and unconscious ways a need to deal with the weight of the past as a force in the present, to explore the tensions of ongoing social transformations, and, often, to seek values that might serve the future. The United States was not a country of one tradition, or one experience, or one relationship to past and present. Rather than establishing a common or dominant voice for the 1930s, the impact of the depression and of "social evangelism" reshaped particular patterns of American culture with an irregular application of force.

## An Agitation of Radical Ideas

The onset of economic crisis found many intellectuals, especially those in literary and artistic circles, predisposed to critical response and prepared to take radical analyses seriously. Dissatisfactions with middle-class culture, explorations of the inequities of wealth and status, and attention to the crueler underside of industrial society had claimed a part in the literary consciousness of Europe and the United States for decades. In the years before World War I, socialist ideas and ideals had been commonplace in the vital intellectual compound of Greenwich Village, and antagonism toward national celebrations of commerce and the businessman had permeated literary attitudes during the 1920s. There was thus no occasion for shock when the prominent critic Edmund Wilson reported that "the writers and artists of my generation" had felt a sense of exhilaration at the collapse of the "Big Business era" and a delight in the fact that "the bankers, for a change, were taking a beating." For writers who were already leaning left, the depression seemed to sweep away "a world dominated by salesmen and brokers" and to open opportunities to build American culture on a different basis.[2]

Earlier events had prepared the way for intellectual discontent to take political form. According to Robert Morss Lovett, nothing had "so shaken the Liberal's belief in the working for equal justice of free institutions" as the executions of Nicola Sacco and Bartolomeo Vanzetti in 1927.[3] A mixed bag of idealists, radicals, and liberals, including Katherine Anne Porter, John Howard Lawson, Dorothy Parker, John Dos Passos, Edna St. Vincent Millay, and William Gropper, had mounted protests to save what they believed were two innocent men being persecuted for their ethnicity and their anarchist beliefs. The failure of the campaign seemed both to shake the liberal faith in American justice and to underline the weakness of intellectuals alone as a political force. Advocates of the Communist party, few though they were in the twenties, did their best to make Sacco and Vanzetti martyrs to the cause of the proletariat (the industrial working class) and to mock liberal intellectuals as sentimental and ineffective so long as they failed to join the workers in organized class struggle. On the eve of the stock market crash in 1929, a bitter textile strike led by a Communist union in Gastonia, North Carolina, produced another radical martyr when Ella May Wiggins was killed by a mob trying to prevent a union meeting. To at least some intellectuals, the injustices of the established order and the claims of the working class provided increasingly compelling reasons to move left.

At the beginning of the 1930s, the attraction of radicalism and of the Communist party was closely tied to the image of the Soviet Union. The drama, excitement, and gripping historical significance of the Russian Revolution were barely more than a decade in the past, and the Soviet Union still carried the aura of a great idealistic experiment. The revolution had presumably provided freedom and inspiration for the arts, and during the 1920s there was a sufficient outpouring of creative and innovative work in Russian painting, theater, and film to give substance to the belief. In politics, the Soviets were understood to be designing a new kind of state on egalitarian principles through practical application of the Marxian "science" of society. When the Russian economy in its relative isolation from world markets escaped much of the impact of the early depression, the wisdom of the Soviet course seemed confirmed. The Russian experiment thus appeared to have a place for both aesthetic sensibility and the rational intellect—ways of knowing or of seeking truth that had often seemed at odds in the modern world. Indeed, the example of a system able "to use and to inspire the artist as well as the engineer" could lead even a sober American writer like Edmund Wilson to speak lyrically of the prospects for making "art and science one." Given such a model of idealism and progress, sympathetic intellectuals could easily dismiss reports of Stalin's insatiable appetite for power, news of restrictions on aesthetic freedom at the end of the twenties, and the "atrocity stories of the capitalist press about forced labor and the execution of thousands of peasants" as either biased coverage or passing evidence of the adjustments unavoidable in a new society.[4]

Some were drawn to Marxism by its intellectual appeal, with a spirit that could be both serious and playful: if Sidney Hook and James Burnham wrote philosophical-political essays, a precocious Harold Rosenberg held privately that Marxism was both Talmud and Cabala and "proved that Helen of Troy

. . . was really a loaf of bread," while Lionel Abel suggested a Marxist detective who would "solve crimes by calling upon dialectical materialism."[5] Marxist theory combined a broad framework of explanation and concentrated analytical power, and it allowed ample scope for a certain gamesmanship in the manipulation of ideas. Younger intellectuals, in particular, could claim an immediate sophistication of outlook and understanding as well as a moral edge by embracing Marxism. Many who believed that with the exhaustion of capitalism a proletarian revolution was at hand tended to believe as well that a burst of cultural creativity would accompany fundamental social transformation. Writers and artists wanted to share in the making of this new, and presumably higher, culture. Marxism claimed to have universal application, to be above the limitations of nationality, race, religion, or parochialisms of other kinds. This ethos of universality and nondiscrimination carried powerful appeal for a growing body of intellectuals who defined themselves against such phenomena as 100 percent Americanism and the Ku Klux Klan, and especially perhaps for writers and artists whose own ethnic origins threatened to inhibit their full participation in American cultural life.

An attraction to Marxism, of course, did not necessarily produce common beliefs or movement into the Communist party. Some writers, artists, and intellectuals were notoriously touchy about their independence and eager to put their own slant on ideas. In the early thirties, efforts to create joint projects marking a leftward intellectual movement proved more notable for their foundering than for their achievement. Volumes of essays assessing American civilization from a particular angle were in vogue between the wars, and in 1929 V. F. Calverton, editor of *Modern Quarterly*, had proposed a symposium by writers with leftward views. When more than two years of discussion and planning meetings led nowhere, Granville Hicks, a liberal college teacher moving toward the Communist party, proposed a similar effort by writers who were expected at least to be in sympathy with Marxism though they might yet need to acquire knowledge of it. Another 15 months of exchanges and comments produced a multitude of suggestions but little concrete result, in part because some projected contributors declined or backed out while others nourished lingering doubts.

Late in 1932 a different organizing effort led to a declaration and a pamphlet ("Culture and Crisis") in which 53 intellectuals declared their support for the presidential and vice-presidential candidates of the Communist party. Their statement spoke of the decay and breakdown of capitalism, of the corruption of the major parties and the impotence of the Socialists, and of the Communist party's desire and ability to fight against the ruling classes in the name of equity. The 53 categorized themselves as "intellectual workers" who identified with "muscle workers." The signers included Sherwood Anderson, Newton Arvin, Erskine Caldwell, Robert Cantwell, Lewis Corey, Malcolm Cowley, Countee Cullen, John Dos Passos, Waldo Frank, Horace Gregory, Granville Hicks, Sidney Hook, Langston Hughes, Matthew Josephson, Grace

Lumpkin, Felix Morrow, James Rorty, Isidor Schneider, Lincoln Steffens, Edmund Wilson, and Ella Winter. From a later viewpoint, it is strikingly clear that such a grouping represented a temporary and fragile alliance among intellectuals who would follow quite different tracks. The list combined people who maintained a militant support of the Communist party until the end of the thirties (Hicks, Schneider); who sympathized warmly with the Party as fellow travelers (Arvin, Cowley); who moved into and out of Party favor as its policies changed (Frank); who joined parties sharply opposed to the Communists (Morrow); who became among the best-known independent critics of the Party (Hook, Wilson); and who appeared to move markedly toward the right during the decade (Dos Passos). Anger and frustration over the depression and the insufficiency of governmental response—even at least a loose attachment to Marxism and the idea of a revolutionary restructuring— did not a consensus make.[6]

There was, then, a distinct upsurge of interest among writers and artists in the left and in radical politics, but sympathies diverged in shifting patterns as the decade progressed. Rival left parties, some of them created by policy disputes and power struggles within the Soviet Union and the communist movement, always provided intellectuals with alternatives to immersion in the Communist party. The attentive left intellectual could give considerable energy simply to keeping up with the policy statements and shifting alliances of, for example, the Lovestonites, the Musteites, the Trotskyists, the Social Democrats, and the Socialists. In addition to a menu of specific choices, the existence of multiple parties provided an umbrella of political activity under which many could maintain an independent, or simply a vague, attachment to radicalism. None of this changed the fact that for most of the decade, in shaping both the public and the intellectuals' perceptions of radicalism, the Communists took the lead.

During the first half of the 1930s, the Communist cultural program called for the creation of a proletarian literature that would turn writing to political account. This literature of novels, stories, plays, and poems would presumably depict the breakdown of capitalism in all its economic and social relations and the emergence of working-class consciousness and commitment. Mike Gold, the dominant editor of the Party's leading cultural organ, *New Masses*, wanted "the working men, women and children of America" to produce the bulk of this revolutionary writing, telling the story of their own experience. The "suffering of the hungry, persecuted and heroic millions"—the "real conflicts" of real lives and not the "silly little agonies" of bourgeois bohemians— would be the raw material of a new art.[7]

To encourage the development of younger writers, especially those of working-class background, *New Masses* founded the John Reed Club of New York just after the stock market crash and supported the establishment of chapters in 12 major cities by 1933. Torn as it was between the expectations of local chapters and the demands of Soviet cultural policies, between the assignment of supporting new artists and the task of recruiting a broader range of intellectuals, the John Reed Club organization never quite satisfied anyone for very long. Yet it did offer opportunities for young writers at a time when prospects were bleak. Several chapters started their own magazines of fiction, poetry, and criticism, expanding opportunities for publication. As it turned out, young writers with genuine literary ambitions often balked at fitting into Gold's definition of proletarianism. Both the Reed clubs and the magazines provided a basis for the expression of views that were not always as controlled or as deferential as *New Masses* seemed to wish.

The radical thrust in literature provoked a number of controversies that preoccupied the membership of the John Reed clubs. Writers leaning left could generally unite in rejecting the idea that the creation of art was a sufficient end unto itself ("art for art's sake") and in demanding a consciousness of social issues, but they could not so easily settle the question of just how direct and how explicit a writer's social purpose must be. Some proclaimed the doctrine that "art is a weapon," holding that each work should be of immediate service to the class struggle. Others protested that this doctrine reduced art to its propaganda value, ignoring aesthetic qualities and the complex ways in which artistic insight related to social change. As in many other debates on the left during the thirties, the question of what was happening in the Soviet Union was soon dragged into the controversy. In *Artists in Uniform* (1934), Max Eastman—a Greenwich Village rebel and "once the Bolshevik leader of a generation of young intellectuals" (in Mike Gold's words)—assailed bitterly the political domination of literature in the Communist state. The Soviet writer, Eastman charged, either followed official prescriptions or faced a life of obscurity and misery. Although the immediate impact of this attack was limited, *New Masses* critics found it necessary, not untypically, both to denounce Eastman as a "filthy and deliberate liar" (Gold) and to claim that they proudly accepted the designation "artists in uniform" (Joshua Kunitz).[8] Political direction of the arts was to *New Masses* a matter both of slander and of policy.

Other problems complicated the task of defining a radical literature as well, as in changing forms they continue to complicate cultural debates. Writers disagreed over the place of literary tradition. The proletarian camp of *New Masses*, led by Gold, was sometimes inclined to dismiss all "bourgeois" literature as irrelevant or damaging to radical efforts; a contrary position argued that literary tradition was a part of the writer's heritage, an available body of technique and insight, and a source of aesthetic standards. For some writers, including Newton Arvin, Granville Hicks, and Robert Gorham Davis (who, following Party fashion, adopted the pseudonym Obed Brooks), the historical moment demanded that artists and intellectuals accept the leadership of a radical party, suppressing their individual concerns and their critical function in the name of a greater political good.[9] For others, like Edmund Wilson, notions of intellectual independence and literary responsibility served as a constant check on their willingness to bow before organization or doctrine.

Although contested issues were sometimes engaged in reasoned and civil ways, from the very beginning of the thirties much literary criticism and debate took on a sharp and rancorous tone. This may have been attributable in part to a sense of urgency among critics who believed, as Alfred Kazin put it, that they might help resolve "a crisis in the whole moral order of civilization."[10] But such higher motives were not the whole story. Criticism was subject to pique and personality, and to a jockeying for status within the left as well as in the larger culture. Radical critics struggled with their own pretensions, with the tendency to mimic the wider cultural models they often disdained, and with fundamental conflicts over the significance of ideas. And they had more to worry about. In the quest for a new radical literature embodying positive social ideals, there was always a need for examples.

## Searching for a Left-wing Literature

Among those writers whom the left was eager to celebrate in the early 1930s, two gained particular contemporary stature, James T. Farrell and John Dos Passos. Both defined themselves as radicals at the beginning of the decade, and both demonstrated a full measure of social passion. Each could be seen as a chronicler of human possibilities thwarted and of a social system that had failed. Yet despite efforts to claim their works as symbolic of a revolutionary literature rising in response to the depression, it was soon clear that neither Farrell nor Dos Passos worked from the assumptions of Communist proletarianism or provided politically reliable models for a new radical art. Their concerns were complex, and as each followed his own intellectual and political trajectory, he grew more distant from the competing (and changing) versions of a left aesthetic.

Farrell's *Studs Lonigan* trilogy (1932, 1934, 1935) provided an unrelievedly bleak and detailed depiction of lower middle–class Irish life in Chicago. Begun before the depression, two of the novels in the trilogy had taken full form by mid-1931. The third incorporated a background of depression unemployment, strikes, and political activism while maintaining an established tone and direction. Studs as a character was not devoid of his own feelings and aspirations, yet he was bound by his environment and was able to express himself and to act only within the constricting limits of what he took to be expected, leaving him frustrated and lonely as he drifted toward an early death. Farrell's philosophical training and knowledge of modernist techniques, his familiarity with John Dewey and James Joyce, were not the stuff of Mike Gold's proletarianism. Yet the wastefulness and failure surrounding Studs was quickly identified with the mood of the early thirties, and the sheer weight of dreary specificity in the novels seemed to carry radical import. Indeed, *New Masses* had called on proletarians to write of the lives they had lived, to provide direct descriptions of lower-class experience. Farrell did this, but for his own reasons. His autobiographical character was not the doomed Studs but Danny O'Neill, who moved to center stage in Farrell's novels of the later thirties. Unlike Studs, Danny managed to free his spirit from the constraints of circumstance to confront a wider world.[11]

In his own trilogy *U.S.A.* (1930, 1932, 1936), John Dos Passos conducted a trenchant survey of national ideals and national practice from the beginning of the twentieth century to the depression. Striking in their technical inventiveness, the three novels combine piercing biographical sketches, inward-looking "Camera Eye" sections, more objectively framed narratives of symbolic characters, and "Newsreel" collages compiled from the headlines and stories of the day. This ingenuity of form, combined with openly anticapitalist sentiments, won enthusiastic praise on the left in the early thirties and made Dos Passos a radical celebrity. The enthusiasm and the hype would not last, however, for his work belonged to a particular context and his opinions were at the service of no political party.

The ambition in *U.S.A.*, one scholar has remarked, was to dramatize "that boundless gulf between the legendary promise of what life in America ought to be and the hideous facts" by showing the two in "suspenseful interaction."[12] The dream of individual opportunity, the hope placed in liberal ideals during World War I, the expectation of justice, were all mocked by social realities in Dos Passos's deeply pessimistic extension of 1920s disillusions. Dos Passos later remarked that he had "seceded privately the night Sacco and Vanzetti were executed"; *U.S.A.* was written during his secession and before the arrival of Franklin Roosevelt. He would acknowledge as well that it was "during the early New Deal that I rejoined the United States."[13] The spark of belonging was rekindled after *U.S.A.*, and Dos Passos brought that new light to his continuing exploration of American values. A concern for the fate of individuals that had kept him somewhat wary of the Communist party helped move him by the later thirties into vehement opposition to Stalinism. Digging into American history and traveling the American land, Dos Passos probed for the meaning of the nation and the character of its people. In seeking to define the significance of competing ideals, experiences, traditions, and behaviors for the American present and future, he was far from alone.

Farrell and Dos Passos could attract the effusive praise of Communist critics for a time in the early 1930s in part because their tactics and concerns overlapped those of writers more closely identified with the proletarian camp. Farrell's exhaustive accounting of specific circumstance coincided with a strong pull among writers of the thirties toward detailed and meticulous description, especially of life on the lower levels of American society, or in the workplace, or at the margins. Demonstrating an intimate knowledge of a particular job and a specific setting became at times almost an end in itself, an effort to capture the reality of the workers' world through an inescapable concreteness. It was also a claim to authenticity, a validation of personal experience, reflecting a preoccupation with autobiographical materials that would prove as strong in the 1930s as the 1920s. And buried within this testimony (or sometimes awkwardly pushed toward the surface) lay deeper concerns: anxieties about the transformations wrought in a society becoming increasingly industrial and urban; a cognizance of people and practices being left out or left behind; and a dismay over the gaps between images and realities. Such concerns embodied dilemmas of identity and meaning that pushed writers in opposite directions, toward the denial of all values and toward the ungrounded assertion of ideals.

Although the passion for close description was often steeped in the spirit of "social evangelism," such writing illustrated quite clearly the inherent tensions between a broad notion of social consciousness and a specific political program. To describe workers' lives and the impact of the depression did not in itself carry any defined political message, as the *New Masses* critic E. A. Schachner recognized when he suggested distinguishing between proletarian novels and revolutionary novels. The idea of social description as a radical weapon seemed even more attenuated when the people being described were not industrial workers but sharecroppers, or service workers, or migrants, or drifters. Such groups were neither the common entities of Marxist analysis nor the projected shock troops of revolution. The radical novelist Josephine Herbst would put it simply: "The poor aren't proletariat."[14] In a trilogy of her own published during the 1930s, Herbst followed the decline of a middle-class family from the late nineteenth century into the depression, while attempting to hold out a positive prospect in the rise of radical alternatives. In retrospect, she remained interested in her own use of language but suggested that "the period was overwhelming and there was not enough of a solid body of intellectual or literary life behind anyone to help much."[15] This lack of context affected all radicals, but it touched those writers seeking to explore the roles and perspectives of women with special force, since concerns based on gender found little encouragement in the Party's organized political program. Direct affirmations of radical politics thus did not come naturally for many left-leaning writers, adding to the difficulties of turning "social evangelism" to a defined purpose.

In "proletarian" novels of one kind, a direct challenge to Communist aspirations seemed inherent in descriptions of lives so wretched as to allow little room for the volition and hope of politics. Matching the dark mood of certain films in the early thirties, the "bottom dogs" novels presented a world bereft of any values worth affirming and lacking in genuine prospects for action.[16] Edward Dahlberg's *Bottom Dogs* (1930), which provided the flagship for the type, dealt with distinctly marginal characters in a style that D. H. Lawrence pronounced in his introduction to the book, "the last word in repulsive consciousness." A "lady barber" and her fatherless son; the peculiar residents of a Jewish orphanage; the denizens of flophouses and freight cars and the "Y"— all inhabit a world of disgust and decay described through an imagery of mud, rats, grease, and rot. Another "bottom dogs" novel, Tom Kromer's *Waiting for*

*Nothing* (1935), records in flat unpolished prose the hunger, exhaustion, and brutality that dominated the lives of unemployed tramps and stiffs: a man on the road with a starving baby is desperate enough to rob, but too poor to acquire the power a gun would give him; a boy trying to hop a freight train falls to a meaningless death beneath its wheels; the narrator waits for hours to get a bowl of soup, and the man serving the soup drips sweat into the bowl. As Kromer's title makes clear, these are lives without redemption. In Nelson Algren's *Somebody in Boots* (1935), the despair of politics seems explicit: the main character finally can "not trouble himself . . . about any better or happier world." The future can only be like the present in the land of the bottom dogs; the characters have nowhere to go and no hope of anything new.

At an opposite pole from the rejection of all ideals stood an unwavering assertion of Party-sanctioned principles combined with the search for a credible call to action. For such efforts, the militant labor strike provided a ready frame. In *Marching! Marching!* (1935), Clara Weatherwax delivered a strike novel that followed closely the guidelines for proletarian writing laid down by Communist critics while remaining at a safe distance from the realism of experience. Amid stilted attempts to be literary and an awkward handling of common speech, the novel constructs a self-conscious endorsement of ethnic equality and cooperation as the basis for worker solidarity, and it aspires toward a stirring climax through the collective action of a radical strike. Whether the message is convincing is another matter. At the close of the book, the workers march in unison, singing their militance, feeling their own power, yet they are about to be met by police, bayoneted, gassed, and slaughtered by machine guns. Nothing points toward any other outcome. Although martyrdom might appeal to some, it hardly seemed a lure that would bring workers flocking to the radical cause; the assertion of socially unrooted ideals provided little foundation for meaning or action. *New Masses* awarded the book a special literary prize.

In *Land of Plenty* (1934), Robert Cantwell wrote much more effectively about factory work and explored the dynamics of a strike without a formula. At the beginning of the book, a power failure plunges a lumber factory into darkness. The middle-class managers are left frantic, immobile, and confused by this symbolic equivalent to the nation's economic collapse. The workers, secure in their intimate knowledge of the factory and their machines, can move about freely and avert hidden dangers. Their skill, their pride in their work, their concern for one another, and their interdependence are all affirmed, and values such as these could presumably reestablish the smoothly functioning factory economy mucked up by the owners and managers. When the workers spontaneously stop work and crowd around the plant offices chanting "Come on out!" the novel reaches its positive crest and the young protagonist feels a profound sense of "excitement and strength." Yet as Cantwell follows the strike past its zenith, social and family tensions rapidly emerge, the workers' organization breaks apart, and the strikers are put to rout. At the end of the book, the young man is left huddled in the rain with one or two others who have escaped, knowing his father has been shot and his girlfriend badly clubbed, waiting for the night. Now the darkness speaks not to the power of workers but to their misery, and it will "set them free" only in the sense of hiding their flight.

Defeat and degradation were not the prescribed outcomes for political activism, and Cantwell's novel aroused considerable controversy on the left. Radical critics like Granville Hicks declared that the characters had bungled the strike or questioned Cantwell's expertise on strike tactics. Such comments implied that for the novelist at least, the labor dispute should be understood as a show that could always be staged successfully to deliver the right effects. This attitude pointed toward a dilemma that commonly frustrated radical efforts to turn social consciousness toward a meaningful left literature. As was evident in their descriptive practice, many left-wing novelists were driven by a desire to capture the harshness or complexity of actual conditions while tearing down the cultural facades constructed to obscure the real.[17] If the depression provided one impetus, the urge to reveal cloaked realities looked as well to literary modernism's concern with the authentic and its attack on the fabrications of middle-class gentility; to the concept of false consciousness resident in Marxist analysis; and to skepticism toward the invention of new "realities" by commerce and advertising and Hollywood. Those writers who struggled to combine the truths of experience with service to a political cause frequently produced the kind of proletarian novels that one scholar describes as a "strange mixture of native realism and sudden dips into ideological editorial or melodrama."[18] Communist critics who made it clear they were not interested in hearing about differences among workers or failed strikes without radical promise—critics who gave their prizes to Weatherwax images of the revolutionary masses—seemed to demand not authenticity from writers but their cooperation in the construction of one more social fiction.

Novels written by those most deeply engaged with radicalism sometimes revealed more curious tensions: they tended to leave their conscious political claims struggling for credibility against seemingly half-conscious efforts to embrace the past, to search for wider social meanings, and to attach personal experience to established images of American identity. Jack Conroy first recorded his experiences in an autobiography and then, at the instigation of a publisher, turned the manuscript into a novel. In *The Disinherited* (1933), Conroy described through the adventures of his narrator-hero Larry Donovan the demands of laboring in the mines, in railroad-car shops, in rubber-heel and automobile factories, and in iron bridgework. Moving from youth to adulthood, Conroy's Larry presumably develops an increasingly perceptive understanding of economics and politics so that the story can end with his decision to become a radical labor organizer. Yet as a sympathetic commentator later remarked, Larry's decision reflects Conroy's desire for a "proper proletarian ending" but is "not in any way a result of personality," "psychological necessity," or "intellectuality."[19]  Conroy himself would later insist that ideological gestures were not important to his purpose, declaring that he considered himself "a witness to the times" fulfilling "Whitman's injunction to 'vivify the contemporary fact.'"[20]  In his witnessing, Conroy sought revolutionary potential and spoke with much fellow feeling, but he also showed workers exhausted by their jobs, turned into "automatons" and "snarling ogres," and bearing the shadows of death.  Moreover, Larry repeatedly confronts the prospect that workers will always settle for a "full gut" and are drawn to the myths of success (myths that Larry himself has to struggle to reject).  Conroy's version of the "contemporary fact" revealed realities often missing from images of a unified working class.

There was a searching going on in Conroy's writing that his conscious choices could not still.  In patterns oft repeated in the 1930s, Conroy's hero migrates from place to place, looking for a way to feel at home, a sense of comfort and community.  The decision made at the end of the novel represents an effort to find a home in radical politics by force of will, to summon a faith in the present and future potential for a community of workers.  Yet Conroy continually turned his gaze to the past.  The book's title, and its dedication to "the disinherited and dispossessed of the world," suggested a heritage and estate now lost, raising implicit questions about American history and identity that were endemic to the thirties.

The mining town of Conroy's Missouri childhood, as he chose to construct it, had striking ties to the rural past and American clichés.  There is the father, half-farmer and half-miner, who takes a dangerous job setting off explosives to free the family from the evil of debt and sends the son to a school that will help him rise; the saintly mother who after the father's death works unceasingly doing washing and ironing to hold the family together; the crusty miner with an "evil eye" and a heart of gold, secretly delivering groceries to help in the mother's cause; and the young aunt, "a good Christian girl" who "never went to dances," who longs to know what a certain roguish boy might be saying about her.  There are images as well of the family's house at the top of the hill, bigger than its neighbors; of days acting out Robin Hood and adventures from ancient Rome (the levity of which keeps the son from his appointed work and—shades of McGuffey's *Readers*—leads directly to an accident that makes the mother's burdens heavier); of the winsome Bonny Fern, whom the boy admires from a distance and imagines himself rescuing from (of course) a "fate worse than death."  Perhaps it could be argued that such images were merely intended to serve as emblems of a somewhat more innocent time for the narrator and the nation that could stand in contrast with the harsher patterns of industrial society. (The garden crops that were the object of the father's agricultural passion are rapidly destroyed when he dies in an industrial accident.)  Yet at the end of his novel, Conroy returns to the countryside, and the "masses" who are about to organize are farmers.  Were farmers, then, the real Americans of whose former estate contemporary workers had been disinherited and dispossessed? Could the wandering individual and the uncertain nation find direction and identity by turning for sustenance toward their rural roots? Although unable to face directly the tensions these questions suggest, Conroy seemed compelled, whatever his politics, to seek a future steeped in inherited values and a half-mythological American past.

Evidence of similar attractions and needs appeared in other unlikely places, including the pages of Mike Gold's *Jews without Money* (1930). Gold tells an autobiographical story of growing up in a Jewish neighborhood on the Lower East Side of New York—a world of tenements and summer heat; of sweatshop gloom and stench; of bedbugs, litter, and flies. Announcing his conversion to communism in the final pages, the book's narrator hails the "Workers Revolution" as the "true Messiah" and the bringer of "hope", yet this sudden ending, like the affirmation it attempts to provide, has little grounding in the experience described. Gold made the recurring question of how an immigrant culture could relate to America a more prominent theme, exploring answers rooted in exploitation, imitation, resistance, and wonder. More than once Gold hinted that his ethnic experience, in fact, ran parallel to that of the wider nation. On an outing in a park, the mother displays a deep knowledge of mushrooms, allowing an urban community to lay claim to its rural or village roots. This mother in her devotion inspires the son's revolutionary conviction, suggesting a rural heritage for radical commitment combined, as in Conroy, with a reliance on the family as a moral and emotional touchstone. Gold cannot resist adding a claim to a frontier experience as well with his declaration that the Hester Street of his boyhood was "like the Wild West." Indeed, Gold had earlier shown the importance he attached to a connection with the national past in his choice of a name. Born Itshok Isaac (later Irwin) Granich, he had by his own account named himself after a Corporal Michael Gold, an aging Civil War veteran who, in living on the Lower East Side among immigrants, tied that Jewish neighborhood to American history.[21]

In part because Conroy and Gold did not achieve complete literary success, their novels offer unplanned testimony to the cultural tensions of the 1930s. The conflicts that pushed to the surface were not theirs alone but reflected the wider stresses and inherent doubts of a culture struggling to comprehend its own transitions. Efforts to construct a compelling vision joining what America had been with what it might be, the search for stable principles of community and personal identity, necessarily became tangled with assumptions, hesitations, loyalties, and convictions only sometimes functioning at the level of conscious recognition. The notions of class and ethnicity central to the stories Conroy and Gold were telling, for example, suggested divisions and differences of fundamental importance within the larger society. Yet both Conroy and Gold looked toward a unified national culture as an ideal, presumed at some level a characteristic or mainstream experience in the American past, and tried through radical faith to envision workers and the Jewish poor within an encompassing culture of the future. The effort to erect radical conclusions above thinly fictionalized personal narratives often fell flat because the writers involved were unable to reconcile distinctive experiences with a unifying social ideal, to make promises of community a credible outgrowth of multiple traditions and contentious actualities.

There were other obstacles as well. The tendency to seek ethical and emotional foundations in rural contexts suggested lingering uncertainty over the benefits of industrial progress and the triumph of the city. For all the advantages, real and proclaimed, of modernity, was modern society more brutal, exhausting, and impersonal, less natural, less virtuous, and less humane? Radical politics encouraged a conscious critique of factory conditions, of hierarchy and managerial authority, and of inequalities of wealth and power, yet communism advocated a collective consciousness on the basis of class that was dependent on industrial structures and impatient with the personal. As Conroy embraced the saving force of worker organization and Gold preached revolutionary communism, the paradoxical emphasis they placed on the family as moral center indicated an uneasiness with all large-scale institutions of industrialized society—not only corporations and the state but also labor unions and political parties. As radicals celebrated the collective interest, the very prominence of autobiography in their work suggested that they were continually drawn toward the attractions of individuality. For Conroy and Gold, divided feelings and competing values were both a product and a sign of that larger uncertainty over American identity and direction that led them to be at once passionate in their criticisms of American society and eager to claim an ownership of its traditions.

The question of how to think about specific experiences and values within a larger cultural framework posed one of the central intellectual problems of the 1930s. Was there an inclusive idea of cultural order, with concomitant assumptions about economic and political relationships, that could accommodate the insistent variety of region, class, ethnicity, religion, association, and behavior? The mixture of literary efforts clustered together awkwardly under the label of proletarianism illustrated the difficulty of the question, sometimes through the denial of all social possibility, sometimes through the failure to forge connections between worldly experience and radical ideals. Perhaps, then, it is understandable why many who had raised the banner of proletarianism (the critics perhaps more than the writers) easily left that concept behind in the mid-1930s and welcomed as a soothing balm a fundamental shift in Communist policy.

The early thirties had belonged to the so-called third period of international communism, a time when the imminence of capitalist collapse and proletarian revolution were deemed to require a militant purity in the Communist party. All who were not Communists were enemies of the working class; fascism was simply an indication of the "final crisis" of capitalism; and under the extraordinary theory of "social fascism," liberals and socialists were lumped together with fascists to be condemned in the same breath. In theory, there could be no Communist cooperation with writers and artists not committed to support of the Party. By mid-decade, however, it was clear that Hitler was not about to fade away, and growing concern in the Soviet Union with the expanding fascist threat led over a period of months to a sharp reversal in policy. From 1935 onward, the Communist party embraced the notion of a "Popular Front," a policy that demanded cooperation with bourgeois and liberal forces to oppose the power of fascism. Class struggle was now a muted theme; socialists and liberals were potential comrades; nationalism, rather than an exclusively internationalist emphasis, would now be all the rage.

From a cultural point of view, the new slogan "Communism Is Twentieth-Century Americanism" was a declaration of contradictions resolved that, like a slick advertising campaign, tapped fundamental emotions while promising smooth fulfillment. If there were loyalties to the past, concerns over meaningful values, anxieties about national identity, there was now a promise that Popular Front politics would blend continuity and patriotism with radical purpose, easing the painful burdens of thought and choice. To demonstrate their sympathy with the radical cause, writers would no longer be asked to emphasize "workers" and the social divisions that term implied; praise could now be lavished on the "people," affirming a message of unity rich in historical resonance. Antifascism and "twentieth-century Americanism" provided radical writers and their allies with a reformulated cause that made it easier for them to bury their contradictions, or to live with them.

## Radical Contenders, Modernist Defenders

In literature, the shift to a Popular Front strategy meant for some that problems associated with Communist attitudes toward writers and their work could be solved. Presumably the conscientious radical critic could now drop dogmatic tests of service to the working class and give ample weight to aesthetic values. Literary tradition could now be seen as a resource, and sympathetic bourgeois writers were targeted for recruitment rather than attack in hopes that they would lend their names to the proper organizations. Yet if the Popular Front eased relationships between radical and liberal writers and, indeed, did its best at times to erase distinctions between them, it gave up much of the cultural aspiration and the interest in new voices that had attracted a number of younger writers to communism in the first place. The John Reed clubs were summarily dumped in 1935. Richard Wright, astounded at the news, got no answer when he inquired what would "become of the young writers whom the Communist Party had implored to join the clubs" and who were now being discarded; with some exaggeration, Malcolm Cowley later declared that the decision launched "a new war between literary generations."[22] Into the closet went the dream of a new kind of literature and high talk about the radical writer's special relationship with a working-class audience. The idea of proletarian culture rapidly became something of an embarrassment to the Communist party as it threw on the rhetorical garb of a new political stance.

Nor did Popular Front policies make the fundamental tensions between literature and politics disappear. For those who had resisted a restrictive proletarianism for its willingness to make literary standards subservient to political expediency, the sudden Popular Front enthusiasm for liberal writers simply repeated the same pattern. The struggling journal *Partisan Review* gave clear voice to these concerns. Founded in 1934 as the organ of the John Reed Club of New York, *Partisan Review* had quickly established a prickly relationship with its senior partner in the Communist cultural camp, *New Masses*. Two of *Partisan*'s editors, Philip Rahv and William Phillips, had gradually constructed a sharp critique of low aesthetic standards and excessive politicization within "orthodox" proletarian writing and criticism, though always within the framework of an appeal for a more sophisticated radical literature. After the disbanding of the Reed clubs, Rahv, Phillips, and Alan Calmer continued for a time to publish *Partisan Review* independently, expressing growing skepticism about the Party's new strategies. The three young critics found in Communist efforts to attract well-known writers to the Popular Front little more than an unseemly celebrity-chasing that imputed radical value to the manufacture of publicity. Works could now be touted according to a different political standard, but for any such standard to dominate the evaluation of writing brought the integrity of all literary judgment under attack.[23] The tone that began to emerge in this criticism, and in writers like Wright and Farrell, as the Popular Front raised its banners of Communist-liberal cooperation was a tone that would turn by decade's end to a dirge of hope disappointed, of opportunity lost, of radicalism betrayed. There had never been a common set of assumptions on the left about the relationship between literature and radical politics. By 1936 the splits were widening, and the differences of the early 1930s were giving way to hostility and recrimination.

The Popular Front strategy in literature found particular embodiment in the League of American Writers, an organization created in 1935 following the Communist-sponsored First American Writers' Congress. The league limped along for a year until the outbreak of the Spanish Civil War in 1936 infused all Popular Front initiatives with new vitality and purpose. As Hitler and Mussolini lined up behind General Franco's effort to overthrow the existing coalition government of the Spanish Republic, and as the Soviet Union moved toward an alignment with Republican forces, the civil war turned into a practical and symbolic demonstration of the need for radical-liberal cooperation to resist fascism. The reluctance of the United States and other democratic governments to intervene in Spain only reinforced the appeal of the Popular Front for those who saw in the civil war a high moral cause. Volunteers from several countries, including a number of intellectuals and writers, joined the fight directly (those from the United States formed the Abraham Lincoln brigade); friends who remained at home could not fail such commitment.

Ernest Hemingway became perhaps the most prominent American writer associated with the cause when he helped raise funds for the Republic, served as a correspondent covering the Spanish war, and then used his experience in writing *For Whom the Bell Tolls* (1940). Yet Hemingway also illustrated the limitations of the Popular Front strategy from both a Communist and a more broadly radical viewpoint, for he was but a temporary ally and not a reliable convert to the politics of the left. Liberals, meanwhile, from Waldo Frank to Lewis Mumford and Van Wyck Brooks, were often wary of Party control, and the policies of the league between 1937 and 1940 were frequently shaped by the tensions between left-liberal writers who had joined the organization and the Communists who had founded it. Nevertheless, the compromises and contradictions of coalition politics seemed of little note during the late 1930s compared with the importance of the issues at hand. Members of Popular Front organizations, including the league, generally gave clear support to the idea of collective security against fascism, to the notion that the Soviet Union was the leader of the antifascist cause, and (less reliably among the liberals) to the proposition that Soviet and Communist actions had to be viewed sympathetically—meaning, in practice, that they could only be praised, justified, or excused.

Such conceptions never held the field alone. A quite different view of the Stalinist state and Communist practice gained vigorous expression during the later 1930s within a circle of left intellectuals who gathered around a new incarnation of the resilient *Partisan Review*. Lacking funds and insecure about its purpose and direction, the magazine had ceased publication in 1936. Before it appeared once again at the end of 1937, a number of factors had combined to make *Partisan Review* a bolder magazine with a heightened import.

Just as the outbreak of the Spanish Civil War in 1936 provided a defining focus for advocates of the Popular Front, the beginning of the Moscow Trials in the same year marked an unfolding of issues and events central to the development of the anti-Stalinist left. The trials were public displays designed to lend credibility to Stalin's charges of a conspiracy against his regime by traitors and fascists. Prominent among those accused were many of the "old bolshevik" leaders of the Russian Revolution whose prestige marked them as potential threats to Stalin's authority, in particular, the already exiled Leon Trotsky. Trotsky's credentials as a theorist in both politics and culture made him not simply the leader of small parties of devoted followers in Europe and the United States but a person claiming interest and respect (if not loyalty) within a much wider sphere. The nature and circumstances of the charges against Trotsky prompted the formation of the American Committee for the Defense of Leon Trotsky, an organization that joined anti-Stalinist radicals and liberals in an ironic parallel to the Popular Front. During the spring of 1937 the defense committee organized an independent "Commission of

Inquiry into the Charges against Leon Trotsky in the Moscow Trials"; John Dewey agreed to head the commission, in part because of his negative reaction to Communist efforts to oppose and obstruct any inquiry. The commission hearings in April at Trotsky's refuge in Coyoacan, Mexico, provided a forum for responding to Stalin's charges that was beyond Soviet control, and the findings of the commission were evident in the title of its report, *Not Guilty*.[24] Disputes over Trotsky, the Moscow Trials, the accompanying Soviet purges, and the integrity of socialist ideals divided the literary left in the United States throughout the later 1930s, provoking bitter struggles over the nature of the Soviet state.

The coalescence around the Trotsky defense committee of resistance to Popular Front domination of the left provided the context in which ideas about a new *Partisan Review* began to stir. During 1936–37 Phillips and Rahv came into contact with an assortment of other writers and intellectuals who had grown, or were rapidly growing, distrustful of Communist behavior and Stalinist aims. Three friends who had attended Yale together would ultimately join Rahv and Phillips as editors of the revived *Partisan Review*: the energetic Dwight Macdonald, the more scholarly F. W. Dupee, and the abstract artist George L. K. Morris, who provided financial support. The sixth member of the editorial board, Mary McCarthy (who had met Rahv through the defense committee), tied *Partisan Review* to a circle of young women writers whom she had known at Vassar, including Elizabeth Bishop, Eleanor Clark, and Muriel Rukeyser. Bolstered by the support they gave each other, the editors worked during the summer of 1937 to line up contributions from sympathetic intellectuals, including Sidney Hook, Edmund Wilson, James Burnham, Lionel Trilling, James T. Farrell, John Dos Passos, Meyer Schapiro, and Lionel Abel. Communist publications, meanwhile, began a vigorous attack on the emerging magazine, accusing its supporters of Trotskyism, of excessive intellectualism, and (quite accurately) of a critical attitude toward the Communist party and the Soviet Union. When in December 1937 the new *Partisan Review* announced in its opening statement that the magazine would be radical but "unequivocally independent," the editors confirmed that it would stand apart from the Popular Front. If *Partisan* had once been associated with the Communist party, the editors declared, the magazine now rejected such association in the conviction that "the totalitarian trend is inherent in that movement and that it can no longer be combatted from within."[25]

The term "totalitarian" was still new in the late 1930s, and its use was evolving rapidly. In 1937 the *Partisan* editors certainly meant to suggest by the term a Communist effort to assert centralized authority, to restrict opinion and debate, and to apply a political test to the evaluation of literature. Within a matter of months, *Partisan Review* would move further to include within its deployment of "totalitarian" a comparison that was growing ever more common among critics of Soviet policy across the political spectrum, a comparison that linked Stalin's communism with Hitler's fascism, and the Soviet Union with the Nazi state. Skirmishing between anti-Stalinists and the Popular Front came to a head in the summer of 1939. Two incipient groups formed by anti-Stalinist intellectuals, both including people from the *Partisan Review* circle, issued public statements criticizing Popular Front mystifications and explicitly linking Stalin with Hitler.[26] The response was emphatic, for the entire rationale for the Popular Front depended on the claim that the Soviet Union was the leader of world opposition to fascism. Some 400 persons signed a letter declaring any suggested similarity between the Soviet Union and fascist states a "fantastic falsehood" and listing ten reasons why the two were fundamentally opposed.[27] Unfortunately for such declarations, the letter had barely appeared when on 23 August, news of a Nazi-Soviet nonaggression pact broke upon the world, opening the way for the Nazi invasion of Poland on 1 September.

Stalin's covenant with Hitler delivered a devastating blow to the prestige of the Soviet Union among many left intellectuals who had supported the Popular Front. Over subsequent weeks and months, a stream of radicals and prominent liberal "fellow-travelers" who had followed the Communist lead turned their backs on the Party, sometimes with public repudiation of their former beliefs. Anti-Stalinists proclaimed themselves vindicated and at times proved vindictive, as when James T. Farrell suggested to the retreating Malcolm Cowley that someone should establish an "Institution for the Moral Rehabilita[t]ion of Betrayed Stalinist Charlatans, Dupes, Hatchet-Men and Literary Hacks." Yet the wiser among them understood their own loss and the wider blow to all socialist ideas, as did Farrell when he commented in his diary that the pact would "do severe damage to Marxism and revolutionary ideology."[28] The intellectuals on the left who had condemned the Moscow Trials and questioned Communist behavior in Spain had often done so out of a genuine commitment to radical ideals. However much they might try to separate those ideals from Stalin and the Communist party, their own capacities for continuing belief were challenged by the haunting specter of communism allied with fascism, by the Soviet Union's attack on Finland and its seizure of territory elsewhere, and by the assassination of Trotsky in 1940 at the hands of a Stalinist agent. The prominence the Soviet Union had claimed as a socialist experiment made its political conduct a problem for the entire left, difficult for some to dismiss or to explain within a framework of radical conviction.

The strange bedfellows of the 1939 pact would become bitter enemies with Hitler's attack on the Soviet Union in the summer of 1941, and Stalin would find new allies of convenience in Churchill and Roosevelt. For most intellectuals, however, the crucial events had already occurred, and the political evolution under way would not be easily reversed. Attempts during the second half of the 1930s to reassess what was vital and what was dead in Marxist thought turned by the beginning of the 1940s toward disputes within an eroding non-Communist left over ideas once taken as fundamental. Some, including Philip Rahv, began to question the radical potential of the proletariat, with the international experience of the thirties providing negative examples; anti-Stalinists within the *Partisan* circle divided over whether World War II was to be opposed on radical grounds or whether such opposition was an irresponsible denial of the evil of fascism; and radicals and former radicals engaged in a vigorous exchange over whether Stalin had corrupted the Russian Revolution or whether authoritarian tendencies were inherent in Leninist ideas. The pattern of fundamental importance, perhaps, was simply that a group of intellectuals with substantive roots in the left carried into the postwar period a conviction that the Communist party and the Soviet Union represented "totalitarian" oppression, a betrayal of genuine radical ideals, and a threat to democracy and free thought around the world. As their anti-Stalinism merged with a wider anticommunism by the early 1950s, and even fell into apparent affinities with more conservative antiradicalisms, the balance of ideas in American culture would be temporarily skewed. The experience of intellectuals with Stalin and the Communist party in the 1930s would cast its lights and shadows well into the future.

The shaping of ideas and ideals was occurring on other ground as well. An orienting process in literature as important as that in politics was coming to a head for the *Partisan Review* circle toward the end of the decade. At the rebirth of the magazine in 1937, the editors recognized modernist writing as the most advanced literature available, yet they clung to their hopes for a new fiction and poetry that would combine aesthetic sophistication and radical ideas in ways that reached beyond the limitations of modernism (limitations that Edmund Wilson had helped define in his 1931 study of major modernist writers, *Axel's Castle*). The era of the Popular Front soon put an end to such hopes for pathbreaking radical innovations. *Partisan Review* came increasingly to associate modernist writing with high literary standards and intellectual sophistication, in contrast to what it took as the crass endorsement of popularity and propaganda within the Popular Front. Moreover, modernism retained—or had regained—a critical bite for *Partisan*'s editors that allowed them to see in modernist literature, and by extension in themselves, a radical marginality that was nevertheless firmly rooted in an "intellectuals' tradition" of resistance to conventional culture. Dwight Macdonald thus noted that "in a reactionary period," modern literature had "come to represent again relatively the same threat to official society as it did in the early decades of the century." And *Partisan Review* commented editorially, "It is coming to be something of a revolutionary act simply to print serious creative writing."[29]

The claim that a "reactionary period" was at hand referred not only to the state tyrannies of Stalinism and of fascism but also to fears that in moving toward war the United States would itself accept social and cultural repressions in the name of nationalist unity, suffering an intensified bout of the patriotic fever that had gripped the nation during World War I. Those around *Partisan Review* had both intellectual and personal reasons to resist any such trend. For the most part they were Jewish, the children of East European immigrants, whose own entry into American intellectual life was situated within a broader cultural migration among second-generation Jews. Suspicion and hostility toward non-Protestant immigrant and ethnic groups remained strong in the United States between the world wars, and anti-Semitism was commonplace on the streets and in the universities. Young Jews staking a claim to broader participation in American intellectual life knew these obstacles and sought in varying ways to resist the normative assumptions that provided ethnic bias with its popular support. An advocacy of modernist writing became one of these ways.

By the end of the 1930s, modernism had come to represent for the *Partisan* circle not only a tradition of cultural challenge and a standard of aesthetic sophistication but also a cosmopolitan model of inclusiveness, cross-fertilization, and enrichment. The *Partisan* critics were aware, of course, that the social views expressed by individual modernist writers were sometimes highly objectionable to them: Rahv and Phillips had condemned sharply T. S. Eliot's anti-Semitic remarks of the early thirties. But they saw a quite different pattern in the literature itself and in modernism as an aesthetic movement. In an elegiac essay on the fall of Paris to the Nazis in 1940, Harold Rosenberg mourned the loss of the "laboratory of the twentieth century." Paris had provided a home for an international culture of modernism, "the opposite of the national in art," and its role could be defined in distinctly cosmopolitan terms: "No folk lost its integrity there; on the contrary, its artists, renewed by this magnanimous milieu, discovered in the depths of themselves what was most alive in the communities from which they had come."[30] This capacity of modernism to provide a sense of commonality across cultural boundaries while encouraging at the same time a richer expression of particularity made it seem a tradition accessible to all, a tradition that could be claimed by any group or individual as a counterforce to restrictive definitions of the "national." The *Partisan Review* intellectuals wanted the experimental and inclusive spirit of modernism, as they defined it, to permeate American culture, encouraging a sophisticated literary and artistic life in which they could freely participate absent the presumptions of nativism. They thus reacted strongly when others who seemed caught up in cultural preparations for war mounted a public critique of modern literature and of errant intellectuals.

The skepticism, the resistance to "official" culture, and the openness to multiple influences that the *Partisan* intellectuals were affirming as central virtues of modernism carried an opposite significance for those seeking to promote a sense of national unity and purpose. In the coming struggle against fascism, it was not the democratic idealism of World War I (despite its patriotic excesses) that would pose the more dangerous threat but the patterns of disillusionment, separation, and wariness that had gripped American thought since the 1920s. To Archibald MacLeish—poet, Librarian of Congress, and friend of President Roosevelt—contemporary intellectuals had become *The*

*Irresponsibles* (1940), slow to carry their talents "to the barricades of intellectu-al warfare." Rather than meeting their "obligation to defend the inherited cul-ture," too many had been seduced by the appeal of "objectivity and detach-ment," a remark that encompassed both aesthetic modernism and trends in social science, philosophy, and the professions.[31] Van Wyck Brooks went fur-ther in "Primary Literature and Coterie Literature" (1941), contrasting more wholesome writers of the past who had developed the "great themes" with "secondary" writers, including the modernists, whose brilliant technique ill disguised a lack of positive substance. Anxiety about an exclusionary nation-alism seemed thoroughly justified when Brooks declared that "primary" liter-ature followed the "biological grain" and contributed to "race-survival," whereas proper content was impossible for writers who "spent their lives in countries not their own."[32]

*Partisan Review* published a series of strong, and in some cases highly polemical, responses to such ideas. A Chicago friend of Rahv's, Morton Dauwen Zabel, compared the "patriotic orator" MacLeish to Hitler and Goebbels. Intellectuals who exercised a "critical faculty" offered the best hope for the present, he insisted, while the danger came from those who sought salvation "through appeals to race, blood, and religious hatred, through contempt for intellect and thought." Dwight Macdonald linked Brooks as well with the "specific cultural values" of Hitler and Stalin. Yet few of the *Partisan* circle went so far. The stronger theme framed a critique of Brooks's "anti-modernism," his "bellicose" allusions to Americanism, his "snobbish mystifi-cation" of some "secret Yankee language." Praising the literature of the 1920s, William Phillips condemned the rising "epidemic of literary nationalism" with its "militant provincialism." Macdonald denounced the "note of xenophobia" and the "chauvinistic leanings" in Brooks, while Lionel Trilling remarked that Brooks wanted "religion and not literature at all."[33]

To the *Partisan* circle, the "Brooks-MacLeish Thesis" threatened the free exercise of intellect and supported an idea of American culture that seemed to imply, especially for those who were Jews, their own exclusion. The promo-tion and defense of literary modernism associated with the writers and critics surrounding *Partisan Review* toward the end of the 1930s thus embodied a striking combination of values. Modernism challenged the intellect, reveled in difficulty, and demanded sophistication and learning, in many ways extending the claims of an elite culture and raising obstacles to access; at the same time, modernism could stand for cosmopolitanism, an openness to talent, and a dis-solution of barriers based on birth or ethnicity. The "highest" culture could also be, from some perspectives, the most meaningfully egalitarian.

The *Partisan* circle was not alone in discovering that an advocacy of literary modernism could embody useful combinations of intellectual and cultural val-ues. The challenge from Brooks and MacLeish helped strengthen an alliance both curious and natural between the New York–centered, largely left-wing *Partisan* critics and a group of southern writers frequently identified during the 1930s as conservatives or reactionaries. The core of the southern group had come together from 1922 to 1925 at Vanderbilt University in Nashville to publish *The Fugitive*, a poetry magazine that won considerable critical attention and acclaim. John Crowe Ransom, Allen Tate, and Donald Davidson stood at the center of the enterprise, with Robert Penn Warren and others contributing along the way. Working through constant interaction and mutual criticism, the *Fugitive* poets formed an intensely intellectual group, little interested in politics, acquainted with modernist poetry, and encouraged from a distance by Tate's literary hero, T. S. Eliot.

Ransom, Tate, Davidson, and, more peripherally, Warren again played a central role in a quite different intellectual project at the end of the 1920s: the development of a collection of essays by "Twelve Southerners" published in 1930 as *I'll Take My Stand*. Variously provoked by mockeries of the South during the publicity circus of the Scopes trial, by H. L. Mencken's scornful attacks on the region, and by developmentally minded enthusiasts of a "New South," the organizers of the symposium launched a self-conscious attempt to invent and claim a cohesive southern tradition. According to the introductory statement of principles, all of the authors supported a "Southern way of life" against the "American or prevailing way," with the distinction best captured in the phrase "Agrarian *versus* Industrial."[34] And indeed, the 12 generally shared a willingness to challenge materialist values and the doctrines of progress. Their separate essays raised questions about the degradation of work, art, and tradition under industrial dominance and looked to southern experience for a contrary model. Yet what was meant by industrialism, agrarianism, or the South was neither rigorously nor commonly defined; both at and beneath the surface of the essays, the 12 differed substantially in their political, racial, and regional sentiments. In part because of these differences, later commentators have often found it easy to downplay the more embarrassing assertions in *I'll Take My Stand* to emphasize the humanistic concerns of the authors, to compare their social critique to that of Marx or Thoreau, and to find in them prophets of a later environmentalism. Contemporary reviewers were less kind, frequently dismissing the book as out of touch with the world or as an exercise in literary nostalgia. Those on the left who labeled the authors reactionaries held up the mirror to Ransom's own conviction that agrarianism and communism stood at opposite poles.

Quiet for more than two years after the publication of *I'll Take My Stand*, several of the contributors, including Ransom, Tate, and Davidson, turned toward agrarian activism in the spring of 1933, a moment when quite disparate ideas seemed to have some prospect of public influence. At the center of the agrarian campaign that followed lay a belief in the fundamental importance of individual land ownership, a model of self-sustaining agriculture, and a desire to decentralize wealth and property. The campaign soon proved no less susceptible to internal tensions and external events than the other movements that changed course or ran aground in the middle thirties. By 1936 agrarianism was disintegrating as intellectual, organizational, and personal difficulties took their toll and as literature again claimed precedence for important members of the circle.[35] Robert Penn Warren, always lukewarm toward agrarian projects, was helping to launch the *Southern Review* at Louisiana State University. John Crowe Ransom, who had stood philosophically and personally at the core of the group, acknowledged disillusionment and moved in 1937 to Kenyon College in Ohio, where he would invest himself in editing the *Kenyon Review*. Ransom, Tate, Warren, and Cleanth Brooks, a former Vanderbilt student who became Warren's colleague at Louisiana State, soon emerged as major proponents of what Ransom referred to in a book title as *The New Criticism* (1941), a form of textual analysis put on display especially effectively in Brooks and Warren's *Understanding Poetry* (1938).

The southerners' turn toward a concentration on these newer literary pursuits coincided with the reappearance of *Partisan Review* as an anti-Stalinist magazine, and almost at once the two intellectual circles found ways to express a degree of mutual respect. This respect did not depend on shared political ideas, though both groups now stood in opposition to the Communist party. Neither did it depend on a common critical outlook. The "New Criticism" tended to emphasize an intense concentration on the text or work of art itself, finding value in its particular aesthetic expression and formal composition. Consequently, the New Critics deemphasized historical and biographical understanding and argued that artistic evaluation must remain separate from moral and social judgments. The *Partisan* critics, by contrast, honored Marxian insights and bowed toward Freud, looked outward from the text to the world, and made the exploration of moral and social meanings central to their work. Where the southerners and the New Yorkers found elements of commonality was in their commitment to literature and ideas, their seriousness about literary standards, and their appreciation for literary modernism.

The limited alliance made sense not just on narrow grounds but because of wider similarities between the impulses and experiences of the two circles. Each was wrestling after 1937 with a frustration of earlier political hopes: the southern New Critics were turning away from agrarianism, while the *Partisan* intellectuals were concluding that the Communist party was the enemy and not the agent of their cultural and social aspirations. Each rejected more particularly a confining version of the patriotic. In September 1936 Ransom remarked to Tate: "What is true in part for you . . . is true nearly in full for me: *patriotism* has nearly eaten me up, and I've got to get out of it."[36] The *Partisan Review* circle, in turn, had little stomach for the Popular Front's version of "twentieth-century Americanism" and the campaigns to which it was linked. These choices remained consonant with a longer experience. Both southerners and New Yorkers had struggled early in their careers to escape the limiting force of particularist traditions. The opening editorial of *The Fugitive* had declared that the magazine "flees from nothing faster than from the high-caste Brahmins of the Old South," and Tate had spoken of the young poets' effort to leave behind the "old atavism and sentimentality."[37]  Many in the New York circle, for their part, shared an experience that a young Alfred Kazin labeled a struggle against the "sentimental chauvinism," "timidity," and "parochialism" of immigrant Jewish culture.[38]  In their quite different ways, both groups had come to resist narrowing definitions of group or national culture, and literary modernism was a part of that resistance.

That they should be wary of narrowness made sense for the wider processes of cultural adjustment that were under way. Just as second-generation Jews sought to enter and sometimes to reshape American cultural life, southern writers still moving out of the economic and cultural penumbra of the Civil War staked their own claims to broader participation. The southern process was well advanced. Indeed, the 1930s have been identified by some as "the high point, the culmination, of the South's literary history."[39]  This writing ranged across a variety of types, most not influenced by agrarian ideas and relatively few carrying the flag of "social evangelism." In an extraordinary burst of creativity that won him little immediate reward, William Faulkner published seven novels between 1929 and 1942: *The Sound and the Fury, As I Lay Dying, Light in August, Absalom, Absalom!, The Wild Palms, The Hamlet,* and *Go Down, Moses.*  Thomas Wolfe wrote voluminously during the 1930s; Lillian Hellman crafted some of her best plays; and Katherine Anne Porter was at her peak. James Agee completed his first two books; Eudora Welty began her first novel; Carson McCullers wrote *The Heart Is a Lonely Hunter* (1940); and Zora Neale Hurston published *Their Eyes Were Watching God.*  Erskine Caldwell made a popular splash with *Tobacco Road* (1932) and *God's Little Acre* (1933); Margaret Mitchell gained fame for *Gone with the Wind*; and toward the end of the thirties Richard Wright wrote the stories that would become *Uncle Tom's Children.*  Robert Penn Warren and Allen Tate each published both poetry and a novel during the thirties. Although no common outlook or style bound these works together, many were linked by the nature of their recurring themes: an attention to the meanings of southern identity, a concern with the relationship of the past to a changing present, and a mulling over of transitions evident within the South demonstrated a keen awareness among southern writers of the region's evolving relationship to a larger culture.

Transitional experiences of their own provided literary material for a growing number of Jewish writers during the 1930s. Like their southern counterparts, they often wrote about "local" cultures that were being left behind and about the prospects and costs of entering a wider world. Mike Gold's *Jews without Money*, a case in point, combined remembrance and aspiration. Henry Roth's *Call It Sleep* (1934) delved into urban immigrant life through the psychological struggles of a young boy, with modernism and James Joyce clearly holding sway over Roth's proletarian sympathies. Daniel Fuchs in the three novels of his Williamsburg trilogy (1934, 1936, 1937) offered a precisely detailed and generally bleak picture of Brooklyn Jewish neighborhoods and their restricted possibilities.[40]  Nathanael West's anxieties over the cultural impact of the movies looked past ethnicity, but Budd Schulberg's less sophisticated and more popular *What Makes Sammy Run?* (1941) turned a sharp gaze on the untempered ambition that could turn poor Jewish boys into Hollywood producers. In *The Unpossessed* (1934), Tess Slesinger worked from her experience within a particular circle of radical young intellectuals in the early thirties to explore different transitions involving both ethnicity and gender. Delmore Schwartz was publishing stories and poems by 1937, and Saul Bellow was just beginning to write. Although not yet at a developmental "high point," the quantity and quality of writing by American Jews was clearly on the ascent.

When *Partisan Review* intellectuals and southern New Critics rejected what they saw as a restrictive, antimodernist nationalism in Brooks and MacLeish, they were thus trying to hold the door open to more complex definitions of literary culture that could accommodate the subject matters, themes, and voices still emerging in America. This was not a matter of conscious group advocacy. The variety among southern and Jewish writers encouraged no collective assertion, even had the critics been inclined to promote some notion of commonality (as they were not). Rather, the *Partisan* circle and the New Critics were defending their own response to the tensions between particular cultural backgrounds and general cultural participation. They were upholding explicit and implicit claims that within the evolving legacy of modernism, multiple traditions might not simply coexist but might enrich a broader aesthetic. And they were affirming once more the importance of intellect, of learning, and of standards to the ongoing construction of a culture worth claiming. For both circles, the defense of modernism involved a wider set of ideas that spoke to social transition and cultural aspiration more successfully than any imaginative framework offered by communism, by agrarianism, or by the nationalism of a "secret Yankee language." Such ideas would gain considerable influence within the academy after World War II. Yet by the end of the 1930s, a different vision of how particular cultures might relate to the American whole was already demonstrating a more popular appeal.

*six*

---

# *Facts, Photos, Values, and Myths: American Culture and the Social Report*

The heightened social consciousness that Frederick Lewis Allen saw as characteristic of the 1930s found expression during the early part of the decade in a wave of writing that sought to lay bare the harshness of depression existence and the enduring inequities of the American system. Proletarian novels contributed their energies to this surge, but they did not typify its central directions, either in their genre or in their presumptive ties to an explicit political program. Fiction yielded pride of place within the wider tide to direct social reporting, and radical agendas influential at the beginning of the decade provided just one source of motivation for social writing, one distinctive flavoring. If the larger body of work was indeed driven by a central urge, it was the impulse to document and describe, which could serve equally well a variety of intellectual ends. By the close of the decade, this impulse was flowing lustily into cultural channels few advocates of "social consciousness" could easily have foreseen.

With the slide into depression, reportage rose to new prominence as established critics and novelists joined journalists and aspiring activists to delineate the human circumstances bespeaking the national condition. Theodore Dreiser and John Dos Passos belonged to one delegation, Waldo Frank and Edmund Wilson to another, that visited Harlan County, Kentucky, in 1931–32 to investigate violence and abuse directed at striking coal miners. (Both delegations were sponsored directly or indirectly by the Communist party, and in a pattern that became familiar during the early thirties, some participants, including Dreiser and Wilson, came to feel they were being "used" by the

Party and stiffened their spines in resistance.) Other writers chronicled life on the breadlines or in the hobo camps; laid before their readers the details of a lynching; explored the worst oppressions of urban or rural poverty; described a Hooverville, a works program, a boxing match; or recounted through individual examples the reactions of common citizens to the depression. These journalistic reports demonstrated a desire to capture and record the details of social experience that would be evident throughout the decade in broadcasting, in photography, in documentary films, in social science reports, in the theater, in the arts, and in combinations of these forms. For those who believed that the discovery of unpleasant realities indicted an entire political and economic system, it was easy to assume for a time that investigating and describing, in themselves, were suffused with radical meaning.

Whatever the convictions of its practitioners, social documentation and description carried an appeal during the early 1930s that was not dependent on specific principles or ideas. Even for intellectuals, like Wilson, who claimed to welcome the collapse of capitalism, the depression often brought the shock of disorientation, a disruption of the predictable, a threat to understanding and control. The urge to witness and report fed on a sense that to capture reality would be to gain some power over it. Against the uncertainty of the times, the writer could array the apparent certainty of social "facts." Observation and description carried an ordering power that presumed to be relatively neutral, but neutrality was not a requisite. If anxiety gave rise to anger or found expression in a fascination with violence—matching a dark motif in the films of the early depression—such emotions could be legitimized as the hallmarks of social passion. The apparent solidity of facts provided a personal and cultural anchor, even when the vessel of their meaning was turning with every crosswind and struggling for clear direction.

The eagerness to convey facts observed at first hand prompted a rush to explore layers and locales of American society beyond the accustomed reach of public attention. Exploration led to discovery. Writers whose own background had largely sheltered them from the harsher functionings of prejudice and power found every exposure to such realities more momentous as a result. When the Harlan County delegation that included Frank and Wilson appeared in Pineville, Kentucky, local authorities—who believed they knew interfering outsiders when they saw them—threw two members of the delegation into jail when they tried to speak publicly, transported the whole group to the state border that evening, and provided some of them with a beating before sending them on their way.[1] Even when writers did not themselves become subject to the circumstances they tried to describe, their efforts to investigate and report often turned up evidence of conditions that warranted their surprise and indignation. It was a short step to the belief that the insights they were gaining into American social relationships confirmed the value of their approach.

If writers sometimes unearthed a strain of violence and brutality in American society or laid bare the presence of injustice, these were not the only themes to emerge from their explorations. They also wrote, for example, about waste, a topic that accumulated a host of meanings in the depression context of the 1930s. Inescapable evidence of the human waste caused by unemployment encouraged recognition of the constriction and misuse of human resources that was a normal fate for some social groups. The continuing waste of land and water gained prominence through the devolution of the Great Plains into the Dust Bowl; a traveling Malcolm Cowley offered a typical lament that some of the "richest agricultural lands on our continent" were also among those "most impoverished by a drought."[2] The waste inherent in corn being burned for fuel, milk being dumped on highways, and farm animals being destroyed—all in a land where millions were going hungry—made for a situation both infuriating and poignant. The painstaking description of depleted lives and squandered resources became one of the characteristic strains of depression writing.

Yet this theme of waste, like many others that came to the fore, had broad American roots and was tied exclusively to no single political stance. Commentators of varying persuasions condemned waste, called for good stewardship, or appealed to efficiency, yet they made quite different assumptions and drew quite different conclusions about what such standards implied. Radical or left-liberal writers commonly interpreted improvidence as a commentary on the failings of capitalism: Stuart Chase and George Soule rejected capitalism "not because it was exploitative or oppressive but because it appeared wasteful and inefficient."[3] Intellectuals enamored of expertise and planning, as well as those battling social class or seeking a higher culture, looked to socialism or communism for a world that was more efficient as well as more just.

Liberals explored the waste of human and natural resources just as avidly, while trusting for remedy to ameliorative modifications in the existing political and economic framework. A zealous concern with efficiency and an interest in conservation—firmly established in at least one branch of progressivism before World War I—provided liberals with a ready language by which wastefulness became a justification for reform, not revolution. With the coming of the New Deal, the federal government took the lead in responding to unemployment and claimed a conservationist mantle with programs ranging from the work of the Civilian Conservation Corps to the planting of trees as windbreaks on the plains. Pare Lorentz made his lyric documentary films on the Dust Bowl and soil erosion, *The Plow That Broke the Plains* (1936) and *The River* (1937), under the auspices of the New Deal.

Political conservatives, meanwhile, had their own established notions about efficiency, and they were quick to attack unemployment spending for wasting money on make-work jobs and handouts for the lazy. Mining this vein, the wealthy R. R. M. Carpenter complained in 1934 that "five Negroes on my place in South Carolina refused work this Spring . . . saying they had easy jobs with the government."[4] At a popular level, "WPA" was said to stand for "We Piddle Around" or "We Putter Around"; migrant Okies were charged with singing "Merrily we dole along"; and jokers declared, "There's a new cure for cancer, but they can't get any of it. It's sweat from a WPA worker."[5] The very same New Deal programs that radicals dismissed as an inadequate response to the waste of human resources stood for conservatives as landmarks of liberal profligacy.

The meaning of every theme in the social writing of the 1930s thus remained subject to competing cultural definitions and claims. Writers struggled to establish those meanings in which they believed, often by seeking to trigger a sympathetic emotional response, sometimes by preaching an explicit political lesson. Reaching beyond the immediacy of particular arguments, this effort to find and establish meaning involved both a need to reexamine national identity in a period of crisis and a standing concern among intellectuals with defining their role and social position. Since the early part of the century, a network of critics and thinkers had aspired self-consciously to avoid intellectual isolation and specialization. Many longed to influence attitudes and events even as they cultivated their claims to independence and perspective. The social report encouraged writers to seek out direct experience, to lay claim to a hardheaded confrontation with reality. At the same time, it invited the creation of a distinctive slant—either through the tone and structure of the material or through direct interpretation—that nourished the hope of influence while preserving the possibility of independence. The crafting of message and stance gained added import from the nature of the issues at stake. As the more astute always knew, their subject in the social report was never social conditions or particular incidents alone, but the character of the American people and the prospects for American culture.

The majority of commentators who set out to describe America in the worst years of the depression quite naturally assumed that all was not well in the land. They were drawn toward evidence of lives and values askew and accepted as a matter of faith the need for change. Often sharply critical of a self-centered individualism, they responded to varying notions of human kinship and community that suggested a collective social responsibility. Yet many continued to be deeply interested in the question of individual character and alert for signs of self-reliance among the Americans they met. And with hardship a given, evidence of spirit and fortitude in a people could easily turn into an argument for their culture's strength. Indeed, if some social reports suggested in the valley of depression a country cut off from its past and uncertain about its future, such reports moved preponderantly over the thirties toward a confluence with established myths and cultural themes, merging present experience into an ongoing national identity. With a balance that shifted as the decade progressed, social reporting combined accusatory exposure and cultural celebration, the mission to reform and the desire to affirm.

## *In Need of Direction*

As a literature of social description began to appear in response to the depression, works with competing emphases quickly demonstrated both the power and perception of the social report and the pliability of the form. In keeping with their attitude toward proletarian fiction, Communist critics proved particularly eager for writers sympathetic to the revolutionary cause to advance explicit political doctrines and agendas. Meridel LeSueur, who made her first contribution to *New Masses* in 1932 when she was in her midtwenties, was offered Party guidance almost as a public scolding. In "Women on the Breadlines," LeSueur described the experience of sitting day after day among the old and the young in the women's section of the Minneapolis free employment bureau, with few prospects, a boredom relieved only by the many faces of suffering, and choices limited to the various forms of humiliation. She saw in the question of what happened to women who were unemployed and hungry one of "the great mysteries of the city": "There are not many women in the bread line. There are no flop houses for women as there are for men. . . . They obviously don't sleep in the [hobo] jungle or under newspapers in the park. . . . What happens to them? Where do they go?" LeSueur suggested in part that destitute women tended to hide away and be overlooked in the "social statistics." The young were rejecting marriage and children, living alone and clinging to what fun they could grasp against the prospect that even in finding work they would face "the suffering of endless labor without dream."[6]

The bleakness of this picture served realism well, and certainly LeSueur raised significant questions about women and the depression, but the dominant tone did not correspond with the Communist party's tactical guidelines for writers. Although allowing that the piece was "able" and "informative," the editors regretted in a published note that it was "defeatest [*sic*] in attitude, lacking in revolutionary spirit and direction which characterize the usual contribution to *New Masses*." What the essay apparently needed and the editors hastened to add—was an upbeat assertion that women could advance their cause by attaching themselves to the organizations of the Communist party. As in the radical novel, *New Masses* wanted to see in social reports a direct political appeal, whether or not the call to arms had any integral relation to the material presented or to the writer's perceptions.[7]

Sometimes the subject matter or an author's approach made developing a political message relatively easy. The heightened interest in the description of specific depression contexts and experiences encouraged attention to ethnic, racial, and cultural settings that had often received limited acknowledgement in earlier American writing, and the efforts of the Communist party to appear as the champion of less-favored groups invited a political framing for any such discussion. The young Richard Wright handled his opportunity deftly in reporting for *New Masses* the reaction of Chicago's black community to Joe

Louis's knockout of Max Baer in 1935. There had been a celebratory rush into the streets and a strong sense of black unity; an exhilaration that surged past customary behavioral barriers, producing a "mingling of fear and fulfillment"; and an awareness of the symbolic power of Louis as the "concentrated essence of black triumph over white." Capturing effectively a dramatic and revealing moment of black empowerment, Wright's piece concluded smoothly that this "wild river" needed to be "harnessed and directed" by the Communist party. This was not a message that suggested to African-Americans that the Party would solve all of their problems. Indeed, there was a potential for criticism of reigning Communist doctrines in the fact that the emotions Wright described sprang from an identity based on race not class. Yet the piece did emphasize that people who have been frequently oppressed harbor a potential for social "dynamite" that might be channeled toward radical politics. No added editorial note was needed, for Wright's explicit political message called for the Party to do precisely what it was already trying to do.[8]

The advent of the New Deal and its activist response to the depression posed an immediate threat to the political appeal of radicalism. John Spivak fought back with a report on the dire conditions among farmworkers in California, framed as a letter to President Roosevelt on behalf of a pregnant 15-year-old Mexican-American girl who had heard that Roosevelt was "doing things for poor workers." The girl presumably wanted to send a letter to the president to ask for a removal of the farmer's charge for electric lights so that she would not have to have her baby in the dark. Yet ultimately, the individual case provided little more than a dramatic focal point. There was really no interest in the girl's personality, in her choices, or for that matter, in the Mexican-American culture from which she came. The heart of the piece lay in the assertion that "nobody else seemed to care" about farmworkers except the Communists, the "red agitators" who "terrified" the "business men and bankers and farmers" who were the direct agents of oppression. Spivak borrowed the wet handkerchief of melodramatic "human interest" reporting to wring out the verities of pre-1936 Communist journalism: the omnipresence of class interests and class conflict; the evils of the existing social and economic system; and the futility of ameliorative reforms when radical change was necessary.[9]

Interspersed with the reports most closely tied to Communist politics, other works of social testament shared a dismay over human conditions but often revealed a different structure of assumptions and concerns. In 1932, with the depression at its worst and Roosevelt not yet in office, Edmund Wilson chose to end his *American Jitters* with the description of "a man in the street" who seemed "able-bodied and self-dependent" and who could have come from any social level or profession. Now this emblematic figure wandered without direction through a once-prosperous neighborhood, looking "dazed . . . as if life had come suddenly under a shadow which he could see no way of getting out of and had no means of accounting for."[10] Wilson's typical citizen was not identified or identifiable as either bourgeois or proletarian. The partial reassurance that common folk still appeared "able-bodied and self-dependent" reflected a desire to believe that the American commitment to individual self-reliance remained strong, though at present frustrated. The nation's confusion might justify taking a close look at radical ideas, as it did for Wilson, yet the image he chose to emphasize after many pages of descriptive report cherished no vision of proletarian solidarity or revolutionary potential.

Sherwood Anderson in early 1933 went a bit further, but with an essentially similar spirit, in writing to a friend, "When you see at first hand what is going on here it's hard not to become a rampant red and cry anything but this. . . . It is not only the hunger and destitution—it's something gone out of America—an old faith lost and no new one got."[11] Anderson could understand a turning toward radical politics in order to do and believe in something, but his was hardly a stance of firm principle and proletarian conviction. What Wilson and Anderson most stressed was the lack of orientation and purpose, the sense of drift, that seemed to them the national mood in the early 1930s. They were not necessarily describing a society and a system so fundamentally diseased as to require a revolutionary cure.

Within a year, different themes were emerging from social reports, and suggestions of a broken or interrupted culture were growing scarce. In early 1934 John Dos Passos described in *New Masses* a national gathering of representatives from the radical "unemployed councils," emphasizing that those present were a geographical, ethnic, and occupational mix reflecting "a real cross section of the U.S.A., . . . the real shivering miserable and alive U.S.A. of the workers, farmers, producers and would-be consumers." Befitting its publication in a Communist magazine and the nature of the gathering described, Dos Passos's piece voiced the disappointment of the unemployed with an early New Deal diet of anticipation and bureaucracy, and it rehearsed a political refrain on the importance of "organization, solidarity, and nerve." Yet what Dos Passos most wanted to report was the positive spirit of people cooperating to do something for themselves through the councils. And what fueled this spirit? For Dos Passos, it was the desire to be "respected citizens again," as well as the demand for "something more" among the young, who had grown up during the "frigidaire and washing machine millennium." The convention, whose "real" U.S.A. was also "Whitman's and Lincoln's U.S.A.," took its "big drive" from young people's "wants and ambitions." The moving spirit within this radical organization of common folk, it seemed, was a well-established American quest for opportunity, participation, and prospects, which had more to do with campaigning for jobs than with the overthrow of capitalism.[12]

In describing cooperation among common Americans to protect their immediate interests and to demand scope for personal ambition, Dos Passos might indeed have claimed association with the frontier politics of "Lincoln's U.S.A." Certainly he was eager to affirm in the unemployed a resilience and endurance often associated with the pioneering tradition. And in a 50-item catalog of groups and occupations, Dos Passos celebrated a diversely "alive" America in a fashion and tone that were indeed Whitmanesque. He was not alone in reaching for such themes. By mid-decade a growing number of writers were winding their way around the country and turning out newspaper pieces, magazine articles, and books detailing their observations and experiences. The evolving patterns of exploration and discovery themselves became a shaping force for social reporting, encouraging the flow of perception into well-worn channels of cultural meaning.

To set out on a journey of exploration, to travel across the land, was to evoke themes of discovery and pioneer trek deeply embedded in the national culture and to reaffirm their significance for understanding America. Writers often moved outward from industrial cities into the South or the Midwest or the West, as if the roots of the country's institutions and the best barometers of its condition could only be found in rural areas and small towns linked with the past. The investigative tour, designed to probe the state of a system and a people, called to mind the decades during the early nineteenth century when examining the American experiment attracted a wave of European travelers. Perhaps not since then had intellectuals shown the compulsion so evident in the 1930s to search out the character of the country through firsthand observation. Finally, the literary commonplace of the journey as metaphor suggested a quest for understanding and identity that gave the pilgrim's observations wider resonance. As national tradition, character, and identity became more and more wrapped up in the findings of the social reports, certain motifs claimed ever greater prominence as positive themes. None were more important than the idea of resilience or endurance, suggesting both character and continuity, and the idea of variousness or heterogeneity, seen as a source of democratic vitality.

In *Puzzled America* (1935), Sherwood Anderson provided a benchmark of sorts in the progress of the social report. Originally published as letters from the field in *Today* magazine, the accounts of his travels exhibited mixed reactions and described a nation complex in its patchwork of experience. One man he encountered had lost his job early in the depression and remained unwillingly dependent and idle—he was a man "whose civilization had got through with him before he was through with it." Anderson observed the persistence in such people of an "undying so-American optimism" that he declared "pathetic." Yet he could not help thinking of these Americans, "They are O.K. They can sure take it." If one side of Anderson's mind insisted that he condemn the human waste involved and tolerate no illusions, the other could not help but admire the persisting desire for self-sustaining work and the ability of Americans to "take it." Through a sometimes reluctant appreciation of the resilience of ordinary Americans, a reason to honor the national character—to suggest that, like their pioneer or immigrant ancestors, living Americans had the will to endure—found its way into the marrow of the social report. On another stop, Anderson was moved to go further and to acknowledge that the civilization that discarded could also build. In Civilian Conservation Corps camps and in the projects of the Tennessee Valley Authority he found "something I have been hungry to find, men working at work they love, not thinking of money or promotion, happy men, laughing men." Rather than speaking as he had in 1933 about something lost, Anderson now emphasized, in the words of a friend about the TVA, that "something new in American life is begun back there."[13]

Although continuing to heed personal suffering and to chart "pathetic" illusions, Anderson edged the balance in his commentary toward direct affirmation of American endurance, complexity, and vitality. The growing strength of such positive themes in social reporting would be given added momentum by two political developments of the mid-1930s. The first took shape as the rising power of German fascism prompted a renewed appreciation for American strengths and democratic values across much of the political spectrum. Stalin's turn toward a Popular Front strategy against fascism led the Communist party to downplay its emphasis on an internationalist class solidarity. Communists and their allies now encouraged efforts to turn national traditions and multiple group identities toward Popular Front purposes, opening the way for left-wing versions of cultural celebration. Meanwhile, many liberals and conservatives (as well as some anti-Stalinist radicals) defined the situation differently, stressing the need to oppose the centralized regimentations of both fascism and communism. This orientation tended once again to stir positive attention to American cultural traditions and a desire to affirm democratic ideals. The second development of the mid-1930s was that the New Deal, with its wide programmatic range, began to claim a major share of descriptive attention that (as Anderson's pleasure in finding laughing workers suggests) proved dominantly positive. New Deal activism seemed to demonstrate that the American system could come alive to a major challenge and uphold the viability of democracy against fascist and communist alternatives. A part of that activism put reporting to work within federal programs themselves.

## Along the American Road

The New Deal altered the implications of social reporting. The reports of the early thirties had most frequently intended to show the extremities of social conditions and the inadequacies of governmental response. Both the products of left journalism and the stream of reports based on social workers' case studies (beginning with Clinch Calkins's *Some Folks Won't Work* in 1930) were in this sense intended as oppositional writing. The New Deal reversed the polarities of the form to claim documentation and report as tools of national administration and, ultimately, of celebration. Within a few months of Franklin Roosevelt taking office, Eleanor Roosevelt toured the southern Appalachian region at her husband's request to examine conditions of numbing poverty and, over many objections, to call attention to such misery as a spur to reform. Eleanor would serve many times as Franklin's conduit for direct experience. To similar ends, whole teams of observers and reporters were organized by ranking administrators in many New Deal agencies, making the gathering of information and impressions a significant governmental process. Within this framework, reports might still describe misery, corruption, or injustice, and they might still testify for change, but their force was directed toward strengthening the New Deal, not challenging it.

Perhaps the best-known band of traveling observers was organized by Harry Hopkins, head of the Federal Emergency Relief Administration (FERA) and later of other New Deal agencies. In July 1933 Hopkins commissioned Lorena Hickok, a veteran news reporter and feature writer, to serve as his chief investigator. "What I want you to do," Hopkins explained, "is to go out around the country and look this thing [relief] over. I don't want statistics from you. I don't want the social-worker angle. I just want your own reaction, as an ordinary citizen."[14] Hopkins sought not predigested information, of which he had plenty, but direct reports on how the relief effort was working, a sense of how people were feeling, a reading on the country's condition. Hickok delivered such direct reactions with reliability and frankness. Finding political corruption or incompetency, she could declare that "Texas is a Godawful mess," or that Florida seemed "chock full of politics and petty graft." Mostly she wrote about the great mix of Americans with whom she talked: "One by one, sometimes bold, sometimes hesitant, sometimes demanding, sometimes faltering, they emerged—individuals. People with voices, faces, eyes. People with hope. People without hope. People still fighting. People with all courage squeezed out of them. People with stories." A 1937 introduction to a planned book on her experiences was dedicated, in defiance of conservative epithets, to "the 'chiselers' and the 'shovel-leaners'" of New Deal work programs, not as representatives of a class or group but as American "individuals."[15]

Hopkins launched a more extensive investigation into the conditions of the unemployed in the second half of 1934, recruiting some 15 experienced reporters whom Hickok coordinated, each of whom was assigned an industrial territory. Ernestine Ball and Martha Bruere, for example, reported on Upstate New York; Lincoln Colcord and Louisa Wilson explored the automobile industry centered on Detroit and Cleveland; Edward J. Webster dealt with St. Louis, Kansas City, and Texas; Martha Gellhorn specialized in the textile industry in the Carolinas and New England; others concentrated on mining regions and on Chicago, New York, Boston, Pittsburgh, and Birmingham. Hickok herself toured the West during 1934. The number of women among the FERA reporters was matched by a strong cadre of women among federal relief officials, testifying both to Hopkins's willingness to employ women and to an established assumption that social work and welfare issues were appropriate public spheres for women's activity. Although conditions had improved marginally during the first year of the New Deal, the investigators went into a land still under a heavy cloud of depression, and their job asked them to concentrate on one of the darker sides of American experience. Carrying with them assumptions based on their own middle-class backgrounds, on current social and economic beliefs, and on prevailing cultural biases, the reporters provided assessments that gave voice to important tensions over ideas and social values within American culture, many of which they could not fully resolve.

The reporters confronted a mountain of evidence that work and success were hollow dreams for significant numbers of Americans, and they struggled to rescue their own sense of American norms, their confidence in the power of professionalism and expertise, and their belief that science and technology worked generally to improve society. An assertion that professional standards could ameliorate at least some social ills was evident in the contrast drawn repeatedly between local politicization, corruption, and inefficiency, and the effectiveness of federal relief management under Hopkins. Although the reporters may often have been accurate in their observations, they left little room for the possibility that "corrupt" systems at the community level might sometimes deliver aid more responsively than structures with firmer rules and bureaucratized management. A recognition that trained social workers within FERA programs sometimes lacked good sense and that relief recipients often complained most about inflexible rules did not alter the thrust of the reports. The sharpness of FERA reporters' comments on local relief administration invested professional control with a socially redemptive efficiency, emphasizing the inherent waste of nonprofessional welfare nearly as much as the wasting lives of the unemployed.

On a wider scale, the application of specialized knowledge within the American economy was often seen as a root cause of unemployment, though the reporters did not frame their remarks in ways suggesting they saw any irony in the treatment of expertise as both cause and cure. They tended to believe, as the closest analysts of their reports have put it, that the United States was "caught in the throes of a historic change" from basic industrialism to a "highly technological" society that created "a minimum demand for people with low technical skills."[16] A substantial segment of those on relief—people who had worked in mills and mines now fading toward obsolescence, the unskilled of urban slums, or those who had been tenants or marginal farmers—seemed unlikely ever to find decent jobs in the emerging economy, thus remaining dependent and enduringly poor, a burden and a threat. This prospect of built-in frustration ran against the grain of most FERA reporters' continuing belief in hard work, ability, and character as central American values. (Martha Gellhorn, one of the gloomiest, turned toward advocacy of birth control for the poor.)[17] Yet unhappiness with the discarding process and its potential for cultural disruption produced little challenge to a sense of inevitability or to the association of technology and expertise with social advance.

Dominant cultural stereotypes sometimes contributed in an unfortunate way to easing intellectual and moral tensions over the idea of a permanently underemployed population: established biases reinforced the perception of a logical overlap between the economically rejected and ethnicity or race. FERA reporters repeatedly judged members of particular groups to be lacking in initiative because they fell short of a proper passion for work, self-reliance, and higher living standards. Mexican-Americans and Hispanic-Indian people in the Southwest, African-Americans in Detroit and the South, French-Canadians in northern New England, rather than suffering from the stigma of relief or finding it inadequate, seemed to the reporters "perfectly contented" and "willing to stay on relief the rest of their lives."[18] Writing from Arizona, for example, Hickok went on at length about the failings of the "Latin and Indian" temperament: "They don't 'want' things. They haven't any ambition." The Spanish side was "easy-going, pleasure loving. It isn't in their makeup to 'get out and hustle.' And the Indian in them certainly wouldn't make them ambitious." What Hickok took to be inherent racial and cultural differences presented a problem that struck her as central to the relief effort. For many whites, "with white standards of living," relief as it currently existed was "anything but adequate," and they were "growing restive." For "Mexicans—or, East of the Mississippi, Negroes—with low standards of living," relief was "adequate and attractive." There were "so many Mexicans and Negroes on relief that, with a limited amount of money, we are compelled to force the white man's standard of living down to that of the Mexicans and Negroes."[19]

Hickok acknowledged that if "Mexicans and Negroes" did get work it was likely to be "at wages so low that they are better off on relief." She pointed out that some FERA administrators believed that requiring the ethnic poor to take whatever work they could find would simply be "forcing these people into peonage," and she condemned the gouging of employers, particularly farmers, ranchers, and housewives. In discussing the effect of the depression in throwing marginal and tenant farmers off the land and sending them unprepared to the cities, Hickok also spoke of whites, particularly rural poor whites of the South, in much the same terms she applied to ethnics: they were "lazy"; they were heirs of an inadequate culture with low living standards; and as a fellow reporter put it, they were "deficient in initiative and resourcefulness."[20] Hickok thus recognized injustices or acknowledged a range of conditions affecting the experience and behavior of particular groups but nevertheless remained ready to advocate a federal relief policy of differential distribution, just as she accepted a system slipped quietly into place in Tucson that provided four different levels of payments for people of different groups and classes.[21]

The FERA reporters defended both directly and indirectly what they took to be normative cultural values. They found it difficult to acknowledge minorities and poor whites as representative citizens or to accept the values and character traits attributed to them as legitimately "American." The identity of the nation rested primarily with those who had "white standards of living" in diet, clothing, and shelter; with those of self-reliant character whose initiative and ambition made relief an embarrassment, and unemployment a torment; with those whose capacity to "'want' things" fired the urge to produce and consume. The political context was quite different, yet the sense of the nation's driving force appeared strikingly similar to Dos Passos's theme of "wants and ambitions" in *New Masses*.

Hickok's Arizona report found house payments, baby food, and support for aging parents legitimate matters of concern for "white collar clients," while the inability to hire household help and a son withdrawing from college became signs of the depression's toll. The reporters worried continually about the effects on both middle- and working-class families when the father lost his place of responsibility, when the family became dysfunctional, and when the necessity of seeking relief began to break down any expectation of self-support. Hickok argued for the least possible disruption of a family's "normal life." Relief levels that lowered a middle-class family's standard of living too much would "ruin its morale" or "make a rebel" out of the family head. By the same token, if the income of poorer families was raised "beyond whatever [it] has been before or beyond what it has any chance of becoming normally, we are damaging the morale of that family." The test of "morale" pointed toward a conclusion that middle-class families suffered most from the depression and needed the greatest aid.[22] Such ideas made it a logical objective for federal policy to rescue the steady earners of predepression years, especially those who belonged to a broadly conceived middle class; to save families by buttressing male providers as family heads; and to support those whose character and habitual expectations were presumably at the heart of "American" identity.

Yet both ideas and results within the FERA and other New Deal programs were complicated, pulled between the idea of life before the depression as a worthy norm and the desire for reform, between established patterns of social hierarchy and concepts of fairness. The work programs that Hopkins and others championed in preference to direct relief aimed explicitly toward the preservation of outlooks and skills. Despite this emphasis on conserving, however, and despite the presence in relief programs of segregation, discrimination, and political manipulation whether or not Hopkins approved of such inequities, work projects in practice often reached beyond preconceptions to reshape as well as preserve. By treating minority and majority people with a degree of equality not in accord with local practice, early FERA programs had already shaken the political and cultural order in some communities, as the Hopkins reporters discovered. Work relief might be advocated for its conserving force and defended in a language of traditional values, but when packaged with an expanding federal authority and a rule-oriented professionalism, it also carried the potential for new social relationships. Moreover, there was a peculiar irony in the notion that those who best represented American ambition and aspiration were also the most vulnerable, an irony rooted in the dilemmas of progress and prosperity. An argument turning the experience of less-favored Americans to positive account was waiting to be made. Indeed, the FERA reports themselves spoke in more than one voice. If stereotyping was painfully apparent, the attention paid to ethnic groups and the displaced moved them toward the mainstream of national discussion and made them a part of the fabric of American life now being woven. Hickok's remembrance of "individuals" and "people with stories" suggested a tapestry that could be valued for the color and variety of its design, not its uniformity. Something of this tone found its way into the work of the Federal Writers' Project. Here the scope of reporting would be broader and the purposes more public.

The Writers' Project was one of four arts projects created under the Works Progress Administration (WPA) in 1935 to employ impoverished writers, musicians, artists, and actors. In keeping with the mix of experimentation and conservation within the New Deal, the projects were both bold ventures in governmental support for the arts and a form of work relief steeped in the social assumptions that justified such programs. Immediately and continually controversial, the projects depended on the support of Hopkins (now head of the WPA), who defended the employment of writers and artists in the most practical of terms: "Hell, they've got to eat just like other people."[23] The Writers' Project at its peak in 1936 had nearly 6,700 people on its payrolls and reached out to every part of the nation. Some ventures begun under the FERA were continued as part of the Writers' Project, including the collection of oral histories from former slaves, the compilation of folklore, and the preparation of histories of specific groups or places. Yet if the project was to provide substantial work relief, and if it was to repel the charge that the New Deal was now creating not just shovel-leaners but pencil-leaners, it needed a task of major scope with claims to public usefulness. Suggestions for a set of American travel guides inspired by the Europe-centered Baedekers had been made in various quarters for more than a year, and in Connecticut relief workers had already produced a state guidebook. These initiatives helped shape the major undertaking of the Writers' Project: the American Guide Series.

The effort to produce a guide for each state that would measure up to centrally established criteria and editorial standards faced a host of obstacles. The people hired by the Writers' Project were generally subject to a means test before they could go on work relief, and most had very limited writing experience, if any. A rich pool of talent existed in, say, New York City or Chicago, even under these conditions, with a considerable political and ethnic diversity. The Illinois project, for example, could claim the left-wing novelists Nelson Algren and Jack Conroy; young Jewish writers in early career like Saul Bellow, Isaac Rosenfeld, and Lionel Abel; and published black writers like Arna Bontemps, as well as those soon to make their mark, including Richard Wright, the poet Margaret Walker, and Katherine Dunham. In North Dakota, however, the project director was 20-year-old Ethel Schlasinger (one of 14 women named state directors in the first round of appointments), who took on the task of producing a guidebook with some 60 assorted workers, not one of whom was an experienced writer and only two of whom helped her with the actual writing. The Writers' Project functioned with whatever assortment of workers a genuine relief program could provide.

The state projects faced frictions between local staff and Washington editors, conservative objections that they were merely New Deal propaganda agencies, political warfare in major cities between Stalinists and Trotskyists, and occasional problems with incompetence and corruption. It was a wonder that some of the projects could be productive at all. Yet productive they were, creating ultimately a guide for every state plus some 330 other books and pamphlets on cities, landmarks, highways, and folklore. Each state guide contains three sections: part 1 offers a collection of essays surveying the state's history, peoples, economy, institutions, and culture; part 2 describes cities; and part 3 takes the reader on a detailed tour down every major highway in the state, providing "mile-by-mile treatment" and describing all points of interest and "all towns and all countryside, attractive and unattractive."[24] Given their common patterns and the limitations of project staffing, the guides might well have become repetitive and dull, but a set of often-resented national editors continually nagged at state projects to keep routinization at bay. The Minnesota project director, Mabel S. Ulrich, recalled that she and her staff had been "baffled by the tendency of all federal editors to regard us as inhabiting a region romantically different from any other in the country." Brushing aside local claims of firsthand knowledge, the national editors demanded the "unique," the "customs and characteristics that differ sharply from those of any other State." The Minnesota draft essay on "racial customs" lacked "color": "Surely there must be folk-dancing and Old World costumes to be observed." The state staff indicated a lack of folklore: "We advise that you interview prisoners in the penitentiary."[25]

With this emphasis on particularity, richness, and variety, the Writers' Project would both build on social reporting and turn it in a new direction. The demand for "facts" became, if anything, more intensive than in earlier reports. Yet the sense of purpose had changed. Despite scattered political efforts to the contrary, the emphasis in project work would not fall on recording immediate social experience or representing a class. The guides did not ask how the American people were doing in facing the exigencies of the moment but, ultimately, how they had done over time. The concern with American direction and identity that affected all social reporting found new expression through a cataloging of towns and peoples and customs; through a recording of local stories rich with the associations of place; and through an inventory of the actions and memories that by accretion constitute a culture.

A process of establishing wider national meaning for the harvest of materials gathered into the guides thus began with their conception and presentation, and it flourished among readers and critics at the end of the 1930s. Lewis Mumford, upon reading the early guides, asserted their central relevance to the question of national identity in calling them "the first attempt, on a comprehensive scale, to make the country itself worthily known to Americans." With an eye toward conservative critics, Mumford declared the series "the finest contribution to American patriotism that has been made in our day."[26]  In the preface to the Washington State guide, Anne E. Windhusen sounded similar themes in declaring the book "an integral part of a dynamic and vibrant picture of these United States." The guides were not about a lost America but an America found; they did not describe a puzzled or a directionless nation but a "dynamic" country with a strong sense of itself. Where early depression social reports assumed a break in the nation's history, Windhusen presented her guide as a testament to continuity: "Against the panorama of the past, the reader will be able to see the moving picture of the present."[27]  The depression seemed ready to take its place as one more experience in the life of a resilient nation. Katherine Kellock emphasized the effects of the projects on the workers themselves, noting the level of "freely-contributed overtime." "It should reassure those who fear to acknowledge shortcomings in the American scene," Kellock suggested, "that close examination of every phase of American life and history by these workers, who above all others had some reason for being dissatisfied, only made them more enthusiastic about their native land."[28]  By this account the mechanisms of social reporting, once geared to breakdown and change, now worked to secure the unemployed as patriots and to affirm the national culture.

More complex assessment led Robert Cantwell toward a positive evaluation of the guides and the country they described. Cantwell was a former proletarian novelist publishing in a magazine sympathetic to the Popular Front—the *New Republic*—and for his tastes, the guides paid too little attention to the ownership of property and suffered in their topical choices from the influence of "bohemianism." Yet in what they did cover, in the mass of detail and the range of stories told, the guidebooks crafted a national portrait distinctive both in its freshness and significance. "The America that is beginning to emerge from the books of the Writers' Projects," Cantwell announced, "is a land to be taken seriously: nothing quite like it has ever appeared in our literature." The guides described an America of "secret rooms, invisible closets, hidden stairways and false halls." They revealed a people with an "odd, clownish, lunatic sense of humor." And most of all, they laid out countless tales of investments lost and plans ruined when "the project failed, the boom collapsed, the railroad went the other way, the authorities got wind of the plot, the current shifted, the bay filled in." This stream of experience led Cantwell, too, toward an appreciation of American resilience and toward a view of the depression as fitting within, rather than breaking from, historical patterns. The guides provided "a catalogue of remarkable instances of Americans' ability to take extraordinary happenings in their stride," and this reminder of past hardships made "some of the horrors of [the country's] present less difficult to endure."[29]

The record of a "capricious and ingenious" people who often "guessed wrong" intrigued Cantwell for a different reason as well. He culled from the guides a "grand, melancholy, formless, democratic anthology of frustration and idiosyncrasy, a majestic role call of national failure, a terrible and yet engaging corrective to the success stories that dominate our literature." It is possible to find in such remarks evidence for a "cult of failure" in the 1930s that made a virtue out of the depression's assault on success. But there is more to Cantwell's outlook than a celebration of tripping up and falling short. The "common generalizations about America and the American temperament" that stressed "thrift, sobriety, calculation or commercial acumen" were hackneyed, inadequate, and boring. It was when a range of stories could be told— when failure and accident, secret rooms and a lunatic humor, added their "engaging corrective" to the mix—that a fuller identity was achieved and America became Cantwell's "land to be taken seriously." Against a depression-battered myth of success Cantwell counterpoised a newer myth: of a country rich in contrasting experiences; of a people disparate in their habits; of an America finding its distinctive character in sheer variety.[30]

Neither the American Guide Series nor the reactions to it were anomalies. By the end of the 1930s, political theory and public parlance were together moving to make an America unified through its differences a common (though not a dominant) idea. Social reporters were still collecting their facts, but they often recorded more of legend, locale, and whimsy than of injustice; they found more "color" and variety in individual stories than pain; and they wrote far more out of affection than out of confusion, rebellion, or anger. From the newspaper columns of an itinerant Ernie Pyle—reporting on Mrs. Berglund and her three daughters living as trappers in Alaska, on New Mexico's "odd laws affecting travellers," and on "A Town That Dreams of Billy the Kid"[31]— to the discursive pages of the most popular roving witness book of the thirties, Louis Adamic's *My America* (1938), the evidence piled up that nothing was so characteristic of the nation as its diversity and its quirks. Against the backdrop of world politics, the denial of uniformity resonated ever more strongly with national affirmation and unifying appeal. As one scholar has commented of Adamic's book, "a lack of pattern was the pattern of choice: it emphasized the values felt to be most American, precious, and threatened—freedom and democracy."[32] With travelers' reports so construed, the revelation of a country disparate and diverse in nature became a proclamation of common loyalty to the nation's traditional political ideals.

## Camera Eyes

The impressions of American life reaching the public during the 1930s were not derived solely, or for many even primarily, from written reports. Radio, with its expanding news coverage and on-the-scene accounts, provided a more immediate contact with certain kinds of events and human interest stories than could magazines or books. Movie theater newsreels allowed patrons to see brief film clips of people and places, presumably caught up in the process of being important. Through the sheer size of the audiences they could attract, these newer media were unmatched in their potential for creating a sense of common involvement and shared experience. Radio and the news-reels remained dominantly tied to entertainment, however, and in their range of coverage and in their concerns they contributed less to the process of social reporting than another medium—photography. Photography was not new, but it underwent something of a popular explosion in the 1930s thanks in large part to the invention of "miniature cameras" (direct ancestors of today's familiar 35mm cameras). Sales of the German-made Leica, first of the new models on the scene, doubled every year during the early thirties despite the depression and the camera's substantial cost, and by mid-decade some 30 other brands of "minicam" were on the market. The rapid expansion of photography as a hobby reflected the relative ease of use and flexibility of the new cameras, a development that also allowed photography to take on new cultural roles in libraries, science, medicine, the arts, and news-gathering.[33]

Perhaps the most striking impact of the new cameras derived from their ability to catch people in the act, to take pictures without subjects being posed or even aware of a camera in use. In 1930 the London *Graphic* introduced some not-always-flattering pictures of political leaders as the work of Dr. Erich Salomon's "candid camera," and an enduring phrase was born. The German photographer's work arrived in the United States the following year to be published in *Fortune* and then *Time*, magazines that belonged to the emerging journalistic empire of Henry Luce. In 1936, having overcome the technological barriers to high-quality, low-cost mass reproduction of photographs, Luce inaugurated *Life* and brought to reality the idea of a magazine based on the abilities of the "minicam." The popular success of *Life* was a genuine phenomenon of the 1930s: American magazines just did not sell a million copies, but on its second anniversary, *Life* announced the "miracle" of selling 2.1 million copies per week. Few versions of American culture and of the world reached more Americans more regularly in the second half of the decade than the one pieced together in *Life*.

The more substantive sections in *Life* presented sets of pictures built around a central topic or idea. Not writers but photographers went out into America to reveal the nation's culture to itself and, with the aid of text and captions, to string particular experiences into versions of American identity. It was the magazine's explicit intent that "the camera shall at last take its place as the most convincing reporter of contemporary life."[34] The first issue of *Life* featured the work of Margaret Bourke-White, who had traveled to the Pacific Northwest to examine New Deal projects on the Columbia River. Bourke-White, at 32, was already a celebrated and exceptionally well-paid photographer, famous for her industrial photography and for her efforts to find unusual angles or vantage points on her subjects. Hired first by Luce in 1929 to work on *Fortune*, she had demonstrated with pictures of the Swift hog-butchering operation in that magazine's first issue that she could make almost anything photographically interesting. The editors of the new *Life* claimed that they had expected from her only "construction pictures" but had found her photographs so compelling that they could not prevent her from "running away with their first nine pages."[35]

Most likely, the editors were impressed not just with the photographs but with what the photographs suggested to them. The collection was presented under the title "Franklin Roosevelt's Wild West" with individual captions that stressed the frontier theme. This in itself implied New Deal continuity with an identifying American experience: the "New West" of the photos centered on the frontier town of "New Deal." The captions went further to suggest a connection between the spirit of the pioneers and the spirit required to endure the depression. "The pioneer mother can trek in broken-down Fords as well as in covered wagons," *Life* declared. "And she can crack her hands in the alkali water of 1936 as quickly as in the alkali water of 1849."[36] The effect was not to deny suffering but to ease its sting by weaving it into a national tradition of meeting hardship with fortitude. Moreover, just as the pioneers had contributed to the building of a great nation, the workers of "New Deal" were helping to construct monuments worthy of that nation: the first cover of *Life* was a Bourke-White photograph of an uncompleted dam at Fort Peck, Montana, taken from far below, its towers looming above two ant-sized workers to stand like Abu Simbel on the Nile.

Roosevelt's "Wild West" was but one stop along the road for a magazine structurally defined to present each week a tour of domestic and international items of interest. Fully as eager for color and uniqueness as any *American Guide* supervisor, *Life* editors appealed constantly as well to human commonality. They seemed convinced that a form of unity must necessarily exist if a circuslike array of characters could all be a part of life, and of *Life*: "French aristocrats, New York stock brokers, Montana barkeeps, gooney-golfers, . . . babies, farmers, sailors, doctors, crowds, a high school class, a one-legged man, a strip-artist, a bearded Russian, The President of the U.S. and the late Sarah Bernhardt."[37] Indeed, the disparateness of both subjects and presentation could be seen as a positive national good, reinforcing those values that sustained patriotic cohesion. In a promotional booklet celebrating its second anniversary, the magazine proclaimed that its features were "helping to safeguard America. For, an intelligent, informed public is not likely to stray from the paths of liberty and democracy."[38] *Life* was prone to cliché, sometimes sensationalistic, and at once pretentious and cute. Yet distributed among the aristocrats, pet fleas, and advertisements were brief pictorial images of American culture and society that added up once more to the suggestion that the nation's character and identity were rooted in its inexhaustible variety.

Photography had another history as a form of social reporting as well, and the New Deal was again quick to turn the tools of imagery and information to public service. The work of Dorothea Lange can stand as a case in point.

Arthur Rothstein's FSA photographs of a cow's skull on dry prairie land took on strong political implications both for those who found them symbolic of the hardship and waste of the 1930s and for those who believed they demonstrated a fakery and manipulation linked to dangerous radical experiments.   As this photograph suggests, Rothstein could also raise his camera to capture the grandeur and beauty of a landscape in which clouds questioned the boundaries between earth and sky.   An alertness to harsh realities and to opportunities for their dramatization, and a fascination with America as a place waiting to be discovered and appreciated, came together not simply in Rothstein but in some of the more distinctive cultural expressions of the 1930s. *National Archives*

Having worked for ten years as a portrait photographer in San Francisco, Lange was moved by the daily evidence of the depression's impact in the early 1930s to go out into the streets to photograph the unemployed.  A 1934 exhibit of the resulting pictures impressed the social economist Paul S. Taylor, who began working with Lange, providing words to accompany her pictures. Together they produced reports for the California State Emergency Relief Administration on the conditions of migrant workers that helped win federal funding for migrant sanitary facilities.  The reports also caught the attention of Roy Stryker of the Resettlement Administration (RA), who promptly hired Lange.   She stood out among a noteworthy group of photographers who worked, after the agency changed names in 1937, for the Farm Security Administration (FSA).  Photography was recruited to document agricultural practices and rural dislocation with a hopeful eye to reform.

The popular conception, shared by many photographers, took it for granted that the camera could provide a unique access to the "facts" of social life: presumably, the "camera eye" would capture an unvarnished reality. Indeed, the bulk of FSA work, providing a largely straightforward documentation of how crops were grown, harvested, and processed, produced photographs that were not noticeably artful and recorded facts not widely interesting. Yet photographers were not without their own ideas or special bag of tricks. Through choice of subject, use of lighting and angles, distractions invoked to shape people's expressions, and selection from multiple shots, photographers could craft the version of reality they set before the viewer. In 1936 Arthur Rothstein stopped by a North Dakota road where he had spotted a cow's skull and, moving it to achieve different effects, took several pictures, the most notable of which showed the skull against a cracked, dry prairie. What the pictures suggested was not in doubt, but a furor over their authenticity threatened Stryker's whole documentary project. Could the camera record reality if the skull had been moved? For some anti-Roosevelt newspapers, the answer was clearly no. The "exaggerated" damage claimed in the "faked 'drought' pictures" revealed "the principal socialistic experiment of the New Deal [the RA-FSA]" as "a ghastly fake, based on fake ideas, . . . promoted by fake methods similar to those used by ordinary confidence men."[39]

The squabble over Rothstein's pictures suggests once again how questions of politics in the 1930s, and behind them issues of national identity, were tied up with an effort to establish acceptable "facts" and control the definition of reality. Opponents who labeled the New Deal "socialistic" were defending their conceptions of limited government, their belief in capitalism and private ownership, and their allegiance to the claims of work, character, and thrift. Photographs or "facts" that did not accord with their outlook could not describe reality as they knew it to be and must, therefore, be "exaggerated" or "faked." Photographer-reporters, for the most part, shared a different perspective, one that found conditions for many Americans severe, contradictions of the myth of success sharply defined, and the need for government remedies abundantly clear. Within their own version of American experience and tradition, the photographers also accepted only certain images and subjects as legitimate representations of the real.

Both Margaret Bourke-White and Dorothea Lange collaborated with writers during the late 1930s to produce books directed toward particular social concerns, combining words and pictures. Bourke-White and Erskine Caldwell, the southern novelist and journalist, published *You Have Seen Their Faces* (1937), an immediately popular and highly praised lament over sharecropping in the South that was hailed as the *Uncle Tom's Cabin* of tenant farming. Sharecroppers had been the objects of widespread attention in the midthirties, through films, documentaries, political organizing, and governmental investigation, and Caldwell's text said nothing that was new. The impact of the book lay in its photographs; here the emphasis created through

"Day labor is used almost exclusively on Hopson Plantation displacing the old tenants on the place. Cotton choppers are hired in nearby towns for 75 cents to $1.00 a day and trucked to the plantation. Clarksdale, Mississippi Delta, Miss." Even as the farm tenantry of the South inspired both cultural exploration and social protest during the 1930s, changes that were part of the larger economic transformation of agriculture in the first half of the twentieth century were altering rural patterns of life. The Mississippi workers photographed for the FSA by Marion Post, who may themselves have been displaced "old tenants," now lived in town and worked for wages. *National Archives*

all the techniques at Bourke-White's disposal fell on evoking feelings of outrage and pity for which many were by now well prepared. In an introductory note, Caldwell and Bourke-White explained that the captions, though printed in quotation marks, were not the words of those pictured but "the authors' own conceptions" of what people should have thought or said. Names and places had also been altered to avoid "unnecessary individualization." The photographs were intended to represent a system, a category of folk, a social issue, not people in their particularity or complexity.[40]

"Part of the family of Alfred Atkinson, tenant farmer of 80 acres near Shannon City, Ringgold County, Iowa, Dec. 1936." The photographs by Margaret Bourke-White in *You Have Seen Their Faces*, as well as those by Walker Evans that would appear in *Let Us Now Praise Famous Men* (1941), seek in their different ways to concentrate attention on the tenant farmers and sharecroppers of the South. This FSA photograph by Russell Lee stands as a reminder that tenantry was not confined to a single region or to a single set of circumstances. The Atkinsons of Iowa, with their varied expressions and their collective presence, would not have succumbed easily to the cultural agenda of either of the later books. *National Archives*

Especially from a later perspective, some of the results seem condescending, palpably shaped to accord with the expectations of an audience steeped in the decade's metropolitan stereotypes of the South. Photographs and captions together appear almost to mock rural evangelical religion. White landowners are held accountable for a brutal racism, while blacks are treated in patronizing fashion. Poor whites are often shown with crooked teeth or in unattractive squinting poses; if not, the captions tend to emphasize their abject condition or their ignorance of better standards. The penultimate photograph displays a beautiful and lined older woman nearly crying, with the caption, "I've done the best I knew how all my life, but it didn't amount to much in the end."[41] It was the authors who made the claim that her life "didn't amount to much." The photographs and captions presented their subjects as pathetic, arousing an easy emotional response and allowing readers to bask unconsciously perhaps in their own social superiority and refined sentiments. This suited at least one notion of what social consciousness should mean. The literary critic Malcolm Cowley, then prominently identified with the Popular Front, declared the captions "exactly right" and the photographs "almost beyond praise."[42] The hardships of tenants and sharecroppers were no invention, but what Bourke-White and Caldwell presented was a prepackaged version of reality honoring fashionable sentiments more than the people involved.

Lange and Paul Taylor established a different tone in *An American Exodus* (1939), a report on the migrations of rural Americans "expelled" from the soil "by powerful forces of man and of Nature." The authors pointedly announced that the quotations accompanying Lange's photographs would only "report what the persons photographed said, not what we think might be their unspoken thoughts."[43] The pictures themselves benefited from Lange's experience as a portrait photographer and conveyed an inescapable sense of respect for their subjects. People's expressions were complex, providing some resistance to the viewer's gaze rather than being subservient to it; few were shown to their disadvantage, and several were in poses that lent them an air of strength or authority. An old man with a crisp white beard stands full-height against a fence, looking very much the patriarch as he speaks of his family being driven away from farming. A young Texan, shown in close-up with a worried expression, has teeth as crooked as any in Bourke-White's photographs but also the black hair and handsome features of a Hollywood hero. Lange allowed multiple photographs of Dust Bowl fields, decaying farms, squatters' camps, and overloaded cars to underscore the seriousness of the migrants' plight, while she upheld in her photographs of individuals a distinct human dignity.

Yet this, too, involved conscious bias. Pare Lorentz noted at the time that Lange had photographed the poor selectively, including no representatives of "the bindle-stiffs, the drifters, the tramps, the unfortunate aimless dregs of a country." William Stott later observed of those in the photos, "Never are they vicious, never depraved, never responsible for their misery"; he extended

Lorentz's insight to argue that "the documentary photographs of the thirties simply do not include those who are poor through laziness or moral dereliction."[44] The text accompanying Bourke-White's pictures attributed to tenants and sharecroppers an in-born original capacity to be striving national citizens. White tenant farmers who were often identified as lazy and improvident (and who were inclined to admit it) had begun life, according to Caldwell, with "many of the same ambitions and incentives" as others, with "normal instincts," with "hope and confidence and the will to work and succeed." Only when the system failed the individual did defeat and frustration get the better of these "slaves of sharecropping."[45] Lange avoided such claims of prelapsarian virtue: her migrants continued to belong squarely within a worthy American mainstream.

Lange and Taylor reached for an epic tone in calling their book *An American Exodus*. Previous migrations had brought Europeans to a new continent and sent streams of people flowing westward. Now, a generation after the end of the frontier, "once more great numbers of landseekers trek west." These new migrants belonged to an old national tradition molded both by dreams of opportunity and by necessity: five tenant farmers pictured together and identified as "native Americans" were presumably true heirs of this tradition. Characteristically, as Taylor hastened to assure his readers, though the migrants might be "driven to relief," they wanted most a "chance for self-support." These were people of sound origin and good character whose fate had been shaped by "forces of man and of Nature" through no fault of their own. The concern must focus, as a subtitle indicated, on the process of "human erosion," on the wasting away of a resource fundamentally sound.[46]

The photographic reports, then, created a version of reality that was far from neutral. There was scant room in this reality for sponging relief recipients lacking initiative and character, or for maliciousness and deceit. (Neither, for that matter, was there room for photographs of people looking too peaceful or too happy. Only the eclecticism of the Washington State guidebook could place a Lange photograph of a worn-down migrant woman opposite a picture of a smiling, healthy-looking fruit picker with a brimming bag of apples.) The tenants and especially the migrants generally offered to the reader shared a presumably characteristic American affinity for hard work and self-reliance, though their prospects had been stunted by the entrapments of their condition. Thus, efforts to provide aid and opportunity would work for the preservation of the national fiber, not contribute to its unraveling. This liberal version of reality contended for public allegiance with more traditional appeals to individualism, supported governmental activism, with the New Deal as a proximate model, and established itself as an outlook that was cultural as well as political.

To the degree that the migrant poor were seen as maintaining their basic worthiness, the evidence of their lives could provide reassurance of the nation's strength. Even more compelling, and now granted elevated recognition, was the ability of common folk to "take it." Lange and Taylor made images of endurance central from the moment their linkage between migration and the pioneer past established an explicit theme. Quite purposefully perhaps, Lange and Taylor placed at the end of their book a photograph of a gray-haired and wrinkled woman who matched Bourke-White's earlier subject strikingly well. But if Bourke-White's tearful woman was made to say that her life "didn't amount to much," Lange's "Ma Burnham," with her matter-of-fact look, had ideas of her own. The family farm was gone now, "but it raised a family." Ma Burnham could declare, "I've done my duty," without a hint of self-pity. Whether drought was "the Devil's work or the Lord's work" she couldn't say; it was simply there to be faced. The forthright gaze of a Confederate soldier's daughter proclaimed that troubles might forever surround but never triumph over *this* American, calling to mind another "Ma" who would stand as a celebration of the type in John Steinbeck's novel, *The Grapes of Wrath* (1939).[47]

In early 1938 Steinbeck had visited California's migrant camps with a *Life* photographer, planning to do an article for the magazine and a book of photographic reporting. His experience gave birth instead to the novel that stands as his best-known work. When a film version of *The Grapes of Wrath* appeared within a year, Steinbeck's story was given a powerful visual life that linked words and pictures as firmly as any photojournalism. The family at the center of the story, the Joads, is forced from the land by a combination of poverty, tractors, erosion, and drought. Joining the "Okie" migration, they make their way to California as part of a tattered Dust Bowl procession. There they find a beneficent nature, but this promised land is badly corrupted by human institutions and behavior. There is no fresh start in the illogic of food being destroyed while people starve, in the brutality and crassness of landowners and their minions, or in the steady intensification of the family's plight.

In some respects, the novel represents an amalgam of themes from the social writing of the 1930s. The specter of waste testifies to a system askew as piteous destitution is cast against images of agricultural fertility and boundless productivity. Like Jack Conroy, albeit more artfully, Steinbeck romanticizes an agrarian culture though acknowledging its day has passed, attacks the distorting mechanical forces of industrial society, and leads his protagonist, Tom Joad, toward a conversion to radical politics that the narrative does not make credible. In keeping with a critique from the left, the "big men," banks, and capitalism draw harsh treatment, while the worth of the common people is strongly affirmed. Even so, the most positive segment of the book is reformist rather than radical: the Joads find temporary security and community in a government migrant camp where the people cooperate for the common good and the director is benevolently paternal. (In the film version, he looks a lot like Franklin Roosevelt.) All of these themes had their place. Yet none of them was so powerful perhaps, or so important to the popular success that discomfited Steinbeck, as the celebrations of the Joads' character and endurance.

The moral center of the family is Ma Joad. Throughout the westward trek, it is Ma whose steadiness and clarity of purpose stave off every threat of personal and social decay. At the end of their journey, the Joads remain people of integrity, seeking self-reliance, looking for the chance to work hard and to honor the values of property, family, and community. They are consummate models of the worthy poor, firm in character and noble in their fortitude. Indeed, Tom's ultimate declaration of activist intent is largely submerged by Ma's assurances of endurance and continuity: "We're the people that live. They ain't gonna wipe us out. Why, we're the people—we go on." Ma Joad, like Ma Burnham, can certainly "take it." In 1938 Steinbeck had used a Lange photograph of a young Okie mother nursing her child on the cover of his pamphlet "Their Blood Is Strong," the picture delivering essentially the same message as the title. In the final scene of *The Grapes of Wrath*, the Joad daughter, Rose of Sharon, who has just lost her baby, gives her breast to a starving stranger, extending the notion of family and affirming the will to life. At the end of a decade of depression, what seemed to strike a chord for the nation was Steinbeck's celebration of survival and endurance, his homage to the strength of common Americans.

The *Grapes of Wrath* reinforced through fiction and film a message central to some of the best photography of the period. Meantime, beside this emphasis on the strength of the people, an equally vigorous attention to their variety, to the heterogeneous nation of *Life*, continued to flourish. One theme did not wholly exclude the other. Lange and Taylor, for example, divided their book into regional sections, noted the "many variations" of agricultural change, and placed the California migrants "at the end of a long immigrant line of Chinese, Japanese, Koreans, Negroes, Hindustanis, Mexicans, Filipinos" who had come "to serve the crops and farmers." Yet they were also committed to a unifying "sharpness of focus."[48] For many of the popular photographic collections published between 1938 and 1941, it seemed an article of faith that simply glimpsing together disparate people, places, and experiences would provide valuable insight into the nation's identity.

When Bourke-White and Caldwell published *Say, Is This the U.S.A.* in 1941, they noted that their American materials might seem "hopelessly jumbled" but insisted that "somehow, regardless, the meaning succeeds in making itself known."[49] Thus, they were free to describe various cities in captions containing nothing but a list of names or nouns, leaving it to the reader to construct a whole from the sum of these parts. And they could tell without commentary a story of searching for the booking agent Dmitri Senoff after learning that he might be visiting an injured Chinese acrobat, with a blond young woman directing them to call Murphy Hospital, which turned out to be Mercy Hospital, and with the hospital, upon receiving an inquiry about a "Chinese act," connecting them with the laundry room. Such combinations of confusion, humor, ethnic groups, and stereotypes presumably said something significant about what it meant to be an American. From a string of such stories, combined with photographs of Hutterians, farmers, elephants, and Odd Fellows, a national meaning would make itself known. The authors, of course, might permit themselves a clue in a final photograph of the Statue of Liberty shot from a position at its base.

## Social Reporting and National Myth

The writing and reporting spurred by an aroused social awareness in the 1930s did not always lead where early practitioners might have expected. A widening scope, political shifts, and multiple voices brought changes of balance and variations of function. Ultimately, the legacy of reporting depended less on the first wave of reaction to the depression than on the directions in which the stream of awareness moved and on the myths and themes that were able to establish their explanatory power over time.

Social reporting in certain respects reflected steadily the distinctive social concerns of the 1930s. For many reporters, there existed a ready bridge between concentration on the problems of the depression and the questions of American spirit, character, and values that spoke to issues of national identity. The way such questions were explored was never neutral. Whether those concerned with the meaning of America tapped the historical and mythic past or examined the furrows and fragments of the present, they often worked from an assumption that shaped the very nature of critical social reporting, an assumption that the reality of America could not be known through the received culture of the metropolitan centers. Thus, whatever the coloration of the reporter's intent, the process of seeking the "facts" during the 1930s tended to bring forward people and circumstances that would otherwise have been obscure, to give importance to experiences and events normally little remembered. The effect was often to widen the cast on the historical stage by seeking to capture the concreteness of multiple contexts and disparate lives.

Tenant farmers and migrants stand as examples of people drawn into an uncharacteristic prominence. Fewer tenant farmers in the South actually moved off the land during the 1930s than during the 1920s and 1940s.[50] Although the depression (especially before 1933) added to their problems, clearly a long-term process was at work. Yet only in the 1930s did the displacement of tenants become a matter for sustained cultural attention. The depression, the New Deal, and radical activism created a climate in which not only immediate conditions but problems endemic to ongoing economic transformations could be pushed into the spotlight and treated as matters of public urgency. At the same time, the reporters paid scant attention for most of the thirties to those whose relatively secure social positions were not fundamentally at risk. Writers alert to social concerns seldom dealt with businesspeople, industrialists, or large farmers except to show them as villains, or with professional and middle-class families except to examine their decay. Social reporting carried a substantial bias against attending to social groups closely associated with traditional formulas of progress and success.

Yet this did not mean that the values associated with individual responsibility, personal achievement, and upward mobility had been nudged into the cultural shadows. The vitality of the myth of success was evident in the popularity of the how-to-succeed books of the thirties, in the glossy triumph of *Fortune*, with its profiles of business leaders, and in the results of opinion surveys revealing the continuing force of individualism. Many social reporters thus found themselves, whether by intent or indirection, standing in opposition to all or part of the traditional success myth, with its relatively monolithic notions of American culture and its antireformist associations. The challenge for social writing was to establish credibility for a revised complex of values, to inspirit competing myths, to foster belief in other versions of the nation's principles and character. An eager push toward redefinition came from the radical left. Yet neither early attempts to construct a credible myth of proletarian character nor later efforts to claim an all-American leftist tradition ever gained broad cultural resonance. Although active in many spheres, radicals were unable to create interpretations of the depression experience or versions of national identity that could reach beyond limited circles.

The newly prominent cultural ideas that won a wider allegiance by the mid to late 1930s were the themes of American endurance and heterogeneity. In building at least a partial challenge to the traditional myth of success and its extended implications, these themes borrowed widely to provide a many-layered cultural appeal. They drew especially on the agrarian myth, an older American ideal that stood in logical tension with consecrations of self-made success, and on the saga of a hard frontier experience that had molded the nation's character. At the same time, the two themes drew on values shared with the success myth itself, establishing cultural connections that were of fundamental importance. The repeated assertions that those who were down-and-out remained "able-bodied and self-dependent," that relief recipients were "individuals," that the unemployed wanted to work, and that migrant families maintained their dignity and desire, delivered the message again and again that those forced to suffer by the depression were made of an approved American fiber, that their resilience and endurance were the characterological kin of success. The theme of heterogeneity could easily incorporate recognition of hard work, aspiration, or wealth, but it may have reached deeper as well, to the underside of the myth of success, where the false starts, curious ventures, and repeated attempts that Cantwell found in state guidebooks acknowledged the quirkiness and risk-taking that accompanied an energetic individualism. Each theme wove established values into a new fabric, combining older meanings with those reflecting an altered social context.

If their rootedness in American culture provided one element in the persuasiveness of particular themes, another part of their appeal derived from their capacity to embrace the tensions of the thirties, to maintain a balance

Dorothea Lange's photograph "Migrant Mother" has become one of the most widely reprinted images of the 1930s. Commentators have emphasized the dignity that Lange allows her subject and the woman's continuing strength. The photograph manages to hold in balance a depiction of genuine hardship, a suggestion that independence and character remain intact, a celebration of endurance, and a justification for assistance. The continuing appeal of this cultural (and implicitly political) balance may contribute to the photograph's popularity. *National Archives*

between the desire for continuity and the call for change. The depression suggested to many a break in the nation's history, a sense of collapse and disorientation. In one way or another, many of the cultural impulses of the thirties reached out for some claim of continuity. The theme of endurance offered assurances that the nation would remain intact because Americans were a people who could "take it" and persevere. References to the pioneers linked present hardships to past ones and implied that depression would be overcome within a continuum of national experience and national character. At the same time, the theme of endurance pointed toward responsiveness and change; an attention fixed on those who were asked to endure provided both a demonstration of human need and a rationale for action. If the destitute were citizens of the kind who had built America—if they were of independent agrarian stock, people committed to family and work, people of dignity and solid character—then the fault for their condition could not be theirs, and a society true to itself surely needed to respond.

Because the hardships of the needy were linked to the idea of their worthiness, the theme of endurance carried with it a particular understanding of the depression that encouraged governmental action. This understanding and its implications became part of the theme's potent appeal not just for the thirties but, indeed, for later decades. Perhaps no photograph has been chosen more frequently to represent the 1930s in texts than Lange's "Migrant Mother," a portrait of a woman with two young children, who turn away from the camera, and with a baby in her arms. The clothes of all the subjects are shabby, and the woman's face reflects a deep weariness and concern, yet her expression is complex, her features handsome and strong, with no suggestion of decay in ability or will. We suggest, however subtly, with each reprinting of this photograph that the depression was akin to an act of nature beyond the responsibility of its victims. We allow to stand as a representative of American experience a woman who comes from the land, who has made the westering trek, and whose character and identity have held together under pressure. Quite probably we imply that if government bears any blame, it is not for doing too much but for doing too little. For us, as for the 1930s, there is explanatory and mythic power in the theme of endurance, combined with at least a mild challenge to things as they have been, and as they are.

Notions of heterogeneity subsumed another set of cultural tensions by managing to be both pluralistic and directed, affirming and rebellious. Those who made variety the essence of the American whole generally delivered an optimistic message, yet in the very act of doing so, they also disassembled the coherence of the success myth and promoted other forms of cultural union. Works with an appetite for variety told not one story, based on one social model, but many stories. In treating progress and success as just a single American theme, they implicitly challenged the logic of conservative individualism, its assumptions of cultural universality, and its right to guide public policy. Those who praised the *American Guides* often did so with the explicit understanding that talk of failure as well as success affronted more restrictive versions of Americanism. In declaring the guidebooks a contribution to patriotism, Lewis Mumford proclaimed: "Let that be the answer to the weaklings who are afraid to admit that American justice may miscarry or that the slums of Boston may be somewhat this side of Utopia. Let it also silence those who talk with vindictive hooded nods about the subversive elements that are supposed to lurk in the WPA." [51] The upbeat pages of *Say, Is This the U.S.A.* had room for several photographs of African-American children with captions lamenting the denial of opportunities they faced, and *Life* exhibited a sporadic, sensationalist conscience of its own. Even when the display of differences had a celebratory cast, the concept of heterogeneity maintained a capacity for rebellion and redefinition that challenged the unifying myths of success.

At the same time, the emphasis on American variety offered a cohesion of its own in responding to shifting patterns of political and cultural consciousness during the 1930s. The nationalization of the country's economic system, along with the growth of transportation and communication networks, had been under way for decades; during the 1920s, highways, radio, and efforts at standardization had added their force to a process already well advanced. In the thirties the center of political attention moved unmistakably to the national level. The New Deal struggled to develop a governmental framework that could deal with a nationwide economy and encouraged the idea that action on a wide range of social issues was a federal responsibility. Many of those who reported on American society after mid-decade were themselves a part of this process: the Hopkins reporters, FSA photographers, and Writers' Project relief workers were all federal employees, many of whose jobs derived from the sudden need of new federal agencies to know something about the problems they were trying to address.

The nationalization of politics contributed for many to a shift in the nation's cultural consciousness through a process that paradoxically centralized information as it decentralized American identity. Investigating injustice or suffering, gathering folklore or designs, recording the exceptional and the common, all added to a mounting pile of information that revealed a nation multifarious and complex. Local color and custom divided the cultural picture one way; attention to ethnic and religious groups divided it another; social class suggested patterns running through every community and group; and a new emphasis on regionalism inserted an intermediate division between nation and state. The generous embrace of heterogeneity proved convenient and even necessary in providing one way of grappling with this flood of cultural particulars and organizing claims. The theme was no trivial by-product of the decade but one that offered Americans a way to adjust their feeling for what national identity and political nationhood might mean.

By the end of the 1930s, there were other live questions to which heterogeneity could offer a pertinent response as well. Spurred on by the spreading influence of radio, film, and advertising, a few intellectuals, including Dwight

Macdonald and Clement Greenberg, were extending older complaints against commercialization into a new analysis of "mass culture," decrying its central- ized production, its numbing quality, and its threat of uniformity. The theme of heterogeneity, developing at the same time, provided a countervailing intel- lectual claim emphasizing the multifaceted complexity of American life. Within a wider public arena as well, a concentration on the vitality of disparate customs worked to offset popular anxieties about the erasure of particularist identities or the centralization of culture and government. These assurances became especially important as the consciousness of Nazism grew stronger. A nation characterized by variety and difference offered a sharp contrast to the dictatorship, the coordinated propaganda, and the dogmatic single-minded- ness associated with fascism (and, for many, with communism). The associa- tion of heterogeneity with liberty—gaining strength as war descended over Europe—was thus no thoughtless claim. Linked to an enduring patriotic theme, the fragmentation of contemporary experience became a triumph of continuity and commitment. With the dangers of the totalitarian state to be avoided and then opposed, claims that America's disparate particulars con- tained a principle of unifying strength provided the most useful of national myths.

The appeal of that myth would only grow during World War II. Because the Nazi enemy preached so vicious a doctrine of racial purity, the ethnic het- erogeneity of the United States offered an irresistible opportunity for moral- izing contrast. The military platoons in many war movies became models of social diversity and cooperative effort, with each "invariably composed of one Negro, one Jew, a Southern boy, and a sprinkling of second-generation Italians, Irish, Scandinavians and Poles."[52] Imagery far outstripped reality. The thoroughly mixed group at the center of *Bataan* (1943) included an African-American soldier on a footing of rough equality at a time when actu- al combat units remained thoroughly segregated.[53] The merging of hetero- geneity with principles of democracy and freedom had created a myth of such cultural power that it could, like the myth of success, remake social "facts" in the construction of national identity. The same pattern of ideas did cultural service in another way as well. Positive war aims, other than victory, were generally vague or abstract. Yet some explanations of what Americans were fighting for had a striking concreteness, especially when attributed to soldiers. They were simply lists of the kind that might have served as a Bourke-White caption: fried chicken, blueberry pie, the high school team, the kid brother, the girl next door, home. Recitations of various particulars were taken to stand for an American purpose that seemed beyond more cohesive articulation. (The pattern would endure: in a nationalistic advertising campaign 40 years later, an automobile manufacturer would offer as the meaning of America "baseball, hot dogs, apple pie, and Chevrolet.")

The themes of heterogeneity and endurance, then, gained potency in the late 1930s because of the reservoirs of meaning and emotion on which they were able to draw, because of the tensions they were able to contain, and because of the explanatory and justifying services they were able to perform. The development and use of these themes provides a body of testimony on the orienting strategies of the period. They did not, of course, function in the same way for everyone. The same assertions of character and strength among the destitute that made them worthy to receive aid also undermined in some minds the urgency of their plight: regardless of the hardships to be faced, they would, after all, endure. The emphasis on differences of culture and condition, at its worst, could turn prejudice, suffering, and atrocity into bits of diverting pathos for the great American variety show, providing little incentive for challenge or change. Neither endurance nor heterogeneity as a theme was attached to a defined program with explicit ends. Like other cultural ideas, their meaning lay open to contest.

Yet to say this is not enough. Both themes were linked to the evolution of liberal ideas in the context of the depression, found strength in directing older public values toward newly recognized needs, and encouraged a cultural and political responsiveness to broader social change, pointing toward necessary adjustments without timetable or doctrine. Moreover, the uses of both endurance and heterogeneity as themes suggested that people of varying backgrounds and convictions might stand as proper Americans. This did not quickly end the dominance of middle-class whites as national representatives or immediately change social practice, but it did offer a platform and direction for continuing efforts to redefine American identity. (The question of whether there was, when the emphasis fell on heterogeneity and diversity, such a thing as national character or identity could wait for later.) The themes in the social reporting of the 1930s were shaped by the experiences and needs of the moment, but in their roots and in their implications, they spoke of where cultural assumptions had been and where they were going.

*seven*

# Measures of Coherence

In 1936 the young president of the University of Chicago, Robert Maynard Hutchins, publicly lamented the intellectual "disunity, discord, and disorder" that had overtaken the American educational system. Fragmentation and false principle seemed everywhere apparent. The free elective system in colleges and progressive education in the schools had allowed students to follow their "sporadic, spontaneous interests"; these departures from an established curriculum amounted for Hutchins to "a denial that there was content to education." The study of humans in relation to each other and to nature had "sunk under waves of empiricism and vocationalism." In the name of the "scientific spirit," researchers gathered "vast masses of data" in the vain hope of mastering the world, succeeding only in identifying much of social science with "large chunks of such data, undigested, unrelated, and meaningless." Professional schools, wallowing in a vocationalism of their own, offered a narrowly conceived special training that led toward "triviality and isolation," that debased the "course of study and the staff," and that undermined the university's proper emphasis on the search for truth rather than utility. Concepts of democracy, liberalism, and academic freedom were used to defend all "subjects and fractions of subjects" as "equally valuable," producing "a complete and thoroughgoing disorder."

Hutchins offered as an alternative, and a purgative, the unity of a common educational program. General education, he insisted, must "draw out the elements of our common human nature," not dissipate intellectual energy on the "accidents of individuals." Particular structures, habits, and customs would be recognized simply as "details" when there was a proper understanding of essentials. "The truth is everywhere the same," Hutchins declared; "hence education should be everywhere the same." Concentration on those commonalities

191

found "in every time and place" would free education from a preoccupation with change and a disorienting responsiveness to the contemporary. The correct cultivation of the intellect rested on "permanent studies": those that "connect man with man"; those that acquaint students "with the best that man has thought"; those that are "basic to any further study and to any understanding of the world." "Permanent studies" meant books recognized as "classics," the "great books of the western world" of which many were ancient and medieval texts. The absence of familiarity with such texts—"the loss of what has been thought and done by earlier ages"—resulted directly for Hutchins in "the false starts, the backing and filling, the wildness, the hysteria, the confusion of modern thought and the modern world." The study of the classics stood for direction, stability, clarity, unity, and order.[1]

Hutchins was not alone in his preachments. A lawyer by training, he had acquired much of his own enthusiasm for classic texts by teaching an undergraduate "great books" course at Chicago in cooperation with Mortimer J. Adler. Adler shared Hutchins's views and would serve as a leading advocate and interpreter of classic texts for half a century. Other strong Hutchins supporters on the Chicago faculty, stymied by majority opposition, moved to St. John's College in Annapolis, Maryland, to create a model "great books" curriculum, which is still in existence. Many Catholic intellectuals hostile toward the implications of scientific naturalism and modern thought responded warmly to Hutchins's educational critique, to his search for unity and universality, and to his reliance on Aristotle and Thomas Aquinas as touchstones. A Jesuit writer suggested, with an assumption of communal assent, "One cannot but feel that we have won an ally."[2] The educational campaign for "permanent studies" would soon expand within a broader public sphere as well. A network of organized groups would meet regularly to discuss "permanent" texts. Advocates of the classics would devise programs to market "great" ideas to businessmen. And the movement would seek codification through the publication of a set of "great books," including 74 "great" authors and a guidebook to the 102 essential ideas of Western thought. Unity and a stable tradition clearly had their appeal.

Yet negative reactions to Hutchins and the kind of arguments he presented flared quickly. A faculty manifesto at Chicago decried the "reactionary" effort to make education conform to "one particular system of ancient or medieval metaphysics and dialectic." A number of commentators held that the goals and obligations of a university were far too diverse to accept a single educational model. John Dewey complained that Hutchins had "evaded the problem of who is to determine the definite truths" on which claims of permanency and universality were based. A belief in absolutes at the center of education and culture implied an elite with the power to enforce its decisions, Dewey suggested, and that smacked of authoritarianism. Hutchins, in defense, declared that his opponents had been caught up in the intellectual "cults" of skepticism, presentism, scientism, and anti-intellectualism, leaving them with no compass for finding the good or the true. It was this lack of clear orientation, not firm convictions like his own, that prepared the way for total-itarian movements. In the international atmosphere of the late 1930s, educa-tional and philosophical differences could turn quickly into debates over the fate of democracy.[3]

Indeed, the Hutchins controversy reflected both immediate political con-cerns and a broad confrontation over basic cultural and intellectual values. Many of the differences that fueled this confrontation came into play in the novelist James T. Farrell's provocatively titled commentary, "Mortimer J. Adler: A Provincial Torquemada." In labeling Adler "provincial," Farrell sug-gested a lack of sophistication and an outlook intellectually and culturally con-fined. His negative use of the term assumed the superiority of a contrasting framework of values that supported an openness to multiple influences, a skepticism toward established verities, and an inclination to find significance in complexity, variety, and breadth. These attitudes were presumed to flour-ish in fundamental historical alliance with an emphasis on human reason flow-ing out of the eighteenth-century Enlightenment and with the development of modern science, both of which had provided powerful intellectual models for breaking down the walls of the provincial. More subtly, an ethnic and racial narrowness associated with the "provincial" was taken to be inescapably at odds with the "cosmopolitan" openness and inclusiveness of more sophisticat-ed modern trends.

Religion generally smacked of the provincial for Farrell, and he resisted with special vigor the claims of the Catholic church in which he had been raised. The alliance between neo-Thomist Catholic theologians and intellectuals like Hutchins and Adler insulted all of the cultural values he had come to endorse. By suggesting that Adler might well be the "leading American fellow-traveller of the Roman Catholic Church," Farrell associated both Adler and the Church with the kind of authoritarianism, dogmatism, and repressiveness he found characteristic of Stalinist communism. (Stalinism was in turn under attack as a religion because of its demands for an unquestioning faith.) The reference to Torquemada, a leading figure of the Spanish Inquisition, made explicit the sug-gestion that Adler accepted the principle of repression, as did the charge that "Catholics and fellow-travelers" were using the "historic prestige of medieval and classic philosophers as a camouflage for [their] authoritarianism." In cele-brating the "unity of medieval society," the "new medievalists" idealized the past and embraced the "persecution of heretics." By implication, this extend-ed to the exclusion of all those who did not conform in belief or identity to the unifying ideal (as Torquemada had expelled Jews from Spain). In the "critique of modern thought and science" mounted by Adler and his allies, all of modern thought became "heretical" and a "blind alley." Their call, Farrell charged, was for a "return to the Absolute."[4]

Farrell's language was his own, but the sharpness of his response called atten-tion to fundamentally competing visions of past and present. The medieval world had stood for many intellectuals as a tangible historical embodiment of

dogmatism, stagnation, and ignorance from which humanity had long struggled to escape. Hutchins, Adler, and their allies offered that same world as a
positive cultural model. In doing so, they turned on its head the assumption
of steady progress during the last several centuries of Western history in what
seemed a blunt rejection of reason, secularism, democracy, and tolerance.
Within a more immediate intellectual context, the advocacy of the permanent
and the universal challenged the "revolt against formalism," the widespread
overthrow of the idea of absolutes that had been central to the development of
ideas since the late nineteenth century.[5] Hutchins's blasts against a directionless scientism and rampant vocationalism in university education had developed into an assault on modernity itself. "The wildness, the hysteria, the confusion" of the modern suggested, for Hutchins, the need to grapple with essential issues of stability, cohesiveness, and order. Many intellectuals who disagreed with Hutchins about both questions and answers were wrestling with
the same issues, even when their intent was to deny the power of these concerns. Directly and indirectly, consciously and by indirection, much of the
thought and culture of the 1930s participated in an extended, loosely jointed
debate over how the modern world might best be comprehended and ordered.

## Unity, Democracy, Stability, and Change

In a thoughtful study of ideas on the left during the depression decade, one
historian has noted with a touch of regret how often intellectuals "translated
the desire for change into an urge for stability."[6] As this remark suggests, the
relationship between change and stability in public thought holds considerable importance for the 1930s. Yet the questions involved are far from transparent. Investigations quickly grow confused if they begin with an assumption that stability and change are necessarily antithetical. "Stability" and
"change" are concepts that depend heavily on context and perception, having
no fixed relationship to one another. The desire for stability may restrain
change, but it may also encourage active attempts to reshape a social or cultural environment. Writing about the labor activism of the 1930s, for example, Robert Zieger has declared that "workers wanted stability," that "at the
heart of [their] militancy" lay the desire to escape the "favoritism, arbitrari-
ness, and cruelty" of unfettered managerial authority over their lives by
achieving the protections of a union contract.[7] To bitter opponents of collective bargaining, stability might mean upholding existing structures of power,
but to advocates of unionization—or of such measures as antilynching laws—
stability could result only from change. To treat the desire for stability as a
necessarily conservative impulse sapping the strength from the desire for
change would simplify and distort a complex of varying cultural meanings.

Moreover, attitudes toward stability and change stand in a contingent relationship to ideas of order: they shape, and are shaped by, fundamental assump-

tions about social, political, and cultural cohesion. During the 1930s a number of different patterns for thinking about the ordering of culture provided frameworks for understanding, for creativity, and for advocacy. None of these patterns was tied exclusively to a particular political orientation; all could be put to varying uses. The lines between them were not sharply drawn, and evocations of more than one ordering idea might appear in a single person, or institution, or work. As newer concepts of cohesion and stability, or ideas previously limited in their appeal, gained greater intellectual prominence, they did not replace more firmly established notions so much as they grew up beside them, creating a continuing tension that manifested itself in some of the central disputes of (and about) the thirties. Patterns of assumption and thought linked to three main ordering ideas—unity, multiplicity, and heterogeneity—played an energetic role in the culture of the 1930s.

The strongest pattern of belief as the decade began held that a culture ought to be unified, at least in its public expressions, around particular principles, values, and behaviors. For the most part, competing political camps of the early thirties offered appeals based on competing conceptions of unity. Herbert Hoover's references to "the American system of life" and "the American manner of life," combined with his horror at any mixture between economic systems, expressed his strong intellectual and emotional investment in assumptions of a fundamental unity. During the early days of the New Deal, Franklin Roosevelt and his allies relied on constant appeals to an ideal of moral oneness. A spirit of cooperation and "neighborliness" was expected to serve as a primary force in overcoming the disunity and the economic difficulties that an exaggerated individualism had created. If in one view departures from principle and precedent threatened the cohesiveness of "traditional America," in the other change was a necessary and desirable corrective that would achieve a new stability.[8]

Much of the political left as well, through various permutations of theory and practice, appealed to an ideal of unity. If present society was the setting for class conflict and human degradation, the future yet to be won would eliminate the historic divisions of class and establish the blessed harmonies of a classless society. The cataclysmic change of revolution, in some of the "orthodox" Communist declarations of the early 1930s, became an essential precondition for stability: disruption, division, and upheaval could be embraced precisely because they would lead toward a compelling unification. With international issues pushing to the fore in the later 1930s, the Communist party and the Popular Front gave primacy to calls for antifascist unity and were quick to heap scorn on leftists who refused to abandon critiques of Stalinism for what they defined as a greater collective good. Left parties, and particularly the Communists, also worked hard to create comprehensive social and cultural worlds for their members, offering what seemed to many a life of principled commitment and common purpose. So strong was the attraction of this integrated life that, as Mark Naison has noted, separation from the group came as a hard blow for those Communists who "found sustenance in the Party's utopian visions, whether of socialism, interracialism, or anti-fascist unity."⁹

The policy of "interracialism" reflected the Communists' attempt in the early 1930s to turn ethnicity and race into a force for unity through an ideal of complete nondiscrimination and the presumptive harmony of a radical culture in the making. Whatever the practice of Party members, the recognition of differences was in theory not allowed. A competing ethnic ideal, often on the other side of the political spectrum, lay behind the continuing urge in many quarters to identify what was valuable in American culture with the dominance of a relatively homogeneous, white, Protestant tradition. In university and college life, the desire to preserve this tradition as the basis for a stable and cohesive culture expressed itself during the early 1930s in a vigorously renewed emphasis on "spiritual values"—those eternal truths taken as applicable to all that were nevertheless thought to have been embodied best in the narrow world of the nineteenth-century Christian college. This "religious-conservative impulse," as David Hollinger notes, was "self-consciously reactionary" yet sufficiently deep-rooted to earn praise from the *New York Times*.[10] At a less genteel level, local evasions of New Deal antidiscrimination policies on work relief and bitter opposition to antilynching laws made it clear that many Americans still looked to white supremacy as a central principle of cultural coherence. The very different notions about ethnic relations that asserted hierarchy and white Protestant preeminence in the one case, and a complete erasure of ethnic differences in the other, supported opposing attitudes toward change, yet both shared the assumption that a desirable and lasting culture must rest on a single ideal.

Intellectuals and artists often constructed their own "metaphors" of cultural unity during the 1930s, some of which have already entered the discussion in different contexts: the harmoniously integrated societies modeled in the Democracity and Futurama displays of the New York World's Fair; the American past as it was depicted in Colonial Williamsburg or in many New Deal murals; the cohesive American culture defined by Constance Rourke; and customarily the "primitive" or nonindustrial cultures described by anthropologists.[11] Another process of metaphor construction was under way in the vigorous efforts to generate a popular taste for aesthetic "culture" in the interwar period, frequently under the heading of "appreciation." A number of forces were at work: the popularizing of the highbrow arts (or the creation of the "middlebrow") has been described as a response to the burgeoning number of high school and college graduates after World War I, as a product of the search for status and a winning "personality," and as part of a consumption-oriented process of marketing commodities of all kinds.[12]

In combination with fulfilling such other needs, the "appreciation" movements promised at their core that there was indeed a unified cultural tradition available, one both elevated and accessible, profound and reassuring. Most musical guidebooks, the great majority of recordings, and especially the wide-

ly popular radio symphony broadcasts that began in the 1930s tended to identify "classical" music with a rather narrow repertoire of eighteenth- and nineteenth-century orchestral music. As Joseph Horowitz has noted, the demands
of marketing "great" music called for a "compact, homogenized repertoire
bulk," and the same limitation conveyed the impression of a cohesive, con-
trollable, and timeless musical culture.[13]  Avoiding confrontation with the
twentieth century or with American materials, yet able to be cultivated as
immediately and permanently valid, a unified cultural construction of this
kind served not simply as art or ornament but as an antidote to fears of decom-
position (musical or otherwise).

Defining a compact repertoire bulk of its own, the "great books" crusade at
a popular level became another of the "appreciation" movements, offering a
stable culture, suitably packaged, that could defy the vagaries of the present.
Hutchins's intellectual and educational critique that made "permanent studies" the cure for "disunity, discord, and disorder" developed the appeal in
more sophisticated form.  As should now be apparent, the Hutchins reformers shared their belief that a worthy culture required fundamental coherence
with dozens of other efforts to create unifying metaphors or movements in the
1930s.  No doubt many of these efforts to preserve or to assert a particular version of cultural unity provided a focus that helped counter feelings of disinte-
gration and drift, feelings prompted immediately by the depression and more
broadly by the social, economic, intellectual, and cultural restructurings of
modernity.  And in part because the urge toward models of wholeness did
remain the strongest intellectual pattern, different conceptions of unifying
cultural principles competed and conflicted with each other throughout the
1930s.  But they also shared the field increasingly with other ideas of how
American culture might function that laid far less emphasis on an integrated
ideal.  These newer ideas about the grounds for a stable culture grew in part
out of the patterns of thought against which Hutchins rebelled and from
which many of his opponents took their bearings.

For several decades before the 1930s, American intellectuals had demonstrated growing resistance to all forms of absolutist thought and to any belief
in permanent truths of the kind Hutchins hoped to reaffirm.  Darwinian ideas
had made change, not permanence, central to conceptions of the natural
world.  By the early twentieth century, evolutionary assumptions were contributing to an accelerated deterioration in the authority of religious doctrine,
revealed truth, and abstract law.  Concomitant with the rising prestige of the
natural sciences, intellectuals placed greater weight on empirical evidence.
Forceful groups in spheres ranging from philosophy and literature to politics
and law identified themselves with a "realism" that presumably looked at
human life and the workings of institutions as they really were, not as abstract
or ideal models had made them out to be.  Emerging fields in the study of society claimed designation as the "social sciences" and sang the praises of "scientific method" (codifications of which would become more sacrosanct in the

social than in the natural sciences). As the processes of professionalization encouraged an increasing emphasis on methodology, objectivity, and exactitude, many social scientists found it easy to brand the work of their predecessors "unscientific" and to dismiss those who continued to seek ethical justification and moral purpose.[14]

Developments in logic and theoretical mathematics reinforced from a different angle the challenge to absolute truths advanced by empiricism. Demonstration that the geometry based on Euclid's axioms was not the only coherent geometry possible led intellectuals in the 1920s and 1930s to contemplate an indeterminate proliferation of non-Euclidean systems (wrongly, it would later appear). If even mathematics and logic represented formally enclosed systems dependent on the prior acceptance of seemingly arbitrary principles, then no structure of belief could lay unassailable claim to a singular truth. For those most persuaded by non-Euclideanism and empiricism, Christian ethics and American ideals were equally bereft of any adequate foundation. Systems of thought or methods of inquiry could claim validity not by reference to larger ends but only insofar as they seemed to describe the actual functioning of society. The majority of social scientists by the early 1930s believed that attending to values and morals obstructed sound investigation.

The momentum that had developed in the critique of absolutism was by this time spinning off extreme versions of the quest for objectivity and "scientific" method, stirring up further intellectual division. Hutchins's assault on the newer ideas carried bite in part because he had himself been an avid legal realist who was now undergoing a reverse conversion. His charges of pointless fact-gathering in the social sciences echoed the complaints against narrowness and excess being voiced by philosophers and social scientists who nevertheless remained committed to naturalistic, antiformalist ideas. For intellectuals who assumed the study of society should speak to needed reforms, a noncommittal objectivism failed to satisfy. Some, like Adolph Berle, Jr., and Charles Merriam, rejected a gathering of data that did nothing to solve definable problems. Others attacked an unproductive infatuation with measurement and statistics. And John Dewey for one argued that a legitimate understanding of scientific method demanded more than a preoccupation with inert facts. At the end of the decade, Robert Lynd framed the fundamental concern in the title of his book, *Knowledge for What?* (1939), in which he criticized the narrow purview of academic specialists and attempted to articulate a more comprehensive social outlook. Such critiques, whatever their particular biases, took on added import as scientism and objectivism were measured against the domestic and international challenges of the 1930s.

Democratic government, according to the descriptions regnant among intellectuals early in the decade, functioned in ways that did little to inspire its vigorous defense either as an effective means for responding to economic collapse or as a desirable alternative to dictatorship. As part of the skeptical dissection of all frameworks of value during the 1920s, the democratic assumption that individuals could determine rationally their own best interests and then express those interests through politics suffered both theoretical and empirical attack. Scholars like Harold D. Lasswell applied still-new psycho-analytic concepts to argue that most political choices were in fact irrational expressions of subconscious needs. Walter Lippmann and others, through examinations of the American system in practice, demonstrated to the satis-faction of many not simply that democratic processes had been corrupted but that democratic rule was impossible.[15] Thurman Arnold's *Symbols of Government*, published in 1935, rested its argument squarely on such conclu-sions. Although not everyone agreed that self-government was a hollow ideal, the deterioration of the practical and ethical justifications for democracy had proceeded far enough by 1935 to leave a considerable number of intellectuals in an awkward position. Faced with the rising threat of fascism (and, for a growing number, with that of Stalinist communism as well), many were dis-covering in themselves loyalties to an ideal for which they were intellectually ill prepared to provide a rationale. How could those who had turned the pow-ers of science and empiricism against all fixed frameworks of value find a basis on which to champion the values of democracy?

The answer that emerged served an urgent need to protect naturalistic intellectual commitments as well as to defend democracy. Advocates of per-manent truths had been quick to argue that in undermining the foundations of ethical and moral belief, the forces of scientific naturalism had introduced an amoral relativism, paving the way for fascism and leaving themselves unable to demonstrate why one internally successful system was better than any other. On the contrary, the naturalists began to insist in ragged chorus, the assertion of fixed truths represented the greater political threat. For many years John Dewey had argued generally that absolutist ideas provided logical support for authoritarianism in politics. By the mid-1930s Dewey was explic-itly identifying fascism and communism with absolutist thought and linking democratic societies with scientific empiricism. The apparent rigidities of absolutism and the doctrines and forms of dictatorship stood on one side; nat-uralism, science, and democracy, by contrast, could be described as flexible, experimental, and multifaceted. Democracy was worthy of defense because it sustained this openness and experimentalism.[16] Others developed the linkages along somewhat different lines than did Dewey, but by the end of the 1930s a relatively common front had appeared among naturalistic intellectuals. Absolutist claims of permanent truths were natural allies to the frightening juggernauts of social and ideological unity now labeled "totalitarian." American democracy stood worthy of defense because its truths were varied and changing. It promoted compromise rather than a quest for domination. It claimed the virtue of being divided and multiple.

Different conceptions of social order emerged along with these newer argu-ments on behalf of democracy. For a significant number of intellectuals, pos-itive visions of a stable society now placed less emphasis on a comprehensive unity than on multiplicity or heterogeneity. Assertions of principle and studies of political process jointly affirmed these newer outlooks. The political scientist Carl Friedrich, who through the mid-1930s had argued that democracy required an acceptance of common values, was suggesting by 1939 that it might instead be the only form of government in which "agreement on fundamentals need not be secured."[17] In *The Politics of Democracy* (1940), Pendleton Herring celebrated the empirical evidence that democratic institutions allowed the "peaceful resolution of interest conflicts." Under democracy, Herring declared, "we are not forced to believe in unity; we may glory in diversity." Thus, the value of American political parties lay not in "their realization of one view as to what society should be" but in their "flexibility." Concluding his exploration of American politics as a means for "reconciling change with stability," Herring placed his primary emphasis on "adaptation" and multiplicity.[18]

Shifting patterns in the public rhetoric of politics were more than keeping pace with philosophical and scholarly ideas, especially in redefining American society as multiple. Early New Deal talk of cooperation, though it never vanished entirely, had largely given way to an emphasis on delineated groups and to what Ellis Hawley has described as the "concept of counterorganization," which sought balance and stability by pitting "one power concentrate against another."[19] For Secretary of Agriculture Henry Wallace in 1937, the "simple unspecialized society" of the past, presumably characterized by a natural unity, stood in clear contrast with the "highly specialized society" of the present, "composed of powerful organized groups of business, labor, and agriculture."[20] Recognition of these groups, and of multiple divisions in American society more generally, became standard in the changing meaning of the term "interests" during the 1930s. From a label that to an earlier progressive mentality was, in Daniel Rodgers's words, a "smear of no mean force," the term became a descriptive reference to the actual workings of the American political system as an equilibrium of pressures and counterpressures exerted by various groups.[21] By 1940 John Chamberlain was complaining sharply about "philosophical idealist[s]" who made the mistake of "considering the whole as greater than the sum of the parts," while speaking warmly of the "broker theory of the State" and of pressure groups as "the new democratic unit." Chamberlain's preferences had everything to do with a vision of social order and the question of stability: differences tended in time to "tear . . . apart" the "strict" state, he declared, while the state based on multiple interests could "adapt itself to pressure."[22]

This newer pattern for thinking about the nature of the American political order did not stand alone in its emphasis on multiplicity, nor in its understanding of difference as a source of stability. By the end of the 1930s, ideas that tended to define the social and cultural order as multiple had emerged in a number of spheres to rival conceptions based on unity. Boas-derived anthropological relativism, which had been part of the broader critique of fixed truths and absolutist values in the early twentieth century, offered encouragement during the 1930s for the belief that the United States might permanently contain many "patterns of culture." African-Americans resisting communist interracialism, writers and scholars collecting historical and cultural materials on ethnic groups or particular regions, Harold Ickes embracing the idea that Indian cultures should "live on"—all were positing in varying ways notions of an ongoing social order rightly multiple. Moreover, evidence was accumulating rapidly during the 1930s that the assumption of multiplicity as an appropriate ideal was coming to represent for some an intellectual, moral, and emotional commitment fully as powerful as the ideal of unity. Functioning as a positive framework now accepted as integral to national identity, multiplicity linked politics and culture, economics and ethnicity, as when Ickes spoke of "those cultures and interests which, in their aggregate, constitute the United States." When the same framework and the same linkages were made the basis for a negative critique, they provided grounds for charging intellectuals who advocated fixed truths or permanent values—in particular, Hutchins, Adler, and the Catholics—not only with harboring political authoritarianism but also with seeking a cultural uniformity hostile to ethnic multiplicity. Divisions among American intellectuals with a long future ahead of them were developing in part around different ideals of social and cultural order.

Multiplicity as a version of order did not, of course, deny the need for an overall cohesion, nor did it entirely negate the still-potent appeal of unity. Frequently, the expectation of commonality and integration was simply moved down a level, as it were, from the whole to the parts, and the multiple society became conceptually a loose general structure filled with "cultures and interests" that were themselves tightly bound. In models of the American political economy that would grow out of ideas from the 1930s, groups like "Labor," "Agriculture," and "Business" might at times be treated as if they were monolithic entities. And consequentially, elements of the society that remained unorganized or that lacked identity as unified "interests" could seemingly be passed over as insignificant. In some versions of cultural pluralism, the constituent parts of the multiple society were unbreakable units of kinship, tradition, and memory. Under the banner of social diversity, ethnic particularism could turn ironically into a demand that all members of an ethnic group embrace a single version of group identity. Studies of particular American cultures by anthropologists and folklorists often combined resistance to claims of the broader society and a theoretical commitment to multiplicity with powerful ideals of commonality and integration for the group. This tendency to seek unity on a smaller scale has not disappeared. One scholar has recently remarked that "even now, having become far more sensitive to the variety of American society, we still tend to use . . . [a fixed] model of cultural stability as a moral norm, assuming that whatever subculture we focus on is or should be as rooted and prescriptive as the older [Van Wyck] Brooks thought his exurban small-town WASP America."[23]

The interactions between unity and multiplicity as conceptions of order could thus become quite complex. Differences between those promoting a holistic unity and those rejecting such an ideal provided one set of intellectual tensions; efforts to describe the social order as multiple while acclaiming a tight integration within its parts involved tensions of another kind. And just as differing ideals of unity could stand as sharply opposed to one another as the Communist party and the Catholic church, different assumptions about which social divisions carried the greatest significance could engender competing versions of multiplicity. Conceptions of a multiple order based on economic interest groups did not necessarily share the political and cultural viewpoints inherent in frameworks based on ethnicity, regionalism, or religion. Together, contrasting versions of a multi-unit society suggested a complicated web of cross-divisions that left few sharply defined and well-integrated segments of the whole intact. Understandably, then, for some, the intellectual journey away from ideals of a unified social order did not stop at the halfway house of multiplicity but hurried on toward the domain of heterogeneity. This third way of thinking about a reasonable stability and a viable order—emerging unevenly in practice and in theory—rested on the idea that cultural coherence and vitality could sometimes derive not from the relatively fixed definitions of either singular or multiple social entities but from an ongoing process characterized by frequent change, fluid relationships, and a penchant for testing and borrowing.

To some degree, heterogeneity as a principle of cohesion extended the assumptions of multiplicity. Both ordering principles relied on a belief that social divisions, far from being destructive, might balance stability and change. Both grew out of the rejection of absolutism and contributed to a defense of democracy for its lack of restrictive purpose. Yet in arguments that rested on heterogeneity, the sense of discrete social and cultural units largely disappeared. Attention fell less on well-defined institutions, groups, or traditions than on a rather amorphous context of perpetual interactions and on the processes of culture in the making.

For intellectuals seeking the sharpest possible contrast with Nazism and Stalinism at the end of the 1930s, diversity and flexibility became the very essence of American political life. Democracy was not a matter of institutions, Jacques Barzun argued in 1939: "It is an atmosphere and an attitude; in a word—a culture." Whereas fascism meant "uniformity," the "culture" of democracy sustained a tolerance for the "many diverse kinds of order" that accompanied art, science, and free thought. Identifying himself in part with naturalistic assumptions, Barzun insisted that knowledge must be seen as only "a working approximation, a pragmatic handle to reality."[24] The constant need to apply and test knowledge required constant questioning and change. Yet the lack of permanence in this world of flux did not end a legitimate concern with cohesion, stability, and ethical propositions. A culture that allowed science "to destroy traditional values," Dewey declared in 1939, must also have confidence in "its power to create new ones."[25] The pragmatic outlook, as David Hollinger has pointed out, held that "inquiry itself was a discipline that could stabilize and sustain a modern, 'scientific' culture."[26] Critical inquiry as a method was thus central to Barzun's "atmosphere," contributing to an ideal of American culture as at once stable and fluid. Tolerance for "diverse kinds of order" became a newer conception of order that assumed heterogeneity.

The ideas about ethnic relations associated with the values of cosmopolitanism rested on a similar outlook. When Randolph Bourne had given early form to the cosmopolitan position with his essays on "trans-nationalism," he had distinguished his viewpoint somewhat from a particularist pluralism by emphasizing that he was not interested in ethnic cultures frozen by their loyalty to fixed traditions but only in "modern," "contemporary" ethnic cultures undergoing constant change and growth.[27] The larger American culture would evolve through a fluid mixing involving all of these living cultures. By the 1930s cosmopolitan values had won an important following among intellectuals who embraced the ideal of creating a heterogeneous cultural whole that required neither the freezing nor the melting of identities. Applied within the special world of universities, where strong resistance remained, cosmopolitanism was helping to break down by the end of the decade those institutional loyalties to the unity of "Anglo-Saxon" or Christian culture that had generally kept Jews outside such sanctums as philosophy or "English" departments.[28] The ideal of an academic order that was beginning to emerge pointed toward a cultural environment in which not a unity of cultural backgrounds and assumptions but their diversity and heterogeneous mixing would be regarded by many as the grounds for legitimacy.

Within a more popular framework, the unabashed conviction at *Life* magazine that its disparate array added up to a coherent view of the world, the published collections of verbal and visual impression that claimed to capture the character of the United States, the mile-by-mile local color reports of the *American Guides*—all were efforts to represent a "culture" of democracy, strong, alive, and endlessly fascinating in its heterogeneity. The apparent acceptance of variety itself as the paradoxical glue of this common culture testified both to a remarkable faith in national cohesiveness and to the avoidance of difficult questions. Intellectuals might claim their method of inquiry as a grounds for coherence, but whether even this unity should be strongly asserted was a question about which many were chary. Barzun acknowledged that the values and methods he espoused added up to a "formula," yet he insisted that it was, "or ought to be, a flexible one," offering only the "unity of many-sidedness."[29] The question of whether that unity was a sufficient one would trouble some intellectuals over the coming decades as confidence in pragmatism, progress, and scientific method dribbled away. For others, the elaboration not simply of "diverse kinds of order" but of diverse modes of analysis would race ahead, cloaked protectively in an ideal of heterogeneity that allowed the celebration of change while sustaining an (often unacknowledged) assumption of stability on which American intellectuals quietly depended to do their work.

## Ordering the Arts

Different conceptions of what constituted a viable social order provided different ways of thinking about the patterning of inherited traditions, of contemporary events, and of future possibilities. Each ordering idea, in all its applications, involved an effort to make sense out of the world and to hold it together intellectually. Developments in the arts suggest that the need to reformulate ideas of order was deeply rooted in twentieth-century experience. Yet this process of organizational and aesthetic reordering has received only sporadic attention. For the most part, a shaping design for historical treatments of the arts during the 1930s has derived from one of three themes: the appeal of radicalism, the cultivation of nationalism, or the assertion in retrospect of a particular artistic direction. These interpretive frameworks deserve to be acknowledged and examined. Then the inquiry should be extended. Paying heed to the uses of unity, multiplicity, and heterogeneity as frameworks of understanding and meaning during the 1930s can cut across customary efforts to line up the arts politically, socially, and aesthetically, even as it can call attention to patterns in American thought and culture that are frequently overlooked.

Interpretations emphasizing radicalism as central to the culture of the decade have concentrated on efforts to infuse the arts with political meaning. Such efforts can be traced easily in drama, for example, for it stood close to literature in its ability to give social ideas direct verbal expression. Like the proletarian vision in literature, the call for a "Workers Theater" in the early thirties looked toward plays created by workers, for audiences made up of workers, that would function as a weapon in the class struggle. In drama as in fiction, the products created under an explicit proletarian banner were soon assailed as simplistic and ineffective, and their motivating rationale was swept aside with the advent of the Popular Front.

Along with fiction and reportage, the theater also exhibited a broader and more diffuse social consciousness sympathetic to the left. A number of groups appeared—with names like the Theater Union, the New Theater League, the Theater Collective, and Labor Stage—that sought to build a sense of communal purpose and to make drama speak to contemporary issues. The most successful and most lasting of these was the Group Theater, founded by Harold Clurman and Lee Strasberg and including people like Franchot Tone, John Garfield, Lee J. Cobb, Elia Kazan, and Karl Malden. From the platform of the Group Theater, the playwright Clifford Odets leaped to prominence in 1935 with *Waiting for Lefty*, a one-act piece written in support of a New York taxi strike. Odets's later plays, like the careers of many from the Group Theater, suggested persistent tensions between political or intellectual ideals and the desire for recognition and success.[30]

A distinct political interest (liberal more than radical) also colored some of the varied productions of the Federal Theater Project, which under the direction of Hallie Flanagan sponsored drama companies in the majority of states beginning in 1935. While serving primarily as a relief program providing jobs, the Theater Project aimed to make drama accessible, to build audiences across the country, to celebrate American cultural resources as mixed and multiple, and to encourage experimentation and innovation. Plays were presented in several languages, including Spanish and Yiddish; Orson Welles situated *Macbeth* in Haiti and used an entirely African-American cast; *The Mikado* was presented in a "swing" idiom, and *Doctor Faustus* without scenery. In its efforts to make drama relevant and engaging, the Theater Project also created the "Living Newspaper"—a rendering of current issues that normally contained a clear liberal or pro–New Deal message, as in the depiction of a reactionary Supreme Court in "Triple A Plowed Under." Not surprisingly, the same social and cultural ambitions that gave the Theater Project much of its vitality prompted strong political opposition, and in 1939 Congress denied all further funding. Public funding implied political limits.

In the visual arts, an emphasis on radicalism during the 1930s has encouraged special attention to painters who chose workers or the downtrodden as their subjects or who tried to make art a direct servant of politics. Within a strain of urban realism that had its origins before World War I, artists like Reginald Marsh and the brothers Soyer—Moses, Raphael, and Isaac—painted scenes from New York's Bowery District and the worn faces of ordinary people. The "social realists," including Ben Shahn, Philip Evergood, and Stefan Hirsch, made the conditions of the working class their dominant subject and accepted the radical argument of the early thirties that art should deliver an explicit (and often heavy-handed) social message. Some, like William Gropper, devoted themselves primarily to providing illustrations for radical publications, especially *New Masses*.[31] In the later 1930s the blend of aesthetic vitality and social protest achieved by the Mexican muralists Diego Rivera and José Clemente Orozco, working in the United States for part of the decade, became an evident influence on some of the approximately 5,000 artists employed by the Federal Art Project. When George Biddle painted a mural that included sweatshops for the Justice Department, the "listless starvelings imprisoned in the pigeonholes of his tenements were vintage Rivera, in style and import."[32] This form of "social realism" remained sharply constrained, however, within the opinion-sensitive federal program.

The political as an orienting theme has been of little help when it comes to music. For the most part, music became intertwined with social issues in the 1930s only when it was combined with words, and the verbal messages dominated the way such materials were perceived. Thus, when the WPA halted the scheduled production of Marc Blitzstein's opera *The Cradle Will Rock* in 1937, it was because the words conveyed a radical message, not because the music was controversial. Musical theater bubbled with vitality in the 1930s and stimulated such offshoots as *Pins and Needles*, a revue put together by the International Ladies' Garment Workers' Union. Certain pieces from the revue, like "Sing Us a Song with Social Significance" and "Doing the Reactionary," are sometimes recalled for their good-humored, self-mocking wit, but virtually no one remembers the music. Songs may have played a part in union organizing, roused a radical meeting, or stimulated patriotic feeling. But when politics stands in the foreground, music as music is largely ignored.

Politics as a cultural key thus functions like other keys—opening certain doors while proving ineffectual before others. Radical vitality does, to some extent, make the thirties distinctive. Emphasizing this pattern fits comfortably with the common historical assumption that social and political issues were preeminent during the depression. Moreover, the story can be closed neatly in arguing that (conveniently synchronous with the end of the decade) greater prosperity, intellectual and tactical contradictions on the left, and the onset of war drained radicalism of its appeal. The danger of a political emphasis in interpreting the thirties is that it restricts our view of the arts; it confines the cultural experience of the decade within a convenient box and invites limited connection with the past or future.

Nationalism as a thematic center incorporates a wider body of materials, in part because the idea is itself so elastic. Various expressions of a heightened interest in local, regional, folk, and ethnic cultures during the 1930s can appear as emblems of a depression-inspired urge toward national self-discovery. Significant work in the arts can fit quite reasonably within both an extended historical context and a ready nationalistic framework through identification with the continuing quest to establish a distinctive American culture and to claim aesthetic equality with Europe. Popular Front antifascism, prodemocracy sentiments, and celebrations of American tradition—all of which found artistic expression toward the end of the thirties—can become bedfellows together under the coverlet of nationalism.

With nationalism as a guiding theme, the culture of the 1930s puts on a clean face and radicalism blends into the background. "Nationalistic attitudes dominated American visual art in the 1930s," one account suggests, as a majority of artists, perhaps for the last time, tried to reach a broad public through "readily recognizable images and symbols." At the heart of these efforts was "American Scene" painting, a category as flexibly inclusive as the idea of nationalism itself. The urban realists are often gathered within the fold. So are the stylistically independent painters Edward Hopper and Charles Burchfield. And the self-consciously radical art of Shahn and Gropper becomes for some scholars just one more example of the "paint-America compulsion."[33] The American Scene label identified most particularly the midwestern regionalist painters Thomas Hart Benton, Grant Wood, and John Steuart Curry. Benton's powerful figures and historical themes, Wood's *American Gothic*, and Curry's imposing storms became familiar images in the 1930s, frequently linked with the vigorous promotion by some critics of an emphatic (and too often a narrow-minded) definition of Americanism.

In music, the theme of nationalism pulls together various efforts to advocate or to celebrate a strong American musical culture during the 1930s, though there was limited agreement on what such a culture should entail. The interest both in gathering and in creating a music of the folk—inspired partially by the radical emphasis first on "workers" and later on the "people"—reflected a search for distinctive native traditions that often became strikingly nationalistic.[34] Jazz was suspect to defenders of white Protestant traditions for its African-American origins, its lower-class urban ethos, and its indulgence of sexuality and disorder, and it became the object of "persistent denigration" by the émigré German intellectual Theodor Adorno in part because of its popularity and commercialization.[35] Yet enthusiasts regularly praised its indigenous roots and looked to jazz as the most American music of all. For large segments of the population, having a strong musical culture in America meant producing a broad audience for the recognized domain of "classical" music, and there seemed much to celebrate in this regard during the 1930s. Radio offered opportunities for "appreciation," and the combined audience for weekend opera and symphony broadcasts by 1939 had grown to ten million. The largest phonograph company, RCA Victor, saw its record sales increase some 600 percent between 1933 and 1938, with classical recordings an important part of this boom. The Italian conductor of the NBC orchestra, Arturo Toscanini, was annointed the "high priest of the music appreciation movement" and turned into a symbol of national good taste, antifascism, and the personality and values expected of an American celebrity.[36]

Yet for many music professionals, the key to claiming a musical culture of which Americans could be proud lay in composition, and some campaigned vigorously during the 1930s to include native composers on the concert programs of the Federal Music Project and private orchestras. More so than in the other arts, a musical work did not necessarily require a distinctively American content in order to serve a nationalistic purpose. Nevertheless, a number of composers sought not simply to establish their talent within a framework defined by Europeans but to make their music specifically expressive of the culture of the United States. Roy Harris insisted that American composers had a "unique rhythmic sense," and he tried to embody his ideas in such pieces as the overture *When Johnny Comes Marching Home* (1935), his *First Symphony* (1933), and his frequently performed *Third Symphony* (1937).[37] Virgil Thomson relied on American hymns and songs in writing the scores for Pare Lorentz's documentary films *The Plow That Broke the Plains* and *The River*. Aaron Copland, seeking to reach a broad audience by expressing himself musically in what he regarded as the "simplest possible terms," drew on native songs and multiple American traditions in such works as *El Salon Mexico* (1933–36), *Billy the Kid* (1938), *Our Town* (1940), and *Lincoln Portrait* (1942).[38] The composer who used American materials most extensively and most creatively, Charles Ives, had done most of his work before 1920, but it was only in the 1930s that a few of Ives's pieces, especially *Three Places in New England* (1908–14), began to receive wider attention.

American materials were also at the center of three very different operas that, appearing close together, seemed to hold considerable promise for national contributions to the form: Louis Gruenberg's *The Emperor Jones* (1933), based on the Eugene O'Neill play; Virgil Thomson's *Four Saints in Three Acts*, with libretto by Gertrude Stein (1934); and George Gershwin's *Porgy and Bess* (1935). In practice, what the varying experience of these productions pointed toward was not an American impact on the traditional realm of opera but a channeling of such efforts toward the commercial musical stage.[39]

During the same period, dance was achieving new levels of significance in the United States, in part by pursuing strongly nationalistic goals. A group of dancers and choreographers who came together in New York at the beginning of the 1930s worked to create a distinctly American gesture and movement, free of the "imperialism of the ballet" and other "transplanted" dance styles.[40] The most influential and productive member of the group, Martha Graham, created works entitled *American Provincials* (1934), *Frontier* (1935), *American Lyric* (1937), and *American Document* (1938). Meanwhile, ballet itself was developing a topical American flavor, especially through the efforts of Lincoln Kirstein's Ballet Caravan. Ballet brought music and dance together, as in the Caravan productions based on music by Elliot Carter (*Pocahontas*, 1936), Virgil Thomson (*Filling Station*, 1938), and Aaron Copland (*Billy the Kid*, 1939). These developments would reach a climax of sorts in the Ballet Russe presentation of *Rodeo* (1942), which combined music by Copland and choreography by Agnes De Mille, and in *Appalachian Spring* (1944), created by Copland and a more ballet-minded Martha Graham.

Graham's sympathies inclined toward the political left, yet that remained largely a footnote to her emphasis on American materials. Nationalism as a theme subsumes a variety of political attitudes, especially during the later 1930s, when Popular Front leftism, prodemocratic liberalism, and a kind of centrist patriotism often seemed to merge. In drama, for example, the need to oppose fascism provided a common subject for Lillian Hellman (*The Watch on the Rhine*, 1941), whose radical affinities had been clearly declared; Robert Sherwood (*There Shall Be No Night*, 1940), whose affection for democracy had been apparent in *Abe Lincoln in Illinois* (1938); and Sinclair Lewis (*It Can't Happen Here*, 1936), whose tale as widely performed by the Federal Theater Project shared the faith in small-town values that also inspired Thornton Wilder's *Our Town* (1938). The ease of this linkage provides a caution. As a lens through which to view the arts, nationalism gives sharp focus to a widespread concern with self-discovery and self-definition during the

Stuart Davis's painting "Abstract Vision of New York: a building, a derby hat, a tiger's head, and other symbols" appeared in the 1932 exhibition "Murals by American Painters and Photographers" at the Museum of Modern Art. The Empire State Building, completed the previous year, soars into the sky (and the future) yet remains strongly rooted in the older structures from which it emerges. The new stands beside the old. Several of the objects in the painting refer to Al Smith, the former New York governor and Democratic presidential candidate who had recently been hired as a publicist for the Empire State Building: the brown derby was Smith's political trademark; the banana on which the lower derby rests alludes to Smith as a "top banana" and to a 1928 campaign song derived from "Yes! We Have No Bananas"; Smith's preference for bow ties is echoed in several bow shapes; and a tipped champagne glass and other symbols suggest his opposition to prohibition. These allusions to a prominent individual blend with references to the historic New York Democratic organization, Tammany Hall, represented by the tiger's head and tail, while the tires and gas pump may refer to contemporary investigations into Tammany corruption involving the transportation industries. The balanced range of contemporary and historical symbols embraces an evolving industrial city and its politics, providing material for an effective artistic composition that itself strikes a balance between representation and abstraction. As Bruce Weber remarks of this painting in *Stuart Davis' New York*, a 1985 exhibition catalog from the Norton Gallery and School of Art in West Palm Beach, "Davis cleverly retained his modernist credentials while handling politically charged subject matter in an original and subtle manner" *Norton Gallery and School of Art*

1930s, and it calls attention to the importance of the decade in the ongoing effort to create or discover aesthetically sophisticated works that were distinctively American. At the same time, it may obscure distinctions, overemphasize a temporary context, and limit consideration of emerging structures and broader directions.

Unlike either radicalism or nationalism as organizing themes, the idea of developmental direction most commonly provides an interpretive spine for studies of particular branches of the arts carried over several decades. Working from firm convictions about which achievements rank as the most important, scholars may configure the past to assert an appropriate governing pattern or to emphasize a chain of contributions toward a particular result. Frequently, the standard of significance derives from American aesthetic accomplishments after World War II. Explaining or tracing the roots of postwar developments may thus become a guiding rationale in discussing the culture of the thirties. In painting, for example, the abstract expressionism of the postwar New York School is widely accepted as a high point of American achievement. Efforts during the 1930s to make art serve a radical purpose contributed little toward this end. Thus, although history texts attuned to politics may use a painting like Ben Shahn's *The Passion of Sacco and Vanzetti* (1931–32) to represent the spirit of the arts in the 1930s, a standard survey of recent American art describes such paintings sharply as "little more than stylized drawing in which paint was merely a fill between contours" and suggests that the social realists were often "not far removed from political cartoonists." The painters of the 1930s taken most seriously in this account, especially Stuart Davis, were engaged before the war with modernist experimentation and abstraction. The WPA Federal Art Project gains recognition because it "supported the budding avant-garde's contention" that abstract art was as "American" as representational art, and because mural work prepared artists to "paint large-scale pictures a decade later."[41]

For some interpreters, the apparent maturation of American culture in the postwar period calls for special attention to the wave of European intellectual émigrés who came to the United States during the 1930s and 1940s. At the end of the thirties, a cluster of European composers, including Igor Stravinsky, Arnold Schoenberg, Paul Hindemith, Darius Milhaud, and Kurt Weill, were working in the United States, and the leading orchestra conductors were dominantly émigrés. European painters teaching and working in America included George Grosz, Hans Hofmann, and Josef Albers. The writers Thomas Mann and Bertolt Brecht, the Bauhaus architects Walter Gropius, Marcel Breuer, and Ludwig Mies van der Rohe, the sociologists, theologians, political theorists, and scientists—all arrived in such numbers, and were of such a quality, as to temporarily shift the intellectual and cultural balance between Europe and the United States. Considering émigré influence on the patterns of American culture may help place artists and intellectuals of the thirties within a wider context. Yet here as elsewhere, arguments based on developmental direction must struggle continually to avoid the distortions of a script read backward from later events.

There is no shortage, then, of organizing themes for thinking about culture and the arts in the 1930s, with each theme leading toward distinctive results. At one level of assumption, however, the most common strategies are not as divergent as they first appear. Disparate interpretations often share an underlying urge to draw from the materials at hand a central unifying pattern. One of the functions of identifying a central theme—whether in categorizing a decade or defining a "tradition"—is to provide an orienting sense of cohesion and unity. Intellectuals and artists of the 1930s were themselves more than commonly aware that their customary frameworks of value were under assault or threatening to crumble. Within this context, champions of cohesive traditions advocated with new urgency adherence to the "permanent truths" or reaffirmation of a modern "Intellectuals' Tradition" of social critique and artistic experimentation.[42] No single tradition or impulse could claim dominance during the 1930s, however, nor should it in later accounts. In the arts as in social and political thought, ordering principles were coming to the fore that did not assume comprehensive unity as an intellectual ideal. Noting the emergence of multiplicity and heterogeneity as vital conceptual patterns provides an enabling perspective on the development of the arts in the 1930s.

The evolution of institutional structures during the period pointed toward a conception of the arts as multiple rather than unitary. Although there was, and is, a powerful urge to maintain a sense of progression in Western aesthetic culture from one dominant style to another, "modernism" has encompassed such a range of efforts to explore new methods and assumptions as to encourage over time a recognition of plural "traditions." In the 1930s the claims of modernist stylistic camps shared attention with the sometimes overlapping attempts to define a specifically American tradition, as well as with popular and scholarly claims for rival traditions of the past or present.

In the fine arts, the opening of new museums in New York announced a transition in the institutional representation of culture. Taking for granted the inadequacies of the Metropolitan Museum of Art, each new museum embodied to some degree a commentary on the notion of a unitary Western tradition and on genteel assumptions about culture, and each sought not only to represent but also to proselytize for an alternative idea of art or a distinctive tradition. The Museum of Modern Art (MOMA) opened its first exhibition at the end of 1929 with a keen sense of the battle still being waged for the cultural acceptance of modern painting, and it did not stop there.[43] MOMA defined art broadly in the course of its exhibitions during the thirties to include photography, film, architecture, and industrial design, suggesting a variety of aesthetic clusters quite alien to established ideas of artistic culture. Neither the breadth of MOMA's interests nor its occasional attention to Americans satisfied all advocates of particular traditions-in-the-making, however. In 1931 the Whitney Museum of American Art, with its special interest in early twentieth-century American painters, opened. By 1937 the Solomon R. Guggenheim Museum of Non-Objective Art had staked out its piece of cultural turf, with its original name broadcasting the tradition it wished to promote. Still, the young painters who had formed American Abstract Artists in 1936 and sponsored a series of annual exhibitions felt that their kind of art was not getting sufficient respect. In 1940 they picketed the Museum of Modern Art to demand more attention, settling in the meantime for displays in such places as André Masson's Museum of Living Art. In a formal, public way through the museums, art came to be represented during the 1930s not as a single tradition but as several traditions.

For music, the concert hall by the early twentieth century had come to function as a museum, and the works performed in concert conveyed the cumulative judgments that defined a cohesive tradition. A major aim for many art music composers was to get into the museum, to advance the tradition of European art music, and to be seen as having done so by educated audiences. Yet the difficulties for listeners that modern music involved, combined with popularizing efforts to limit "classical" repertoire and close the door to the museum, resulted in the advocates of the "new music" creating their own largely separate organizations, publications, concerts, and traditions, as they began to do in the 1920s. Electronic music, to which the French-American composer Edgard Varèse was making significant early contributions in the 1930s, offered a new direction within art music that departed from recognized paths. As political and anthropological ideas combined with the personal interests of composers and scholars, folk music and non-Western music became subjects of serious study offering distinctive traditions of their own. In 1932 Henry Cowell and Charles Seeger taught the first ethnomusicology course in the United States. Although the enthusiasms of the 1920s had faded, jazz took on a second life as "swing" in the later 1930s. A famous Carnegie Hall appearance by Benny Goodman in 1938 was to one leading scholar a benchmark in the increasing acceptance of jazz as concert music, as a "new kind of art music."[44] The realm of musical theater could be added to the list, as could the rising interest in pre–eighteenth-century music that led to the creation of societies supporting "early" music at the beginning of the forties. This was not a musical world of unified tradition or even of neat divisions between "serious" and "popular" forms but a world of multiple tendencies and cross-pollinating clusters in which supporters of particular musics sought—as some have urged partisans of modern music to continue to seek—"museums of their own."[45]

Institutional structures in the arts, of which museums actual and metaphorical provide a prominent example, had developed by the end of the 1930s patterns similar to those traced by interest groups in political thought. In each case, changes in social and cultural organization were connected with the emergence of multiplicity as a viable ordering principle. Rather than seeking a comprehensive unity or a single tradition, many artists and intellectuals were beginning to work, knowingly or not, from an assumption that the cohesion within like-minded groups or more particularist traditions could provide an adequate basis for the stability of the whole. The existence of multiple centers provided an important alternative to the assumption of cultural unity. Yet multiplicity as an ordering idea remained itself too constraining for some. From certain cultural points of view, opportunity, identity, and even stability might best be found through fluid relationships between traditions that could accommodate variety and change. Heterogeneity was, or ought to be, one of modern culture's defining traits.

An emphasis on flexibility of outlook and on the interactions between cultures was often evident among intellectuals who had embraced cosmopolitan values. Just as they rejected both homogenizing uniformity and ethnic particularism as social ideals, they were often skeptical of autonomous traditions in culture and the arts, either singular or plural. A group or national culture seeking richness and definition would do best not to look inward to defend its distinctiveness but to recognize itself as one of many cultures swimming in a broader cultural stream, able at once to be distinct and an evolving part of a dynamic whole. This outlook led some interpreters to suggest that American culture, characterized by diversity and flux, could best find its national distinctiveness through interaction with the modern international culture of the West. Thomas Mann was both "deeply rooted in the German soil" and a general representative of "the intellectual experience of Europe," William Phillips and Philip Rahv argued in 1937; so, too, American writers could best find their national identity by carrying the "particulars of American life into the mainstream of world culture." The greatest promise of America was that it possessed "the most modern, variegated, and plastic" culture in the Western world.[46] Harold Rosenberg extended the theme when he suggested that the culture of modernism owed a special debt to the heterogeneity of early twentieth–century Paris, where "no folk lost its integrity" because artists of every nation found there "what was most alive in the communities from which they had come."[47] The intermixing of cultures was in this view the requisite condition for integrity and continuity, not a disruptive force.

Rosenberg was perhaps still groping toward an explicit statement that the restlessness and diversity of modernism might itself provide the basis for a vital, lasting, and, in a newer sense, stable artistic culture. If the idea had not fully taken shape as a conscious ordering principle by the end of the 1930s, the notion of heterogeneity as central to an understanding of modern culture would emerge in postwar aesthetic theory and criticism to rival vigorously the claims of unity and multiplicity. In *Music, the Arts, and Ideas* (1967), for example, Leonard Meyer insisted that the "paradigm of style history and cultural change" dominant since the seventeenth century—a paradigm assuming a succession of unified styles—has proved inadequate for comprehending twentieth-century arts. In a chapter on "The Aesthetics of Stability," he described a contemporary world in which "an indefinite number of styles and idioms, techniques and movements" coexist in the arts in a "dynamic steady-state."[48] Meyer Schapiro suggested in turn that modern heterogeneity "may be regarded as a necessary and valuable consequence of the individual's freedom of choice and of the world scope of modern culture." To achieve a common style in the present, Schapiro suggested, would require the destruction of "the most cherished values of our culture"—that is, unity, not heterogeneity, may threaten the stability of modern culture.[49] George Roeder in writing about American art has defined modernism as "the unprecedented condition of choice" surrounding artists, not as something ephemeral but as a condition that has already lasted most of a century and promises to last a good deal longer.[50] In these viewpoints, heterogeneity serves as an ordering and orienting idea, placing variety and choice at the heart of an ongoing modern tradition.

Individual artists and playwrights, dancers and composers, often recognized by the 1930s the possibilities of selecting from and recombining disparate elements to create cohesive wholes. Because heterogeneity as an ordering idea developed more rapidly as practice than it did as theory, the readily available frameworks for understanding and assessing such works could not always encourage a very sophisticated analysis of their nature. As a result, the qualities of particular works sometimes remained veiled behind standards associated with a unified tradition or with multiple (and relatively fixed) stylistic categories. Consider George Gershwin's *Porgy and Bess*, first produced in 1935, which has received little serious analytical and critical attention until recently. According to Lawrence Starr, Gershwin's use of popular idioms has alienated champions of a purer art music and a narrowly defined "avant-garde," while rival commentators who fall into a democratic swoon over Verdi's creation of popular hits in his operas have refused to honor the same result from Gershwin. Assumptions about what makes for a coherent work of art are directly involved. Quick judgments of Gershwin's music as a "haphazard combination of amiable elements" owe much, Starr argues, to "the common and often unconscious prejudice in favor of traditional, essentially European, conceptions of stylistic unity, and against the interest in heterogeneity which was one of Gershwin's characteristics as an artist and which links him strongly to major lines of development in specifically American music, arts, and aesthetic thought." Starr's formal musical analysis of the song "Bess, You Is My Woman Now" demonstrates how diverse elements work together in a specific piece and suggests how Gershwin constructed an opera—"the largest and most elaborate of Western musical forms"—out of particular but varied elements taken from American black and white musical traditions.[51] Such an argument represents an effort to confront heterogeneity as a basis for style, as a grounds for coherence, and as an enduring concern in American aesthetic culture.

## Re-cognitions

There were, then, at least three broad ordering patterns at work in the culture and thought of the 1930s. The varying assumptions associated with these conceptual frameworks helped shape the intellectual positions, define the group identities, and mold the aesthetic perceptions of the period. None of these principles of order uniquely represented a desire for stability, and none ignored that concern. Thoughtful people wrestled with the problem of coherence from different perspectives; nearly all were seeking structures of understanding and of meaning that would reflect or help create enduring cultural designs. Those who envisioned their social and cultural worlds as unified, multiple, or heterogeneous differed in their attitudes toward change and in their assumptions about what forms of cultural cohesion were necessary or desirable. In consequence, their perceptions of what constituted disorder, instability, the decay of standards, or a collapse of values varied markedly, and the differences at times created striking obstacles to reasoned discourse and balanced judgment. We would do well to recognize competing ideas of order at work in the culture and thought of the 1930s.

Such recognition may help us, first, to explore particular confrontations and events with a better appreciation for their resonance within the immediate cultural setting. As the likelihood of war became apparent at the end of the decade, intellectuals disputed sharply (and often anxiously) questions involving the shape of American culture and its ability to withstand external threats. The different principles of cultural cohesion assumed in these debates contributed to their tone and magnified their import. Intellectuals gathering at New York University in 1940 witnessed the "indecent spectacle" of Mortimer J. Adler and Sidney Hook intemperately disputing once more the principles behind Hutchins's "permanent truths," with each accusing the other's ideas of paving the way for fascism.[52] In the same year, Archibald MacLeish attacked in *The Irresponsibles* intellectuals who had accepted the premises of skepticism and "objectivity" and who now neglected their "obligation to defend the inherited culture." In a similar vein, Van Wyck Brooks in 1941 praised the unifying tradition of "primary literature," which he contrasted invidiously with the "coterie literature" of modernism. Defenders of modern thought and modern literature saw in such attacks a cultural retreat to the myth of a coherent past. While Morton Dauwen Zabel and Dwight Macdonald compared the condemnatory arguments of MacLeish and Brooks and those of Hitler and Goebbels, Zabel and William Phillips argued that the present might be rescued and continuity preserved not through an abandonment of modern questioning and modernist "provocations" but through the elaboration of this unsettled and unsettling "tradition." Like many other intellectual engagements of the thirties, these end-of-decade disputes took shape in part around the problem of cultural coherence.[53]

If at times conceptual lines were sharply drawn, they could also be blurred or inconsistent. An alertness to differing ordering patterns can underscore once more that for many people in the 1930s, identity and perspective were not acquired whole but assembled from available parts. Competing structures of organization and meaning were available for comprehending politics and ethnic relations, cultural traditions and the arts. An individual might adopt explanations in different spheres that relied on fundamentally different ordering principles. Or within a single sphere (the political, perhaps), a person might gravitate toward affirmation of a unitary public at one moment and toward assertions of interest-group multiplicity at another. Ordering possibilities in tension with one another could be combined in irregular ways. These shifting combinations created intellectual contradictions that may seem to later observers the antithesis of coherence. Yet we must also understand their logic. A plurality of viable ordering patterns during the 1930s created breathing space for those who found themselves continually, and contingently, balancing ideas against circumstance in an effort to make sense of the world.

Attention to competing ideas of order, in the second place, may help us see the culture of the thirties through a wider historical lens. The declining acceptance of older models of coherence and the breakup of what had been taken as unified traditions and fixed principles formed one of the central cultural patterns of the early twentieth century. Depression, the rise of fascism, and the slide toward war sharpened the consciousness of this trend and provided ample cause during the 1930s for fears of collapse and disorder, of peril both domestic and foreign. Yet these same events also stimulated efforts to assert ideals of cohesiveness and purpose. Some of these ideals looked single-mindedly toward the past or toward the future. Other responses rested on efforts to reconcile, at least roughly and for the moment, a desire for continuity and a commitment to change, values long established and values still taking form.

Among the platforms for cohesion most assertively advanced during the 1930s, radicalism and nationalism hold a prominent place. As organizing themes for looking at the period's culture, however, both draw attention too narrowly to cycles constrained by the boundaries of a decade, and both emphasize too strongly the pervasiveness of their defining ideas. We need to develop a broader view. Competing structures of order and meaning emerged during the 1930s as parts of an extended twentieth-century process, a process that included the patchwork outlooks of everyday people and passing moments fully as much as it did the sustained intellectual search for coherent cultural viewpoints. Whether the topic is cultural relativism and anthropology, the nature of the American political system, the values associated with success, notions of ethnicity and culture, ideals of education, or institutional and creative structures in the arts, it is evident that different frameworks for comprehending the world were being tested against one another and against the problems at hand. Fragmentation to some was reconstruction to others. The intersections and contradictions between ideas provide evidence of a people engaged in an ongoing struggle for comprehension, for at least tentative forms of stability that might accommodate and control the pressures of broad historical-cultural change. Recognizing such a struggle calls for us to lift our eyes beyond the horizons of a decade.

A third benefit of attending to different concepts of order is that we may come to appreciate more fully our own inescapable confrontation with the challenges of coherence and the dilemmas of choice. What assumptions do we make about the meaning of "American culture"? From what sources do we derive our standards for defining and judging a work of art? As changing perceptions of Gershwin should remind us, standards based on conceptions of a unified artistic tradition may do scant justice to works created according to a different ordering idea. Similarly, multiplicity and heterogeneity as principles of order may encourage presumptions of worth that both contribute to and interfere with intelligent understanding. We cannot escape the particular dilemmas that questions of cultural identity and intellectual standards create, because we cannot stand outside the twentieth-century problem of order and meaning.

Being thus caught, we may well find that an alertness to competing ideas of order in the thought and culture of the 1930s can present us with a lesson and a challenge. The lesson is that if we are to see well the varying angles from which Americans of the 1930s approached their world—if our vision is to be sensitive to the shifting lights by which different audiences viewed specific cultural products or ideas—then we must make every effort to see the assumptions about identity and coherence, order and meaning, that filter our own perceptions. The challenge is to recognize that when faced with daunting evidence of complexity in our materials and of limitation in the ideas we bring to bear, we must neither evade the problem of order nor deny its significance.

In evaluating younger writers who were struggling to match the achievements of modernist fiction, Philip Rahv found in the work of the late 1930s too little that represented insightful innovation and too much that reflected one-sided imitation. "To know how to take apart the recognizable world is not enough," Rahv insisted, but "is in fact merely a way of letting oneself go." The pattern for the artist of genuine significance was distinctly different: "*At the very same time that he takes the world apart he puts it together again*." To do otherwise was to "dissipate . . . our sense of reality, to weaken and compromise rather than change in any significant fashion our feeling of relatedness to the world."[54] Rahv's critique gave voice to fundamental concerns of the period that we would do well to respect. Higher education and familiarity with the strategies of varying disciplines make it remarkably easy to take the world apart through analysis. An awareness that reputable ideas of order compete and coexist may encourage at times an evasion of responsibility for reconstruction or, contrarily, a willingness to accept claims of cohesion in almost any form. We may let ourselves go, we may "dissipate . . . , weaken, and compromise," in many ways, when faced with the task of re-cognition. The ferment of ordering ideas in the 1930s reflected a wide array of efforts to preserve or construct frameworks of coherence, identity, and meaning. By attending to these ideas, we may find a fertility and richness in that culture beyond our common expectations. We may also gird ourselves to understand better and face more openly contemporary struggles for coherence—the balancing acts of our own.

# Chronology

1929 New York stock market crash, October-November. The Museum of Modern Art opens in New York.

1930 *Fortune* magazine founded. *Little Caesar* leads the way for gangster films. First national ratings system for radio shows established to serve advertisers. Mike Gold publishes *Jews without Money*. "Twelve Southerners" contribute to *I'll Take My Stand*. William Faulkner's *As I Lay Dying* is published, the first of nine Faulkner books that will be published during the decade. Grant Wood paints *American Gothic*.

1931 *Dracula* and *Frankenstein* come to the movies. Constance Rourke publishes *American Humor*. Writers' delegations investigate violence against striking miners in Harlan County, Kentucky. The Whitney Museum of American Art opens. Lincoln Steffens's *Autobiography* appears. Eugene O'Neill's *Mourning Becomes Electra* is staged. Pearl Buck's *The Good Earth* becomes a best-seller. The Empire State Building is completed, and construction begins on Rockefeller Center. "The Star-Spangled Banner" officially becomes the national anthem.

1932 Bonus Army encamped in Washington, D.C., May-July. Presidential campaign pits Herbert Hoover against Franklin Delano Roosevelt, Jr. Fifty-three intellectuals declare their support for Communist candidates in *Culture and Crisis*. Reinhold Niebuhr publishes *Moral Man and Immoral Society*. John Chamberlain's *Farewell to Reform* is published. Unemployment rate reaches approximately 25 percent in the winter of 1932–33. "Technocracy" has its moment in the public eye. American physicists Harold Urey, Ernest Lawrence, and Carl Anderson complete work related to nuclear structure that will eventually win

Nobel Prizes for all three. The film version of *I Am a Fugitive from a Chain Gang* appears with its bleak ending. Henry Cowell and Charles Seeger teach the first ethnomusicology course in the United States. Amelia Earhart is the first woman to fly solo across the Atlantic.

1933     *Recent Social Trends in the United States* surveys many elements of American life and culture. Roosevelt gives his inaugural address 4 March and his first fireside chat 12 March; the Hundred Days legislative session launching the New Deal lasts 9 March to 16 June. Tennessee Valley Authority created. Frances Perkins becomes the first woman cabinet member as secretary of labor. Walt Disney's *The Three Little Pigs* offers a depression challenge to the big bad wolf. Sidney Hook publishes *Toward the Understanding of Karl Marx*. Mae West's *She Done Him Wrong* shares the theaters with upbeat film musicals *42nd Street*, *Gold Diggers of 1933*, and *Footlight Parade*. First international radio conversation between Walter Lippmann and John Maynard Keynes. Jack Conroy's semiautobiographical novel *The Disinherited* is published. Lorena Hickok begins work as an investigator for Harry Hopkins. George Balanchine and Lincoln Kirstein establish the School of American Ballet.

1934     *Modern Monthly* publishes a "Symposium on Communism." The film *It Happened One Night* earns Frank Capra his first great popular and critical success. Legion of Decency organized to influence film content. Ruth Benedict publishes *Patterns of Culture*. The Indian Reorganization Act is passed. Intellectual and strategic differences within the NAACP lead to the departure of W. E. B. Du Bois. Robert Cantwell's strike novel *Land of Plenty* appears. Virgil Thomson composes *Four Saints in Three Acts*, with a libretto by Gertrude Stein. FBI shooting of "Public Enemy No. 1" John Dillinger symbolizes efficacy of federal law enforcement and J. Edgar Hoover.

1935     James T. Farrell completes his *Studs Lonigan* trilogy. Federal Writers' Project, Federal Art Project, Federal Theater Project, and Federal Music Project are launched. George Gershwin's opera *Porgy and Bess* is produced. Colonial Williamsburg opens to visitors. The Douglas Commercial (DC-3) is introduced and will become the most popular of the new metal airplanes. Committee for Industrial Organization is formed. Movements led by Francis Townsend, Huey Long, Father Charles Coughlin, and the American Liberty League fuel political activism. Communist party turns toward the Popular Front strategy of cooperation with liberals. Social Security Act is passed. Roosevelt issues nondiscrimination order for relief programs. Zora Neale Hurston records African-American customs, stories, and rituals in *Mules and Men*. Thurman Arnold's *Symbols of Government* is published. Clifford Odets's one-act play *Waiting for Lefty* performed.

1936   Presidential election sees Alfred M. Landon thoroughly trounced by Roosevelt. John Dos Passos completes his *U.S.A.* trilogy. *Life* magazine appears. *Index of American Design* is launched under Federal Art Project. Dale Carnegie points the way to success in *How to Win Friends and Influence People*. H. V. Kaltenborn covers the Spanish Civil War on radio. Jesse Owens wins four gold medals in Berlin Olympics and is snubbed by Hitler. Robert Maynard Hutchins promotes permanent truths in *The Higher Learning in America*. Margaret Mitchell publishes *Gone with the Wind*. Frank Capra's film *Mr. Deeds Goes to Town* reaches theaters.

1937   John Dewey leads the Commission of Inquiry into the Charges Made against Leon Trotsky in the Moscow Trials. *Partisan Review* reappears as an anti-Stalinist intellectual magazine on the left. Robert and Helen Lynd publish *Middletown in Transition*. Amelia Earhart disappears over the Pacific. Disney's *Snow White and the Seven Dwarfs* is a hit in theaters and the toy industry. Live radio reports the explosion of the zeppelin *Hindenberg* in New Jersey. Zora Neale Hurston publishes *Their Eyes Were Watching God*. Margaret Bourke-White and Erskine Caldwell combine pictures and words to lament sharecropping in *You Have Seen Their Faces*. ILGWU political-musical revue *Pins and Needles* is produced. The doors open at the Solomon R. Guggenheim Museum of Non-Objective Art.

1938   Edward R. Murrow and others report the Munich crisis from Europe. *The War of the Worlds* broadcast creates fears of alien invasion. Joe Louis knocks out Max Schmeling in the first round of their rematch. Cleanth Brooks and Robert Penn Warren exemplify the New Criticism in *Understanding Poetry*. Benny Goodman band plays Carnegie Hall and promotes jazz as concert music. Twenty thousand television sets are in service in New York City. Martin Dies becomes chair of the new House Un-American Activities Committee. NAACP legal campaign wins Supreme Court ruling that University of Missouri Law School must admit African-Americans.

1939   New York World's Fair opens in April. Nazi-Soviet nonaggression pact signed 23 August. World War II begins in Europe with German invasion of Poland on 1 September. Soviet Union invades Finland. John Steinbeck publishes *The Grapes of Wrath*. The movie version of *Gone with the Wind* sets box-office records. Nathanael West's *The Day of the Locust* reaches print. Marian Anderson sings at the Lincoln Memorial. Nylon introduced commercially by Du Pont; nylon stockings will challenge the primacy of natural fibers. Albert Einstein sends a warning letter to President Roosevelt that leads to the establishment of the Manhattan Project to develop an atomic bomb. Dorothea Lange's photographs and Paul Schuster Taylor's text examine rural migration in *An American Exodus*. John Dewey's *Freedom and Culture* and Jacques Barzun's *Of Human Freedom* are published. Aaron Copland composes *Billy the Kid*. "God Bless America" becomes a popular song.

1940    Norway, Denmark, the Netherlands, Belgium, and France fall to the Nazis. Germany bombs English cities in the Battle of Britain, which is covered in live reports on American radio. Leon Trotsky is assassinated in Mexico by a Stalinist agent. Edmund Wilson publishes *To the Finland Station*. Richard Wright's *Native Son* appears. Ernest Hemingway's novel of the Spanish Civil War, *For Whom the Bell Tolls*, is released.

# Notes and References

*Preface*

1. D. W. Brogan, "Uncle Sam's Guides," in *American Themes* (New York: Harper and Row, 1949; reprint, Port Washington, N.Y.: Kennikat Press, 1969), 103–4.

*Chapter One*

1. Based on the account of Eileen Barth in Studs Terkel, *Hard Times: An Oral History of the Great Depression* (New York: Pantheon Books, 1970; paperback reprint, New York: Pantheon, 1986), 419–20. Although Terkel indicates that Barth "weeps angrily" and finds it difficult to speak, the emotional power of Barth's recollection is far more evident in listening to the original recording of the interview, Caedmon, tape CDL 5208 (2c).

2. David Burner, *Herbert Hoover: A Public Life* (New York: Alfred A. Knopf, 1979), 248.

3. William E. Leuchtenburg, *Franklin D. Roosevelt and the New Deal, 1932–1940* (New York: Harper and Row, 1963), 2.

4. Jonathan Norton Leonard, as quoted in Frederick Lewis Allen, *Since Yesterday: The Nineteen-Thirties in America* (New York: Harper Brothers, 1940), 64. Extensive discussions of the coal industry appear in Irving Bernstein, *The Lean Years: A History of the American Worker, 1920–1933* (Boston: Houghton Mifflin, 1960); John W. Hevener, *Which Side Are You On? The Harlan County Coal Miners, 1931–1939* (Urbana: University of Illinois Press, 1978); and James P. Johnson, *The Politics of Soft Coal: The Bituminous Industry from World War I through the New Deal* (Urbana: University of Illinois Press, 1979).

5. Quoted in Arthur A. Ekirch, Jr., *Ideologies and Utopias: The Impact of the New Deal on American Thought* (Chicago: Quadrangle Books, 1969), 50.

6. One of the best sources for general statistical information is *Historical Statistics of the United States,* issued and occasionally updated by the Bureau of the Census. This material has also been more popularly published as *The Statistical History of the United States: From Colonial Times to the Present,* introduction and user's guide by Ben J. Wattenberg

(New York: Basic Books, 1976). Statistics will be cited here by statistical series and by page number from *Statistical History*. Thus, changes in crop prices can be traced in series K-496 to K-623, 510–25. These national price averages do not necessarily reflect local or regional conditions. The several oral histories in "The Farmer Is the Man" section of Terkel, *Hard Times*, are more revealing of specific circumstances. See also John L. Shover, *Cornbelt in Rebellion: The Farmers' Holiday Association* (Urbana: University of Illinois Press, 1965); Donald Worster, *Dust Bowl: The Southern Plains in the 1930s* (New York: Oxford University Press, 1979); and Theodore Saloutos, *The American Farmers and the New Deal* (Ames: Iowa State University Press, 1982).

7. Anthony J. Badger, *The New Deal: The Depression Years, 1933–1940* (New York: Noonday Press, 1989), 21–22; *Statistical History*, N-1, 618.

8. Allen, *Since Yesterday* (64) quotes eyewitness testimony to the battle over garbage from Louise V. Armstrong's *We Too Are the People* (1938); Terkel, *Hard Times* (388–91) contains an interview with the former Chicago teacher Elsa Ponselle; Rahv's life is best covered in Andrew James Dvosin, "Literature in a Political World: The Career and Writings of Philip Rahv" (Ph.D. dissertation, New York University, 1977).

9. *Statistical History*, F-176, 236.

10. Ibid., F-3, 224.

11. Ibid., F-563, 263.

12. Ibid., D-86, 135.

13. See the discussion of the unreliability of unemployment statistics and the comparison of various international patterns in John A. Garraty, *The Great Depression: An Inquiry into the Causes, Course, and Consequences of the Worldwide Depression of the Nineteen-Thirties, as Seen by Contemporaries and in the Light of History* (San Diego: Harcourt Brace Jovanovich, 1986).

14. *Statistical History*, B-166, 58.

15. Ibid., B-5, 49; B-214, 64.

16. Ibid., B-167, 59; B-107, 55.

17. Garraty, *The Great Depression*, 109.

18. See the discussion containing this estimate in Badger, *The New Deal*, 39.

19. Garraty, *The Great Depression*, 104–12.

20. See the comments on games and the depression in Warren I. Susman, *Culture as History: The Transformation of American Society in the Twentieth Century* (New York: Pantheon, 1984), 161–64. Susman took his lead in this discussion from T. V. Smith, "The New Deal as a Cultural Phenomenon," in *Ideological Differences and World Order*, ed. F. S. C. Northrop (New Haven, Conn.: Yale University Press, 1949).

21. *Statistical History*, D-49, D-36, D-58, D-60, 132–33.

22. Ibid., D-36, D-60, D-61, 132–33; slightly different figures for the same year are sometimes available even within the same statistical series, as is the case with D-36 (132), for example, where decennial census figures vary from annual figures assembled at a different point. A thorough discussion of workforce participation by women that includes a major effort to assemble statistical tables that add to what has previously been available may be found in Claudia Goldin, *Understanding the Gender Gap: An Economic History of American Women* (New York: Oxford University Press, 1990).

23. See the concise analysis of women and work during the 1930s in Alice Kessler-Harris, *Out to Work: A History of Wage-Earning Women in the United States* (New York: Oxford University Press, 1982), esp. chap. 9, "Some Benefits of Labor Segregation in a Decade of Depression."

24. Ibid., 269.

25. See especially Winifred D. Wandersee, *Women's Work and Family Values, 1920–1940* (Cambridge, Mass.: Harvard University Press, 1981).

26. Goldin, *Understanding the Gender Gap*, 17.

27. In addition to the sources previously cited, see Susan Ware, *Holding Their Own: American Women in the 1930s* (Boston: Twayne Publishers, 1982); and Lois Scharf, *To Work and to Wed: Female Employment, Feminism, and the Great Depression* (Westport, Conn.: Greenwood Press, 1980).

28. See Susan Ware, *Beyond Suffrage: Women in the New Deal* (Cambridge, Mass.: Harvard University Press, 1981).

29. For a broad introduction to the range of social ideas on the left in this period, see "Political and Economic Thought, 1929–1935," chap. 2 in Richard H. Pells, *Radical Visions and American Dreams: Culture and Social Thought in the Depression Years* (New York: Harper and Row, 1973).

30. R. Allan Lawson, *The Failure of Independent Liberalism, 1930–1941* (New York: Putnam, 1971), provides a solid study of one group of intellectuals who tried to construct a political position between the New Deal and organized radical parties.

31. John Chamberlain, *Farewell to Reform* (New York: John Day, 1932), 220.

32. Lewis Corey, *The Crisis of the Middle Class* (New York: Covici, Friede, 1935), 260.

33. John Dewey, "Why I Am Not a Communist," *Modern Monthly* 8 (April 1934): 135–37.

34. For a fuller picture of Dewey's ideas, see Robert B. Westbrook, *John Dewey and American Democracy* (Ithaca, N.Y.: Cornell University Press, 1991), esp. chap. 12.

35. Sidney Hook, *Towards the Understanding of Karl Marx: A Revolutionary Interpretation* (New York: John Day, 1933), ix, 5, 16, 98.

36. Sidney Hook, "Why I Am a Communist," *Modern Monthly* 8 (April 1934): 143–65.

37. T. B. Bottomore, *Critics of Society: Radical Thought in North America* (New York: Vintage Books, 1969), 38.

38. Edmund Wilson, "An Appeal to Progressives," *New Republic* 65 (1931): 235–38.

39. Sherman Paul, *Edmund Wilson: A Study of Literary Vocation in Our Time* (Urbana: University of Illinois Press, 1965), 139.

40. Bottomore, *Critics of Society*, 38.

41. Edmund Wilson, *To the Finland Station: A Study in the Writing and Acting of History* (New York: Doubleday and Co. 1940; paperback reprint, New York: Anchor, 1953), 194, 190.

42. Ibid., 452.

43. On Niebuhr, see Richard Fox, *Reinhold Niebuhr: A Biography* (New York: Pantheon Books, 1985). The discussion here makes particular use of chaps. 6–8.

44. Reinhold Niebuhr, *Moral Man and Immoral Society: A Study in Ethics and Politics* (New York: Charles Scribner's Sons, 1932).

45. Ibid., 277.

46. Quoted in Fox, *Reinhold Niebuhr*, 149.

47. Ibid,. 164.

48. See the accounts of Technocracy in Allen, *Since Yesterday*, 89–92, and in Garraty, *The Great Depression*, 137–40.

49. Jeffrey L. Meikle, *Twentieth Century Limited: Industrial Design in America,*

*1925–1939* (Philadelphia: Temple University Press, 1979), is the most important source for this discussion of streamlining.

50. Ibid., 185.

51. Quoted in Susman, *Culture as History*, 189–90.

52. Francis V. O'Connor, "Introduction" to *Art for the Millions: Essays from the 1930s by Artists and Administrators of the WPA Federal Art Project* (Greenwich, Conn.: New York Graphics Society, 1973), 20–21.

53. Karal Ann Marling, "A Note on New Deal Iconography: Futurology and the Historical Myth," *Prospects* 4 (1979): 421–40.

54. Alfred Haworth Jones, "The Search for a Usable American Past in the New Deal Era," *American Quarterly* 23 (December 1971): 710–24.

55. Lewis A. Erenberg, "From New York to Middletown: Repeal and the Legitimization of Nightlife in the Great Depression," *American Quarterly* 38 (Winter 1986): 761–88.

56. See Meikle, *Twentieth Century Limited*, 170, 228n.

57. See Joseph J. Corn, *The Winged Gospel* (New York: Oxford University Press, 1983).

58. From R. D. McKenzie, *The Metropolitan Community* (1933), quoted in Alan I. Marcus and Howard P. Segal, *Technology in America: A Brief History* (San Diego: Harcourt Brace Jovanovich, 1989), 260.

59. Marcus and Segal, *Technology in America*, 261.

60. See Thomas P. Hughes, *American Genesis: A Century of Invention and Technological Enthusiasm, 1870–1970* (New York: Viking, 1989), 353–81.

61. William E. Wickenden, "Science and Every-Day Philosophy," *Science* 78 (24 November 1933): 468, as quoted in Daniel J. Kevles, *The Physicists: The History of a Scientific Community in Modern America* (New York: Alfred A. Knopf, 1978), 238.

62. John Haynes Holmes, "Religion's New War with Science," *Christian Century* 54 (27 October 1937): 1323; G. K. Chesterton, "A Plea That Science Now Halt," *New York Times Magazine* (5 October 1930): 2; both quoted in Kevles, *The Physicists*, 238–39.

63. "Science—and Other Values," *New Republic* 68 (16 September 1931): 114, quoted in Kevles, *The Physicists*, 239.

64. Kevles, *The Physicists*, 269.

65. *Newsweek* (7 November 1936): 29, quoted in ibid., 282.

66. Kevles, *The Physicists*, 281.

67. Hughes, *American Genesis*, 382–83, 399.

## Chapter Two

1. William E. Leuchtenburg, "The Achievement of the New Deal," in *Fifty Years Later: The New Deal Evaluated*, ed. Harvard Sitkoff (New York: Alfred A. Knopf, 1985), 213.

2. Garraty, *The Great Depression*, 216–18.

3. *Statistical History*, X-580, 1019, X-741, 1038.

4. Franklin D. Roosevelt, speech to the Commonwealth Club of San Francisco, 23 September 1932, in *The Public Papers and Addresses of Franklin D. Roosevelt*, vol. 1, *The Genesis of the New Deal, 1928–1932* (New York: Random House, 1938), 755.

5. Ibid., 647–48.

6. Ibid., vol. 2, *The Year of Crisis, 1933*, 11.

7. Ibid., 61–65.

8. Quoted in Geoffrey S. Smith, *To Save a Nation: American Countersubversives, the New Deal, and the Coming of World War II* (New York: Basic Books, 1973), 41.

9. Alan Brinkley, *Voices of Protest: Huey Long, Father Coughlin, and the Great Depression* (New York: Alfred A. Knopf, 1982; paperback reprint, New York: Vintage Books/Random House, 1983), xi.

10. See, for example, John P. Roche, "Entrepreneurial Liberty and the Fourteenth Amendment," *Labor History* 4 (Winter 1963): 3–31.

11. Quoted from a public statement of 3 February 1931, in David E. Hamilton, "Herbert Hoover and the Great Drought of 1930," *Journal of American History* 68 (March 1982): 871.

12. Quoted in Garraty, *The Great Depression*, 33.

13. The comments from Roosevelt's acceptance speech provoked this reaction from the *Boston Transcript*, as quoted in J. Joseph Huthmacher, *Massachusetts People and Politics, 1919–1933* (Cambridge, Mass.: Harvard University Press, 1959; reprint, New York: Atheneum, 1969), 244.

14. Quoted in Allen, *Since Yesterday*, 162.

15. Jouett Shouse, "The Return of Democracy" (radio address of 1 July 1935), in *FDR's America*, ed. David E. Kyvig (St. Charles, Mo.: Forum Press, 1976), 60–65.

16. Herbert Hoover, *The Memoirs of Herbert Hoover: The Great Depression, 1929–1941* (New York: Macmillan, 1952), 351–56.

17. Charles A. Beard, "The Myth of Rugged American Individualism," in *New Deal Thought*, ed. Howard Zinn (Indianapolis: Bobbs-Merrill, 1966), 10.

18. Allen, *Since Yesterday*, 43.

19. Adolph Berle, Jr., and Gardiner C. Means, *The Modern Corporation and Private Property* (New York: Macmillan, 1932), 125. The thesis is in the title of Alfred D. Chandler, Jr., *The Visible Hand: The Managerial Revolution in American Business* (Cambridge, Mass.: Harvard University Press, 1977).

20. Thomas K. McCraw, "The New Deal and the Mixed Economy," in Sitkoff, *Fifty Years Later*, 58–59.

21. Richard Hofstadter, *The Age of Reform: From Bryan to FDR* (New York: Vintage Books, 1955), 316–17.

22. Roosevelt, address at Oglethorpe University, 22 May 1932, in *Public Papers*, vol. 1, 646.

23. Rexford Guy Tugwell, "Planning Must Replace Laissez Faire," in Zinn, *New Deal Thought*, 85–88.

24. Beard, "The Myth of Rugged American Individualism," 9.

25. Quoted in Badger, *The New Deal*, 200.

26. William W. Bremer, "Along the 'American Way': The New Deal Work Relief Programs for the Unemployed," *Journal of American History* 62 (December 1975): 636–52.

27. Roosevelt, "The Annual Message to the Legislature, 7 January 1931," in *Public Papers*, vol. 1, 103.

28. Quoted in Leuchtenburg, *Franklin D. Roosevelt and the New Deal*, 133.

29. Charles H. Trout, "The New Deal and the Cities," in Sitkoff, *Fifty Years Later*, esp. 139–41.

30. The S in Truman's name is not followed by a period because it was not an abbreviation for any other name. The S by itself was his parents' compromise between two family names beginning with *S*, one from each side of the family. See Robert J. Donovan,

*Conflict and Crisis: The Presidency of Harry S Truman, 1945–1948* (New York: W. W. Norton, 1977), 9.

31. Lyle W. Dorsett, "Kansas City and the New Deal," in *The New Deal: The State and Local Levels*, ed. John Braeman, Robert H. Bremner, and David Brody (Columbus: Ohio State University Press, 1975).

32. Bruce M. Stave, "Pittsburgh and the New Deal," in ibid, 392–93.

33. Charles H. Trout, *Boston, the Great Depression, and the New Deal* (New York: Oxford University Press, 1977), statistics from 193, quotation from 311; Jo Ann E. Argersinger, *Toward a New Deal in Baltimore: People and Government in the Great Depression* (Chapel Hill: University of North Carolina Press, 1988), 64–65.

34. Robert S. Lynd and Helen Merrell Lynd, *Middletown in Transition: A Study in Cultural Conflicts* (New York: Harcourt, Brace, and World, 1937), esp. 487–510.

35. Sidney Verba and Kay Lehman Schlozman, "Unemployment, Class Consciousness, and Radical Politics: What Didn't Happen in the Thirties," *Journal of Politics* 39 (1977): 291–323.

36. Richard Oestreicher, "Urban Working-Class Political Behavior and Theories of American Electoral Politics, 1870–1940," *Journal of American History* 74 (March 1988): 1257–86, esp. 1283–86.

37. Roger Keeran, *The Communist Party and the Auto Workers Unions* (Bloomington: Indiana University Press, 1980), 14–20, quotation 19.

38. Robert H. Zieger, *American Workers, American Unions, 1920–1985* (Baltimore: Johns Hopkins University Press, 1986), 27.

## Chapter Three

1. Quoted in Andrew Bergman, *We're in the Money: Depression America and Its Films* (New York: New York University Press, 1971), xx.

2. Malcolm Cowley's discussion of the Greenwich Village "doctrine" and its wider societal echoes in *Exile's Return: A Literary Odyssey of the 1920s* (1934; reprint, New York: Viking Press, 1951), 59–65 and *passim*, remains a useful and colorful interpretation of changing patterns of values.

3. Robert Sklar, *Movie-Made America: A Social History of American Movies* (New York: Random House, 1975), 204.

4. Charles R. Hearn, *The American Dream in the Great Depression* (Westport, Conn.: Greenwood Press, 1977), 59. Hearn provides the fullest treatment of success as a theme during the 1930s, and the discussion of magazine patterns and variations that follows is based primarily on his work.

5. Quoted in ibid., 60–61.

6. See Warren I. Susman, "'Personality' and the Making of Twentieth-Century Culture," in *Culture as History*, 271–85, and the comments on Carnegie, 165–66, 200.

7. David Riesman, *The Lonely Crowd: A Study of the Changing American Character* (New Haven, Conn.: Yale University Press, 1950, 1961); William Whyte, *The Organization Man* (New York: Simon and Schuster, 1956).

8. Dale Carnegie, *How to Win Friends and Influence People* (New York: Simon and Schuster, 1936), 30, 113–14.

9. Ibid., 80, 223, 221.

10. Ibid., 206, 55.

11. *Time* 26, no. 2 (8 July 1935): 7.

12. *Fortune* 4, no. 6 (December 1931): 120; 4, no. 4 (October 1931): 107; 4, no. 1 (July 1931): 79.

13. See the discussion in Roland Marchand, *Advertising the American Dream: Making Way for Modernity, 1920–1940* (Berkeley: University of California Press, 1985), 320–24.

14. Ibid., 325, 329.

15. Reproduced in ibid., 326.

16. *Fortune* 4, no. 3 (September 1931): 85.

17. Marchand, *Advertising the American Dream*, 63–66.

18. Quoted in Stephen Fox, *The Mirror Makers: A History of American Advertising and Its Creators* (New York: William Morrow, 1984), 117.

19. Marchand, *Advertising the American Dream*, 300.

20. On Gallup and his work, see Fox, *The Mirror Makers*, 138–39, and Marchand, *Advertising the American Dream*, 110–11.

21. *Time* 26, no. 2 (8 July 1935): 34.

22. Fox, *The Mirror Makers*, 122–23.

23. *Life* 1 (30 November 1936).

24. See Marchand, *Advertising the American Dream*, 296–99, on "Unraised Hands and Skinny Kids."

25. Ibid., 248–54.

26. *Statistical History*, H-873, 400 (attendance); H-884/878, 401 (share of recreation expenditures).

27. Sklar, *Movie-Made America*, 176.

28. See the discussion in William Stott, *Documentary Expression and Thirties America* (New York: Oxford University Press, 1973), 41–45.

29. Bergman, *We're in the Money*, 96.

30. Quoted in ibid., 6.

31. Ibid., 6–13.

32. Sklar, *Movie-Made America*, 179–81.

33. Robert Warshow, "The Gangster as Tragic Hero," in *The Immediate Experience: Movies, Comics, Theatre, and Other Aspects of Popular Culture* (New York: Atheneum, 1972), 127–33.

34. Sklar, *Movie-Made America*, 200.

35. Robert Forsythe [Kyle Crichton], "Mae West: A Treatise on Decay," *New Masses* (9 October 1934), reprinted in *"New Masses": An Anthology of the Rebel Thirties*, ed. Joseph North (New York: International Publishers, 1969), quotations from 84.

36. Bergman, *We're in the Money*, 33.

37. Sklar, *Movie-Made America*, 200.

38. Bergman, *We're in the Money*, 102. Interestingly, the effect of the NRA code established to cover the film industry was to aid not the giant production–distribution–theater chain conglomerates but smaller exhibitors and distributors—a reversal of the pattern most commonly associated with the NRA. Under the code, efforts by the larger firms to keep films out of the hands of competitors or to force theaters to rent whole blocks of films to get the better pictures were often restricted. Double features, which the large distributors opposed and audiences liked, were not obstructed by the code. For about two years under the NRA, theaters were prohibited from using lotteries, special ticket deals, and gifts to entice customers (except for gifts of pottery and

glassware protected by the pressure to avoid destruction of another part of the manufacturing economy), but with the demise of the codes in 1935, the whole range of come-ons came rushing back. Meanwhile, popcorn and candy, once unacceptable in self-respecting theaters, became commonplace as it was discovered that their profitability might well keep theaters in business.

39. See the extended argument in Lary May, *Screening out the Past: The Birth of Mass Culture and the Motion Picture Industry* (New York: Oxford University Press, 1980; Chicago: University of Chicago Press, 1983).

40. Garth Jowett, *Film: The Democratic Art* (Boston: Little, Brown and Co., 1976), 220–28, 240–56.

41. Quoted in Richard Gid Powers, "One G-Man's Family: Popular Entertainment Formulas and J. Edgar Hoover's FBI," *American Quarterly* 30 (Fall 1978): 473.

42. Bergman, *We're in the Money*, 87.

43. Powers, "One G-Man's Family" (474), applies these phrases to G-man films alone.

44. Molly Haskell, *From Reverence to Rape: The Treatment of Women in the Movies* (New York: Holt, Rinehart, and Winston, 1974), 130–31, 139.

45. Raymond Carney, *American Vision: The Films of Frank Capra* (Cambridge, Eng.: Cambridge University Press, 1986), 308–9.

46. *Fortune* 4, no. 3 (September 1931): 109.

47. See Margaret Farrand Thorp, *America at the Movies* (New Haven, Conn.: Yale University Press, 1939), esp. 14, 42, 38, 69–71, 76–79.

48. See Sklar, *Movie-Made America*, 189–94.

49. Ibid., 195.

50. Nathanael West, *The Day of the Locust* (New York: New American Library/Signet Classic, 1983), 128, 189–93, 200–201.

51. For this argument and the examples in the previous paragraph, see David Karnes, "The Glamorous Crowd: Hollywood Premieres between the Wars," *American Quarterly* 38 (Fall 1986): 553–72.

52. Thorp, *America at the Movies*, 35–38.

53. Daniel J. Boorstin, *The Image: A Guide to Pseudo-Events in America* (1961; New York: Atheneum, 1987).

54. *Statistical History*, R-104, 796 (households with radios; the census figure is used for 1930); R-4, 783 (residential telephones).

55. The most important sources for this discussion of radio are the first two volumes of Erik Barnouw's history of broadcasting in the United States, *A Tower in Babel* (1966), covering the period through 1933, and *The Golden Web* (1968) covering 1933 to 1953 (New York: Oxford University Press).

56. A new and detailed study of this period in the organizational history of radio has appeared in Robert W. McChesney, *Telecommunications, Mass Media, and Democracy: The Battle for the Control of U.S. Broadcasting, 1928–1935* (New York: Oxford University Press, 1993).

57. Reuel Denney, *The Astonished Muse* (Chicago: University of Chicago Press, 1957), 249.

58. Barnouw, *The Golden Web*, 70.

59. On radio news in the late thirties, see ibid., 74–83, and Alice Goldfarb Marquis, *Hopes and Ashes: The Birth of Modern Times, 1929–1939* (New York: Free Press, 1986), 42–47.

60. Marquis, *Hopes and Ashes*, 40–41.

61. Quoted in Leo Lowenthal, "Historical Perspectives of Popular Culture," in *Mass Culture: The Popular Arts in America*, ed. Bernard Rosenberg and David Manning White (Glencoe, Ill.: Free Press, 1957), 54.

62. Barnouw, *The Golden Web*, 61–62.

63. Paul F. Lazarsfeld, *Radio and the Printed Page: An Introduction to the Study of Radio and Its Role in the Communication of Ideas* (New York: Duell, Sloan and Pearce, 1940), 329–33.

64. Hadley Cantril and Gordon W. Allport, *The Psychology of Radio* (New York: Peter Smith, 1941), vii, 3, 36, 59–64, 20, 259.

65. Lowenthal, "Historical Perspectives," 47–48.

66. Ibid., 49–56.

67. Warshow, *The Immediate Experience*, 28, 24.

## Chapter Four

1. Ruth Benedict, *Patterns of Culture* (Boston: Houghton Mifflin, 1959, 1934), 11, 50, 46.

2. Susman, *Culture as History*, 154.

3. Van Wyck Brooks, *America's Coming-of-Age* (Garden City, N.Y.: Doubleday/Anchor, 1958), 3, 63.

4. Quoted in Joan Shelley Rubin, *Constance Rourke and American Culture* (Chapel Hill: University of North Carolina Press, 1980), 57.

5. Ibid., 68–71.

6. An extended discussion of one pattern of developing knowledge and appreciation appears in Helen Delpar, *The Enormous Vogue of Things Mexican: Cultural Relations between the United States and Mexico, 1920–1935* (Tuscaloosa: University of Alabama Press, 1992).

7. See David A. Hollinger, "Ethnic Diversity, Cosmopolitanism, and the Emergence of the American Liberal Intelligentsia," *American Quarterly* 27 (1975): 133–51; also Hollinger's *In the American Province* (Baltimore: Johns Hopkins University Press, 1985).

8. Harold Ickes, "Foreword" to the "Reorganization Number," *Indians at Work*, 31 July 1936 (3), quoted in Brian W. Dippie, *The Vanishing American: White Attitudes and U.S. Indian Policy* (Middletown, Conn.: Wesleyan University Press, 1982), 271.

9. Quoted in Dippie, *The Vanishing American*, 280–81.

10. Ibid., 301–4.

11. Quoted in Francis Paul Prucha, *The Great Father: The United States Government and the American Indians*, vol. 2 (Lincoln: University of Nebraska Press, 1984), 939.

12. Quoted in ibid., 951.

13. *Congressional Record*, 73d Cong., 2d sess., 22 May 1934, H9267.

14. Ibid., 12 June 1934, H11228.

15. Prucha, *The Great Father*, 964–65.

16. Quoted in ibid., 996.

17. Quoted in ibid., 977. The Indian New Deal is discussed in Prucha, *The Great Father*, 944–92, and Dippie, *The Vanishing American*, 304–21.

18. Prucha, *The Great Father*, 1001–2.

19. Quoted in John B. Kirby, *Black Americans in the Roosevelt Era: Liberalism and Race* (Knoxville: University of Tennessee Press, 1980), 56.

20. For the basic data, see *Statistical History*, A-78, A-79, 12–13; A-176, 22.

21. Mark Naison, *Communists in Harlem during the Depression* (Urbana: University of Illinois Press, 1983), xvi, 45.

22. The comment by P. B. Young of the *Norfolk Journal and Guide* (Virginia) was echoed by other editors participating in "Negro Editors on Communism: A Symposium of the American Negro Press," *The Crisis* 39 (April-May 1932).

23. Harvard Sitkoff, *A New Deal for Blacks: The Emergence of Civil Rights as a National Issue*, vol. 1, *The Depression Decade* (New York: Oxford University Press, 1978), 139–40.

24. Quoted in Kirby, *Black Americans in the Roosevelt Era*, 56.

25. Quoted in ibid., 23.

26. Du Bois's "Segregation" and Walter White's response in "Segregation—A Symposium," both from *The Crisis* 41 ( January and March 1934), are reprinted in *Black Protest Thought in the Twentieth Century*, 2d ed., ed. August Meier, Elliott Rudwick, and Francis L. Broderick (Indianapolis: Bobbs-Merrill, 1971), 159–64.

27. See Ralph J. Bunche, "A Critical Analysis of the Tactics and Programs of Minority Groups," *Journal of Negro Education* 4 ( July 1935): 308–20, reprinted in Meier, Rudwick, and Broderick, *Black Protest Thought*, 183–202; and Kirby, *Black Americans in the Roosevelt Era*, 202–17.

28. Klineberg's findings were published in *Negro Intelligence and Selective Migration* (New York, Columbia University Press, 1935), and *Race Differences* (New York, Harper and Brothers, 1935).

29. Lewin's work is discussed in Sitkoff, *A New Deal for Blacks*, 196–97.

30. Ibid., 202.

31. Ibid., 326–27.

32. Harvard Sitkoff, "The New Deal and Race Relations," in Sitkoff, *Fifty Years Later*, 104.

33. Sitkoff, *A New Deal for Blacks*, 117–21.

34. *Statistical History*, H-1170, 422; the explanation of sources and definitions on 412 also deserves attention.

## Chapter Five

1. Allen, *Since Yesterday*, 250–52.

2. Edmund Wilson, "The Literary Consequences of the Crash," in *The Shores of Light: A Literary Chronicle of the Twenties and Thirties* (New York: Farrar, Straus and Young, 1952), 498–99, 493. This piece appeared originally in the *New Republic* for 23 March 1932.

3. Quoted in Daniel Aaron, *Writers on the Left* (1961; New York: Avon Books, 1965), 189.

4. Edmund Wilson, *Axel's Castle: A Study in the Imaginative Literature of 1870–1930* (New York: Charles Scribner's Sons, 1931), 293, 297; Philip Rahv, "Marxist Criticism and Henry Hazlitt," *International Literature* 2 (1934): 51.

5. Lionel Abel, "New York City: A Remembrance," *Dissent* 8 (1961): 257.

6. On the symposium proposals and the declaration of support for Communist candidates, see Aaron, *Writers on the Left* 260–64, 213–15.

7. Quoted in ibid., 221, 225.

8. Quoted in ibid., 333.

9. Hicks and Davis were in general sympathy with Arvin's opinion that

Communist leaders were "fighting what is really our battle for us" and that the concerns of intellectuals like themselves "must take their places . . . out of the thickest dust along the rim of the arena." Quoted in Walter B. Rideout, *The Radical Novel in the United States, 1900–1954: Some Interpretations of Literature and Society* (Cambridge, Mass.: Harvard University Press, 1956), 226.

10. Alfred Kazin, *On Native Grounds: An Interpretation of Modern American Prose Literature* (New York: Harcourt, Brace, and World, 1942), 405.

11. Farrell's trilogy included *Young Lonigan* (1932), *The Young Manhood of Studs Lonigan* (1934), and *Judgment Day* (1935); these were collected as *Studs Lonigan* in 1938. On Farrell, see Edgar M. Branch, *James T. Farrell* (New York: Twayne, 1971); and Donald Pizer, "James T. Farrell and the 1930s," in *Literature at the Barricades: The American Writer in the 1930s*, ed. Ralph F. Bogardus and Fred Hobson (University: University of Alabama Press, 1982).

12. Iain Colley, *Dos Passos and the Fiction of Despair* (Totowa, N.J.: Rowman and Littlefield, 1978), 119.

13. Quoted in Linda W. Wagner, *Dos Passos: Artist as American* (Austin: University of Texas Press, 1979), 111.

14. Quoted in David Madden, ed., *Proletarian Writers of the Thirties* (Carbondale: Southern Illinois University Press, 1968), xix.

15. Ibid., xx. The three novels in Herbst's trilogy were *Pity Is Not Enough* (1933), *The Executioner Waits* (1934), and *Rope of Gold* (1939). A full treatment of Hearst's life developing a feminist perspective may be found in Elinor Langer, *Josephine Herbst* (Boston: Northeastern University Press, 1994).

16. Using fairly generous criteria, the most extensive scholarly study has claimed approximately 70 proletarian novels revolving around a few central ideas, of which one is the life of the "bottom dogs." The other primary themes are the decay of the middle classes, the conversion to radical belief, and the dynamics of the militant strike. See Rideout, *The Radical Novel in the United States.*

17. Proletarian novels were particularly fond, for example, of contrasting presumably accurate depictions of a strike with owner-biased press accounts that appeared before the public as truth. And any writer during the depression could set suffering against the myth of success, or images of repression against the claim of equality before the law.

18. Frederick J. Hoffman, "Aesthetics of the Proletarian Novel," in Madden, *Proletarian Writers of the Thirties*, 186.

19. Erling Larsen, "Jack Conroy's *The Disinherited or, The Way It Was*," in ibid., 94.

20. Quoted in ibid., 93.

21. Marcus Klein, "The Roots of Radicals: Experience in the Thirties," in ibid., 154.

22. Quoted in Aaron, *Writers on the Left*, 298–99; Malcolm Cowley, in "Symposium: Thirty Years Later: Memories of the First American Writers' Congress," *American Scholar* 35 (1966): 512–13.

23. The history and role of *Partisan Review* in the 1930s is explored in Terry A. Cooney, *The Rise of the New York Intellectuals: "Partisan Review" and Its Circle* (Madison: University of Wisconsin Press, 1986); on responses through criticism to the closing of the Reed clubs and the rise of the Popular Front, see esp. 79–92.

24. The commission's work was recorded in two volumes of material: a report on its hearings was published as *The Case of Leon Trotsky* in 1937; the commission's own judgments appeared as *Not Guilty* in 1938.

25. "Editorial Statement," *Partisan Review* 4 (December 1937): 3–4.

26. The two groups were the Committee for Cultural Freedom, of which Sidney Hook was a primary organizer and John Dewey the official chair, and the League for Cultural Freedom and Socialism, the membership of which included the editors of *Partisan Review* as well as Lionel Abel, James Burnham, James T. Farrell, Clement Greenberg, Harold Rosenberg, Meyer Schapiro, and Delmore Schwartz. As the names of the groups suggested, the most significant difference between them was the league's effort to maintain a positive emphasis on socialist belief and the committee's willingness to leave references to socialism aside in order to appeal to a larger body of liberals. The committee was something of an ancestor to, but should not be confused with, the American Committee for Cultural Freedom of the early 1950s.

27. The text of the letter, with a partial list of signatures, was published under the heading "To All Active Supporters of Democracy and Peace," *Nation* 149 (26 August 1939): 228.

28. James T. Farrell's diary is among his papers in the Special Collections Division of the Van Pelt Library at the University of Pennsylvania, Philadelphia; these and other excerpts are quoted in Cooney, *The Rise of the New York Intellectuals*, 171.

29. Dwight Macdonald, "Kulturbolschewismus Is Here," *Partisan Review* 8 (November-December 1941): 451; editorial reply under "P.R.'s Literary Principles," ibid., 519.

30. Harold Rosenberg, "On the Fall of Paris," *Partisan Review* 7 (November-December 1940): 440–48.

31. Archibald MacLeish, *The Irresponsibles: A Declaration* (New York, Duell, Sloan, and Pearce, 1940), 21, 30–34. MacLeish's argument should also be considered a part of the debate over democratic values, discussed in chapter 7.

32. The Brooks essay was presented orally at a Columbia University conference on 10 September 1941. A published version may be found in Jack Salzman, ed., *The Survival Years: A Collection of American Writings of the 1940s* (New York: Pegasus, 1969), 185–203.

33. Morton Dauwen Zabel, "The Poet on Capitol Hill," *Partisan Review* 8 (January-February and March-April 1941): 2–8, 132–38; Macdonald, "Kulturbolschewismus Is Here," 442–51; F. W. Dupee, "The Americanism of Van Wyck Brooks," *Partisan Review* 6 (Summer 1939): 69–85; William Phillips, "The Intellectuals' Tradition," *Partisan Review* 8 (November-December 1941): 481–90; Trilling's comments appeared along with those of others in "On the 'Brooks-MacLeish Thesis,'" *Partisan Review* 9 (January-February 1942): 38–47.

34. [Twelve Southerners,] *I'll Take My Stand: The South and the Agrarian Tradition* 1930; (Baton Rouge: Louisiana State University Press, 1977), xxxvii.

35. On the agrarian movement of the middle thirties and its relation to Distributist ideas, see Paul K. Conkin, *The Southern Agrarians* (Knoxville: University of Tennessee Press, 1988), 89-126.

36. Quoted in George Core, "Agrarianism, Criticism, and the Academy," in *A Band of Prophets: The Vanderbilt Agrarians after Fifty Years*, ed. William C. Havard and Walter Sullivan (Baton Rouge: Louisiana State University Press, 1982), 125.

37. Quoted in Daniel Joseph Singal, *The War Within: From Victorian to Modernist Thought in the South, 1919–1945* (Chapel Hill: University of North Carolina Press, 1982), 199.

38. Alfred Kazin, in "Under Forty: A Symposium on American Literature and the Younger Generation of American Jews," *Contemporary Jewish Record* 7 (February 1944): 11.

39. Louis D. Rubin, Jr., "Trouble on the Land: Southern Literature and the Great Depression," in Bogardus and Hobson, *Literature at the Barricades*, 96. Rubin mentions many of the works cited in this paragraph as justification for his remark.

40. The three novels, published between 1934 and 1937, were *Summer in Williamsburg*, *Homage to Blenholt*, and *Low Company*. Earning little attention and no money for this work, Fuchs turned, like many another writer of the period, including Faulkner, to writing for the movies.

## Chapter Six

1. Aaron, *Writers on the Left*, 199; the incident was discussed by Wilson and by Malcolm Cowley in print and reported to a Senate committee, as reprinted in *Harlan Miners Speak: Report on Terrorism in the Kentucky Coal Fields Prepared by Members of the National Committee for the Defense of Political Prisoners* (New York, 1932).

2. Malcolm Cowley, from "Transcontinental Highway," *New Republic* (25 February 1931), reprinted as "Drought" in *Think Back on Us . . . A Contemporary Chronicle of the 1930s: The Social Record*, ed. Henry Dan Piper (Carbondale: Southern Illinois University Press, 1967), 14–15.

3. Pells, *Radical Visions and American Dreams*, 71.

4. Quoted in Leuchtenburg, *Franklin D. Roosevelt and the New Deal*, 91–92.

5. James T. Patterson, *America's Struggle against Poverty 1900–1980* (Cambridge, Mass.: Harvard University Press, 1981), 46.

6. Meridel LeSueur, "Women on the Breadlines," *New Masses* (January 1932): 5–7, reprinted in *The American Writer and the Great Depression*, ed. Harvey Swados (Indianapolis: Bobbs-Merrill, 1966), 181–90.

7. Ibid.; the editorial comment is reprinted with the piece.

8. Richard Wright, "Joe Louis Uncovers Dynamite," *New Masses* (8 October 1935), reprinted in North, *New Masses*, 160–64.

9. John L. Spivak, "A Letter to President Roosevelt," *New Masses* (20 March 1934), reprinted in North, *New Masses*, 145–51.

10. Edmund Wilson, *The American Jitters: A Year of the Slump* (New York: Charles Scribner's Sons, 1932), 313.

11. Anderson to Dorothy Dudley (early spring 1933), in *The Portable Sherwood Anderson*, rev. ed., ed. Horace Gregory (New York: Penguin Books, 1977), 474.

12. John Dos Passos, "The Unemployed Report," *New Masses* (3 February 1934), reprinted in North, *New Masses*, 141–44.

13. Sherwood Anderson, *Puzzled America* (New York: Charles Scribner's Sons, 1935), 103–10, 54–65.

14. These were Hopkins's instructions as recorded by Lorena Hickok; see *One Third of a Nation: Lorena Hickok Reports on the Great Depression*, ed. Richard Lowitt and Maurine Beasley (Urbana: University of Illinois Press, 1981), quotation from ix.

15. Ibid., 216, 163, x, ix.

16. John F. Bauman and Thomas H. Coode, *In the Eye of the Great Depression: New Deal Reporters and the Agony of the American People* (DeKalb: Northern Illinois University Press, 1988), 192.

17. Ibid., 193.

18. Ibid., 183–84, 166–69.

19. Hickok, *One Third of a Nation*, 238–39.

20. Alan Johnstone, speaking of West Tennessee, as quoted in Bauman and Coode, *In the Eye of the Great Depression*, 169.

21. Hickok, *One Third of a Nation*, 238–40.

22. Ibid., 242. As noted in the chapter on "Beleaguered Households" in Bauman and Coode, *In the Eye of the Great Depression*, esp. 73–74, contemporary social science studies tended to reinforce the claim of a special depression impact on the middle class. Mirra Komarovsky, *The Unemployed Man and His Family: The Effect of Unemployment upon the Status of the Man in Fifty-Nine Families* (New York: Dryden Press, for the Institute of Social Research, 1940); Ruth Cavan and Karen Ranck, *The Family and the Depression: A Study of One Hundred Chicago Families* (Chicago: University of Chicago Press, 1938); and Robert C. Angell, *The Family Encounters the Depression* (New York: Charles Scribner's Sons, 1936), reported different reactions to prolonged unemployment among working- and middle-class families. Glen H. Elder, in *Children of the Great Depression: Social Change in the Life Experience* (Chicago: University of Chicago Press, 1974), cites evidence based on data from a Berkeley Guidance panel study of 112 families between 1929 and 1933 that middle-class families, suffering a greater "disturbance of habit," exhibited more cases of decaying marriages and male neuroses than others.

23. Quoted in Jerre Mangione, *The Dream and the Deal: The Federal Writers' Project, 1935–1943* (Boston: Little, Brown, and Co., 1972), 4.

24. Katherine Kellock, "The WPA Writers: Portraitists of the United States," *American Scholar* 9 (Autumn 1940): 474.

25. Mabel S. Ulrich, "Salvaging Culture for the WPA," *Harper's* 178 (May 1939): 656.

26. Lewis Mumford, "Writers' Project," *New Republic* 92 (20 October 1937): 306–7.

27. *Washington: A Guide to the Evergreen State* (Portland, Oreg.: Binfords and Mort, 1941), vii–viii.

28. Kellock, "The WPA Writers," 475.

29. Robert Cantwell, "America and the Writers' Project," *New Republic* 98 (26 April 1939): 323–25.

30. Ibid.

31. Ernie Pyle's columns have been collected in *Ernie's America: The Best of Ernie Pyle's 1930s Travel Dispatches*, ed. David Nichols (New York: Random House, 1989).

32. Stott, *Documentary Expression and Thirties America*, 252.

33. See, for example, "The U. S. Minicam Boom," *Fortune* 14 (October 1936): 125ff.

34. Publisher's prospectus for *Life*, reproduced in *Fortune* 14 (December 1936): 55, as part of a four-page ad for the new magazine.

35. *Life* 1 (23 November 1936): 3.

36. Ibid., 9–17.

37. Ibid., 3.

38. Quoted in Marquis, *Hopes and Ashes*, 134–35.

39. Quoted from the Erie, Pennsylvania, *Dispatch-Herald* in F. Jack Hurley, *Portrait of a Decade: Roy Stryker and the Development of Documentary Photography in the Thirties* (Baton Rouge: Louisiana State University Press, 1972), 90.

40. Erskine Caldwell and Margaret Bourke-White, *You Have Seen Their Faces* (New York: Modern Age Books, 1937), disclaimer of captions on reverse of dedication page.

41. Ibid., 47.

42. Quoted in Stott, *Documentary Expression and Thirties America*, 222.

43. Dorothea Lange and Paul Schuster Taylor, *An American Exodus: A Record of Human Erosion* (New York: Reynal and Hitchcock, 1939), 5–6.

44. Stott, *Documentary Expression and Thirties America*, 58–59; Lorentz is quoted by Stott. Stott's work provided a number of leads for this discussion of photography and of social reporting in general.

45. Caldwell and Bourke-White, *You Have Seen Their Faces*, 19, 28, 21.

46. Lange and Taylor, *An American Exodus*, 5, 152.

47. Ibid., 150–51.

48. Ibid., 5–7.

49. Erskine Caldwell and Margaret Bourke-White, *Say, Is This the U.S.A.* (New York: Duell, Sloan and Pearce, 1941), 3.

50. This pattern is cited in Badger, *The New Deal* (185), in the midst of a useful brief discussion of rural poverty and the limited options for federal policy.

51. Mumford, "Writers' Project," 307.

52. Quoted in John Morton Blum, *V Was for Victory: Politics and American Culture during World War II* (New York: Harcourt Brace Jovanovich, 1976), 63.

53. Clayton R. Koppes and Gregory D. Black, *Hollywood Goes to War: How Politics, Profits, and Propaganda Shaped World War II Movies* (New York: Free Press, 1987), 180.

## Chapter Seven

1. Robert Maynard Hutchins, *The Higher Learning in America* (1936; New Haven, Conn.: Yale University Press, 1962), *passim*.

2. Quoted in Edward A. Purcell, Jr., *The Crisis of Democratic Theory: Scientific Naturalism and the Problem of Value* (Lexington: University Press of Kentucky, 1973), 152.

3. Comments expressing opposition to Hutchins are taken from the discussion in ibid., 139–58.

4. James T. Farrell, "The Cultural Front: Mortimer J. Adler: A Provincial Torquemada," *Partisan Review* 7 (1940): 453–55.

5. Morton White's *Social Thought in America: The Revolt against Formalism* (New York: Viking Press, 1949) is a time-honored study on the breakdown of absolutes in American thought. James T. Kloppenberg, *Uncertain Victory: Social Democracy and Progressivism in European and American Thought, 1870–1920* (New York: Oxford University Press, 1986), covers roughly the same period with a different focus and is especially useful for its comparative perspective.

6. Pells, *Radical Visions and American Dreams*, 114.

7. Zieger, *American Workers, American Unions*, 27–28.

8. Hoover, *Memoirs: The Great Depression*, 351, 475, 485. On early New Deal appeals to moral unity, see James Holt, "The New Deal and the American Anti-Statist Tradition," in *The New Deal: The National Level*, ed. John Braeman, Robert H. Bremner, and David Brody (Columbus: Ohio State University Press, 1975), 33–35.

9. Naison, *Communists in Harlem during the Depression*, xx.

10. David A. Hollinger, "Two NYUs and 'The Obligation of Universities to the Social Order' in the Great Depression," in *The University and the City: From Medieval Origins to the Present*, ed. Thomas Bender (New York: Oxford University Press, 1988), 251.

11. This usage of "metaphors" is borrowed from Richard Pells, who speaks of the left's image of the Soviet Union, and the agrarian image of the South, as metaphors used to suggest "a desirable cultural alternative"; *Radical Visions and American Dreams*, 67. On the 1939 fair exhibits, see Meikle, *Twentieth Century Limited*, and Marquis, *Hopes and Ashes*, 202–11.

12. See, for example, Joan Shelley Rubin, "'Information Please!': Culture and Expertise in the Interwar Period," *American Quarterly* 35 (Winter 1983): 499–517.

13. Joseph Horowitz, *Understanding Toscanini: How He Became an American Culture-God and Helped Create a New Audience for Old Music* (New York: Alfred A. Knopf, 1987; Minneapolis: University of Minnesota Press, 1988), 262, and 189–270 more generally.

14. The discussion that follows draws especially on Purcell, *The Crisis of Democratic Theory, passim.* See also Robert C. Bannister, *Sociology and Scientism: The American Quest for Objectivity, 1880–1940* (Chapel Hill: University of North Carolina Press, 1987); and Dorothy Ross, *The Origins of American Social Science* (New York: Cambridge University Press, 1991), which ends its story before 1930.

15. Lasswell's works included *Propaganda Technique in the World War* (1927) and *Psychopathology and Politics* (1930); Lippmann's arguments appeared in *Public Opinion* (1922) and *The Phantom Public* (1925).

16. For one of the fuller statements of these views, see John Dewey, *Freedom and Culture* (1939; New York: Capricorn Books, 1963).

17. Quoted in Purcell, *The Crisis of Democratic Theory*, 214.

18. Pendleton Herring, *The Politics of Democracy: American Parties in Action* (New York: Rinehart and Co., 1940), 26, 421, 435, viii.

19. Ellis W. Hawley, *The New Deal and the Problem of Monopoly: A Study in Economic Ambivalence* (Princeton, N.J.: Princeton University Press, 1966), 187.

20. Henry A. Wallace, *Technology, Corporations, and the General Welfare* (Chapel Hill: University of North Carolina Press, 1937), 71.

21. Daniel T. Rodgers, *Contested Truths: Keywords in American Politics since Independence* (New York: Basic Books, 1987), 176–211.

22. John Chamberlain, *The American Stakes* (New York: Carrick and Evans, 1940), 25–28.

23. Fred Matthews, "Polemical Palefaces and Genteel Redskins: The Debate over American Culture and the Origins of the American Studies Movement," *American Quarterly* 35 (Winter 1983): 549.

24. Jacques Barzun, *Of Human Freedom* (Boston: Little, Brown and Co., 1939), 21, 43, 191.

25. Quoted in Purcell, *The Crisis of Democratic Theory*, 207.

26. David A. Hollinger, introductory note to "The Problem of Pragmatism in American History," *In the American Province: Studies in the History and Historiography of Ideas* (Bloomington: Indiana University Press, 1985), 24.

27. Randolph S. Bourne, "Trans-National America," and "The Jew and Trans-National America," in *War and the Intellectuals*, ed. Carl Resek (New York: Harper and Row/Torchbooks, 1964), 107–33. Bourne notes with distaste the "arrested development" of some ethnic cultures (131).

28. One of the cases most discussed involved the permanent appointment of Lionel Trilling in the English Department at Columbia in 1939. For two differing versions of the circumstances surrounding this appointment, see Diana Trilling, "Lionel Trilling: A Jew at Columbia," *Commentary* 67 (March 1979): 40–46, and Sidney Hook, "Anti-Semitism in the Academy: Some Pages of the Past," *Midstream* 25 (January 1979): 49–54.

29. Barzun, *Of Human Freedom*, 261.

30. The story of the Group Theater is best told in Harold Clurman's memoir, *The Fervent Years* (New York: Alfred A. Knopf, 1945).

31. A Reginald Marsh etching, "East Tenth Street Jungle," and drawings by Gropper and others are included in North, *New Masses*, 34, 136, and *passim*.

32. Karal Ann Marling, *Wall-to-Wall America: A Cultural History of Post Office Murals in the Great Depression* (Minneapolis: University of Minnesota Press, 1982), 57.

33. Charles C. Alexander, *Here the Country Lies: Nationalism and the Arts in Twentieth-Century America* (Bloomington: Indiana University Press, 1980), 177, 179.

34. Sometimes the folk-left provided the context for new songs that sounded positively patriotic, as in the case of Woody Guthrie's "This Land Is Your Land" (1940). Like Irving Berlin's "God Bless America" (1938) and Katharine Lee Bates's "America the Beautiful" (1893) before it, Guthrie's song relies on a catalog of the nation's bounteous natural attributes, and its original refrain was "God blessed America to me." William Stott connects Guthrie and Berlin in *Documentary Expression and Thirties America*, 255.

35. Horowitz, *Understanding Toscanini*, 242.

36. See ibid., 3–4 and *passim*.

37. Roy Harris, "Problems of American Composers," in Henry Cowell, ed., *American Composers on American Music* (Palo Alto: Stanford University Press, 1933; New York: Frederick Ungar, 1962), 149–66. An important advocate of the "New Music" in the 1920s and 1930s, Cowell looked to multiple traditions and included in this volume essays on Mexican, Cuban, and "Oriental" music, reflections by the African-American composer William Grant Still, George Gershwin on jazz and American music, and comments on the future of music by Charles Ives. The range of interest represented in the collection is another cultural marker of the 1930s.

38. Copland's comment, and a discussion worthy of note, appear in Aaron Copland, *The New Music, 1900–1960* (New York: W. W. Norton, 1968), quotation from 160.

39. For general treatments of American music during the 1930s, see the relevant chapters of Charles Hamm, *Music in the New World* (New York: W. W. Norton, 1983); H. Wiley Hitchcock, *Music in the United States: A Historical Introduction*, 3d ed. (Englewood Cliffs, N.J.: Prentice-Hall, 1988); and Barbara Tischler, *An American Music: The Search for an American Musical Identity* (New York: Oxford University Press, 1986).

40. The words are Martha Graham's as quoted in Alexander, *Here the Country Lies*, 234.

41. Barbara Rose, *American Art since 1900*, rev. ed. (New York: Praeger, 1975), 105–8, 114–20.

42. See, for example, William Phillips, "The Intellectuals' Tradition," *Partisan Review* 8 (November-December 1941), which summarizes an outlook and an appeal that had been important in varying contexts throughout the 1930s.

43. Several of the museum's officers came from the ranks of those actively fighting on behalf of modern art: the new president of MOMA, A. Conger Goodyear, had recently been fired by a Buffalo gallery over the purchase of an early Picasso; several trustees came from the Harvard Society for Contemporary Art, organized only the year before; and the young director of the museum, Alfred Barr, had recently taught the first American course on modern art during a one-year career at Wellesley.

44. Hitchcock, *Music in the United States*, 237.

45. The metaphor of concert hall as museum, and the final quoted phrase, are taken from J. Peter Burkholder, "Museum Pieces: The Historicist Mainstream in Music of the Last Hundred Years," *Journal of Musicology* 2 (Spring 1983): 117–18, 133.

46. William Phillips and Philip Rahv, "Literature in a Political Decade," in *New Letters in America*, ed. Horace Gregory and Eleanor Clark (New York: W. W. Norton, 1937), 172–80.

47. Harold Rosenberg, "The Fall of Paris," in *The Tradition of the New* (New York: McGraw-Hill, 1965), 212; the essay was originally published in *Partisan Review* in 1940.

48. Leonard B. Meyer, *Music, the Arts, and Ideas: Patterns and Predictions in Twentieth-Century Culture* (Chicago: University of Chicago Press, 1967), 172, 170.

49. Quoted in ibid., 179.

50. George H. Roeder, Jr., "What Have Modernists Looked At? Experiential Roots of Twentieth-Century American Painting," *American Quarterly* 39 (Spring 1987): 80–81.

51. Lawrence Starr, "Gershwin's 'Bess, You Is My Woman Now': The Sophistication and Subtlety of a Great Tune," *Musical Quarterly* 72 (1986): 429–48. In *Music in the New World*, Charles Hamm remarks that "Gershwin came closer to bridging classical and popular musical culture than any other operatic composer of the twentieth century," and he judges *Porgy and Bess* to be "the greatest nationalistic opera of the century, not only of America but of the world." Wilfred Mellers, in *Music in a New Found Land: Themes and Developments in the History of American Music* (London, 1964; New York: Oxford University Press, 1987), points out that the content of *Porgy and Bess* allows no easy answers or simplistic dreams but faces up to the processes "necessary for growing up" to deal with a complex modern world. A dream of social harmony is no more the basis for the work than a unified musical tradition.

52. On the Adler-Hook exchange, see Purcell, *The Crisis of Democratic Theory*, 218–19.

53. Selections from both the MacLeish and Brooks attacks are perhaps most readily available in Jack Salzman, ed., *The Survival Years* (New York: Pegasus, 1969), 173–203; on the reactions by Zabel, Macdonald, and Phillips, see Cooney, *The Rise of the New York Intellectuals*, 200–206.

54. Philip Rahv, "Souvenirs and Experiments," *Kenyon Review* 4 (1942): 238.

# Bibliographic Essay

---

The political and economic history of the 1930s has received ample attention from scholars. After three decades, William E. Leuchtenburg's *Franklin D. Roosevelt and the New Deal, 1932–1940* (New York: Harper and Row, 1963) remains one of the strongest surveys of the period. Paul Conkin's *The New Deal*, 2d ed. (Arlington Heights, Ill.: AHM Publishing, 1975) set out to "demythologize" the New Deal and continues to be read for its critical judgments. Barry Karl evaluated the achievements of the New Deal against its failings and constraints in *The Uneasy State: The United States from 1915 to 1945* (Chicago: University of Chicago Press, 1983). The essays in Harvard Sitkoff, ed., *Fifty Years Later: The New Deal Evaluated* (New York: Alfred A. Knopf, 1985), offer useful summary evaluations in a number of different domains. A recent survey may be found in Anthony J. Badger, *The New Deal: The Depression Years, 1933–1940* (New York: Noonday Press, 1989). Badger provides an extensive and helpful bibliographical essay on economic and political issues that attends to the development of different historiographical angles on the New Deal; the interested reader may wish to turn to that bibliography. The experience of the depression itself is explored in Caroline Bird, *The Invisible Scar* (New York: David McKay Co., 1966), and Robert S. McElvaine, *The Great Depression: America 1929–1941* (New York: New York Times Books, 1984). John Garraty's *The Great Depression: An Inquiry into the Causes, Course, and Consequences of the Worldwide Depression of the Nineteen-Thirties, as Seen by Contemporaries and in the Light of History* (San Diego: Harcourt Brace Jovanovich, 1986) places the American experience within an international context.

The richest source of statistical information on the 1930s, as on most of U.S. history, is the compilation published periodically by the Census Bureau under the title *Historical Statistics of the United States*. An edition aimed at more general circulation is Ben J. Wattenberg, *The Statistical History of the United States: From Colonial Times to the Present, Introduction and User's Guide* (New York: Basic Books, 1976). The statistics can often be given life through the direct testimony of individuals. The interviews gathered in Studs Terkel, *Hard Times: An Oral History of the Great Depression* (New York: Pantheon, 1970), show the great variety of depression experiences. The Federal Writers Project recorded many life histories during the 1930s, samplings of which have been published in Ann Banks, ed., *First-Person America* (New York: Alfred A. Knopf, 1980), and Tom Terrill and Jerrold Hirsch, eds., *Such as Us: Southern Voices of the Thirties* (Chapel Hill: University of North Carolina Press, 1978). Robert S. McElvaine compiled a selection of letters from workers, mostly written to federal agencies during the thirties, for *Down and Out in the Great Depression: Letters from the "Forgotten Man"* (Chapel Hill: University of North Carolina Press, 1983). A good part of the fiction, documentary work, and social reporting of the 1930s was also concerned with capturing the range and specificity of contemporary experience.

Among works of reasonably broad scope that address the cultural life of the 1930s, Frederick Lewis Allen's lively, on-the-spot journalistic account in *Since Yesterday: The Nineteen-Thirties in America* (New York: Harper Brothers, 1940) should not be neglected, though it is far less celebrated than Allen's parallel account of the 1920s. Charles C. Alexander made nationalism a defining theme of cultural and intellectual life in *Nationalism in American Thought, 1930–1945* (Chicago: Rand McNally, 1969), then turned the same interest to more effective use in *Here the Country Lies: Nationalism and the Arts in Twentieth-Century America* (Bloomington: Indiana University Press, 1980). Richard Pells's *Radical Visions and American Dreams: Culture and Social Thought in the Depression Years* (New York: Harper and Row, 1973) provides an especially useful treatment of the political, economic, and social ideas of the early 1930s and can lead the way into the contemporary sources. In *Hopes and Ashes: The Birth of Modern Times, 1929–1939* (New York: Free Press, 1986), Alice Goldfarb Marquis argues that the newer media were transforming the United States into a mass culture during the 1930s. Warren I. Susman's suggestive essays on the 1930s may be found in *Culture as History: The Transformation of American Society in the Twentieth Century* (New York: Pantheon Books, 1984). Lawrence W. Levine offers his own observations in "American Culture and the Great Depression," *Yale Review* 74 (Winter 1985): 196–223. An older and still interesting interpretation may be found in T. V. Smith, "The New Deal as a Cultural Phenomenon," in *Ideological Differences and World Order*, ed. F. S. C. Northrop (New Haven, Conn.: Yale University Press, 1949).

Women's experience during the decade is the subject of Susan Ware's *Holding Their Own: American Women in the 1930s* (Boston: Twayne Publishers, 1982) and, with a more distinctly political focus, of the same author's *Beyond Suffrage: Women in the New Deal* (Cambridge, Mass.: Harvard University Press, 1981). Working women and their economic and social status are at the center of three books that provide somewhat different angles of vision: Lois Scharf, *To Work and to Wed: Female Employment, Feminism, and the Great Depression* (Westport, Conn.: Greenwood Press, 1980); Alice Kessler-Harris, *Out to Work: A History of Wage-Earning Women in the United States* (New York: Oxford University Press, 1982); and Claudia Goldin, *Understanding the Gender Gap: An Economic History of American Women* (New York: Oxford University Press, 1990). A number of essays dealing directly or partially with women's experience during the labor organizing drives of the 1930s appear in Ruth Milkman, ed., *Women, Work and Protest: A Century of U.S. Women's Labor History* (London: Routledge and Kegan Paul, 1985); the most interesting of these for the purposes of this text is Marjorie Penn Lasky's "'Where I Was a Person': The Ladies' Auxiliary in the 1934 Minneapolis Teamsters' Strikes" (181–205). Winifred D. Wandersee looks toward the relationship between work and the home in *Women's Work and Family Values 1920–1940* (Cambridge, Mass.: Harvard University Press, 1981). An increasing number of women active in the 1930s are becoming the subjects of individual biographies, most of which are easily located. A valuable set of short biographies covering a wider array of women and providing bibliographical references may be found in Barbara Sicherman and Carol Hurd Green, eds., *Notable American Women: The Modern Period* (Cambridge, Mass.: Harvard University Press, 1980).

The symposium in *Modern Monthly* 8 (April 1934) in which several prominent intellectuals discuss why they were, or were not, supporters of communism provides considerable insight into the intellectual choices being made in the early 1930s and into the underlying values that would sometimes reverse those choices at a later date. Reviving interest in John Dewey has been given a boost by Robert B. Westbrook, *John Dewey and American Democracy* (Ithaca, N.Y.: Cornell University Press, 1991). Edmund Wilson's ideas are given context in Sherman Paul, *Edmund Wilson: A Study of Literary Vocation in Our Time* (Urbana: University of Illinois Press, 1965). Wilson's more important pieces of contemporary journalistic commentary are gathered in Edmund Wilson, *The Shores of Light: A Literary Chronicle of the Twenties and Thirties* (New York: Farrar, Straus and Young, 1952). Sidney Hook has given his own account of his life and ideas in *Out of Step: An Unquiet Life in the Twentieth Century* (New York: Harper and Row, 1987), which should be used with caution. Differences between Hook and Max Eastman over the nature of Marxism during the 1930s, as well as the political migrations of John Dos Passos, Will Herberg, and James Burnham, are explored in John P. Diggins, *Up from Communism: Conservative Odysseys in American Intellectual History* (New York: Harper and Row, 1975). Reinhold Niebuhr's ideas are carefully traced in Richard Fox, *Reinhold Niebuhr: A Biography* (New York: Pantheon Books, 1985). An account of the migration of many intellectuals away from the radical or collectivist interests of the early 1930s, in the face of Roosevelt's 1936 victory and the growing threat of fascism, appears in R. Allan Lawson, *The Failure of Independent Liberalism, 1930–1941* (New York: Putnam, 1971).

The phenomenon of streamlining and the wider cultural implications of design are explored thoroughly and creatively in Jeffrey L. Meikle, *Twentieth-Century Limited: Industrial Design in America, 1925–1939* (Philadelphia: Temple University Press, 1979). This discussion can be supplemented with Richard Guy Wilson, Dianne H. Pilgrim, and Dickran Tashjian, *The Machine Age in America, 1918–1941* (New York: Brooklyn Museum in association with Harry N. Abrams, 1986). Questions of design also play a part in Lewis A. Ehrenberg, "From New York to Middletown: Repeal and the Legitimization of Nightlife in the Great Depression," *American Quarterly* 38 (Winter 1986): 761–88. Alfred Haworth Jones considers attitudes toward the past during the 1930s in "The Search for a Usable American Past in the New Deal Era," *American Quarterly* 23 (December 1971): 710–24. Karal Ann Marling analyzes attitudes toward both past and future in federally sponsored post office murals in "A Note on New Deal Iconography: Futurology and the Historical Myth," *Prospects* 4 (1979), 421–40, and discusses such work more extensively in *Wall-to-Wall America: A Cultural History of Post Office Murals in the Great Depression* (Minneapolis: University of Minnesota Press, 1982). Susman, *Culture as History*, and Marquis, *Hopes and Ashes*, as well as Meikle, offer interpretations of the New York World's Fair of 1939.

A view of two of the major technologically based projects of the thirties as parts of a larger history may be found in the chapter "Tennessee Valley and Manhattan Engineer District" in Thomas P. Hughes, *American Genesis: A Century of Invention and Technological Enthusiasm, 1870–1970* (New York: Viking, 1989). Daniel J. Kevles, *The Physicists: The History of a Scientific Community in Modern America* (New York: Alfred A. Knopf, 1978), places the emergence of atomic physics within both a scientific and a social context. Joseph J. Corn explores the cultural enthusiasms associated with airplane flight in *The Winged Gospel* (New York: Oxford University Press, 1983). An introduction to other technological developments may be found in Alan I. Marcus and Howard P. Segal, *Technology in America: A Brief History* (San Diego: Harcourt Brace Jovanovich, 1989).

The New Deal involved not simply politics but cultural symbolism and intellectual debate. Franklin D. Roosevelt's participation is fully documented; his own words are perhaps most accessible through the 13 volumes of *The Public Papers and Addresses of Franklin D. Roosevelt* (New York: Random House, 1938–50). Herbert Hoover's self-explanations and his critique of the New Deal appear in *The Memoirs of Herbert Hoover: The Great Depression, 1929–1941* (New York: Macmillan, 1952). Arthur A. Ekirch, Jr., undertook to assess the larger intellectual influence of the New Deal in *Ideologies and Utopias: The Impact of the New Deal on American Thought* (Chicago: Quadrangle Books, 1969). Ellis W. Hawley concentrated on a limited topic, but with broadly suggestive results, in *The New Deal and the Problem of Monopoly: A Study in Economic Ambivalence* (Princeton, N.J.: Princeton University Press, 1966). Differences among the New Dealers are effectively summarized by Thomas K. McCraw,

"The New Deal and the Mixed Economy," in Sitkoff, *Fifty Years Later*. Daniel T. Rodgers explores the changing meaning of "interests" in the 1930s in *Contested Truths: Keywords in American Politics since Independence* (New York: Basic Books, 1987). An extremely useful collection of contemporary materials appears in Howard Zinn, ed., *New Deal Thought* (Indianapolis: Bobbs-Merrill, 1966), which contains more than 60 selections from a variety of perspectives.

Alan Brinkley explores the cultural implications of some of the leading movements that set out to pressure or to rival the New Deal in *Voices of Protest: Huey Long, Father Coughlin, and the Great Depression* (New York: Alfred A. Knopf, 1982; paperback reprint, New York: Vintage Books/Random House, 1983). The interplay between New Deal programs and local patterns of cultural politics are well examined in a number of studies of particular cities: Charles H. Trout, *Boston, the Great Depression, and the New Deal* (New York: Oxford University Press, 1977); Jo Ann E. Argersinger, *Toward a New Deal in Baltimore: People and Government in the Great Depression* (Chapel Hill: University of North Carolina Press, 1988); and Bruce Stave, *The New Deal and the Last Hurrah: Pittsburgh Machine Politics* (Pittsburgh: University of Pittsburgh Press, 1970). The essays in John Braeman, Robert H. Bremner, and David Brody, eds., *The New Deal*, vol. 2, *The State and Local Levels* (Columbus: Ohio State University Press, 1975), look into the particulars of other federal-local relationships.

Robert H. Zieger, *American Workers, American Unions, 1920–1985* (Baltimore: Johns Hopkins University Press, 1986), offers an excellent overview of labor activism in the 1930s, bringing together insight and common sense. A more traditional source, rich in its bulk, is Irving Bernstein, *Turbulent Years: A History of the American Worker, 1933–1941* (Boston: Houghton Mifflin, 1970). Roger Keeran, *The Communist Party and the Auto Workers Unions* (Bloomington: Indiana University Press, 1980), can serve as one strong example of the kind of detailed study of a particular union, industry, region, or city of which there have been many worthy representatives during the last two decades. Richard Oestreicher raises important questions about the relationship between labor activism, class identity, and politics in "Urban Working-Class Political Behavior and Theories of American Electoral Politics, 1870–1940," *Journal of American History* 74 (March 1988): 1257–86. An earlier effort to analyze related issues based on poll data from the 1930s may be found in Sidney Verba and Kay Lehman Schlozman, "Unemployment, Class Consciousness, and Radical Politics: What Didn't Happen in the Thirties," *Journal of Politics* 39 (1977): 291–323. Among many contemporary efforts to assess American values and sources of identity, Robert S. Lynd and Helen Merrell Lynd's *Middletown in Transition: A Study in Cultural Conflicts* (New York: Harcourt, Brace, and World, 1937) is justifiably the best known.

Charles R. Hearn looks to a host of magazine articles and self-improvement books to examine the fate of the idea of "success" during the 1930s in *The American Dream in the Great Depression* (Westport, Conn.: Greenwood Press, 1977). The most popular and enduring of the success books of the decade was

Dale Carnegie's *How to Win Friends and Influence People* (New York: Simon and Schuster, 1936). Much of the advertising of the 1930s remains directly accessible for those willing to turn the pages of the more successful magazines of the period. Roland Marchand has turned more than his share of these pages and offers a perceptive analysis in *Advertising the American Dream: Making Way for Modernity, 1920–1940* (Berkeley: University of California Press, 1985). Stephen Fox concentrates less on the advertisements themselves than on the nature of the advertising industry in *The Mirror Makers: A History of American Advertising and Its Creators* (New York: William Morrow, 1984).

With the ascent of home video, the movies of the 1930s remain moderately available to fresh viewers. Robert Sklar's *Movie-Made America: A Social History of American Movies* (New York: Random House, 1975) surveys the development of American film while probing for patterns of social implication. Andrew Bergman, *We're in the Money: Depression America and Its Films* (New York: New York University Press, 1971), treats the movies as central to the decade's consciousness. A wealth of contemporary information and observation on the movies may be found in Margaret Farrand Thorp, *America at the Movies* (New Haven, Conn.: Yale University Press, 1939). Molly Haskell's *From Reverence to Rape: The Treatment of Women in the Movies* (New York: Holt, Rinehart, and Winston, 1974) draws attention to at least some patterns in the depiction of women in film. Frank Capra's films have been much discussed. Raymond Carney aspires to a full dissection in *American Vision: The Films of Frank Capra* (Cambridge, Eng.: Cambridge University Press, 1986), which is perhaps overly self-conscious in its use of literary theory. Among other relevant commentaries and analyses, David Karnes, "The Glamorous Crowd: Hollywood Premieres between the Wars," *American Quarterly* 38 (Fall 1986): 553–72, stands out for its suggestiveness about the social and cultural environment surrounding the movies.

Erik Barnouw's history of broadcasting remains a most important source on the development of radio. The first two volumes, *A Tower in Babel* and *The Golden Web* (New York: Oxford University Press, 1966, 1968), carry the story through 1933, and from 1933 to 1953, respectively. Robert W. McChesney, *Telecommunications, Mass Media, and Democracy: The Battle for the Control of U.S. Broadcasting, 1928–1935* (New York: Oxford University Press, 1993), offers a new study of the organizational history of radio in its formative period with an emphasis on political and economic interests. Melvin Patrick Ely leads a trek through the history of what, among other incarnations, was one of the most popular radio shows of the thirties, in *The Adventures of "Amos 'n' Andy": A Social History of an American Phenomenon* (New York: Free Press, 1991). Contemporary scholars, especially in the social sciences, were much interested in the impact of radio. Two of the leading studies were Paul F. Lazarsfeld, *Radio and the Printed Page: An Introduction to the Study of Radio and Its Role in the Communication of Ideas* (New York: Duell, Sloan and Pearce, 1940), and Hadley Cantril and Gordon W. Allport, *The Psychology of Radio* (New York: Peter

Smith, 1941). Daniel J. Boorstin reflects broadly on the implications of modern media in *The Image: A Guide to Pseudo-Events in America* (1961; New York: Atheneum, 1987).

A claim for the discovery of "culture" in the anthropological sense during the 1930s is put forward in Warren Susman's essay, "The Culture of the Thirties," in *Culture as History*. Constance Rourke's role in the discovery and assertion of American traditions of folk culture is explored in Joan Shelley Rubin, *Constance Rourke and American Culture* (Chapel Hill: University of North Carolina Press, 1980). David Hollinger traces the development of a cosmopolitan outlook among intellectuals in "Ethnic Diversity, Cosmopolitanism, and the Emergence of the American Liberal Intelligentsia," *American Quarterly* 27 (1975): 133–51. Two strong studies examine American Indian policy, and the attitudes of reformers and Native Americans toward various policy changes: Francis Paul Prucha, *The Great Father: The United States Government and the American Indians*, vol. 2 (Lincoln: University of Nebraska Press, 1984), and Brian W. Dippie, *The Vanishing American: White Attitudes and U.S. Indian Policy* (Middletown, Conn.: Wesleyan University Press, 1982).

The most complete single-volume history of African-Americans during the 1930s is Harvard Sitkoff, *A New Deal for Blacks: The Emergence of Civil Rights as a National Issue*, vol. 1, *The Depression Decade* (New York: Oxford University Press, 1978). John B. Kirby attends particularly to the attitudes of white liberals and the dilemmas of black leaders in *Black Americans in the Roosevelt Era: Liberalism and Race* (Knoxville: University of Tennessee Press, 1980). The politics surrounding antilynching proposals are discussed in Robert L. Zangrando, *The NAACP Crusade against Lynching, 1909–1950* (Philadelphia: Temple University Press, 1980). Mark Naison explores the complicated relationships between African-Americans and the Communist party in one community in *Communists in Harlem during the Depression* (Urbana: University of Illinois Press, 1983). Some of the debates among African-American intellectuals in the 1930s are evident in the documents included in August Meier, Elliott Rudwick, and Francis L. Broderick, eds., *Black Protest Thought in the Twentieth Century*, 2d ed. (Indianapolis: Bobbs-Merrill, 1971).

The intellectual attraction to left politics was probably strongest within literary circles during the 1930s. The most comprehensive history of radicalism and literature in this period remains Daniel Aaron, *Writers on the Left* (1961; New York: Avon Books, 1965). Walter Rideout's more specialized study, *The Radical Novel in the United States, 1900–1954: Some Interrelations of Literature and Society* (Cambridge, Mass.: Harvard University Press, 1956), also continues to be a valuable source on proletarian literature, though perspectives on this writing continue to change. A number of useful essays appear in David Madden, ed., *Proletarian Writers of the Thirties* (Carbondale: Southern Illinois University Press, 1968). A more wide-ranging set of interpretations reaching well beyond the left may be found in Ralph F. Bogardus and Fred Hobson, eds., *Literature at the Barricades: The American Writer in the 1930s* (University:

University of Alabama Press, 1982). For a recent view concentrating on radical writing by women, some of which remained unpublished during the 1930s, see Paula Rabinowitz, *Labor and Desire: Women's Revolutionary Fiction in Depression America* (Chapel Hill: University of North Carolina Press, 1991). Jack Salzman, ed., *Years of Protest: A Collection of American Writings of the 1930s* (Indianapolis: Pegasus [Bobbs-Merrill], 1967, 1970), offers a sampler giving particular attention to radical writing. On the history of *Partisan Review* in this period, see Terry A. Cooney, *The Rise of the New York Intellectuals: "Partisan Review" and Its Circle* (Madison: University of Wisconsin Press, 1986).

Paul K. Conkin emphasizes economic and social views more than literary analysis in *The Southern Agrarians* (Knoxville: University of Tennessee Press, 1988). Daniel Joseph Singal fits the agrarians within a larger interpretive framework in *The War Within: From Victorian to Modernist Thought in the South, 1919–1945* (Chapel Hill: University of North Carolina Press, 1982), and Richard King concentrates especially on a few major writers in *A Southern Renaissance: The Cultural Awakening of the American South* (New York: Oxford University Press, 1980). A mind made up may be at least partly unmade by Michael O'Brien, *Rethinking the South: Essays in Intellectual History* (Baltimore: Johns Hopkins University Press, 1988). For a provocative argument involving postwar connections between the New York intellectuals and the southern New Critics, see Lawrence H. Schwartz, *Creating Faulkner's Reputation: The Politics of Modern Literary Criticism* (Knoxville: University of Tennessee Press, 1988).

In *Documentary Expression and Thirties America* (New York: Oxford University Press, 1973), William Stott investigates the forms through which the urge to document and report found expression during the 1930s and seeks to define purposes and inclinations as well as to interpret. John F. Bauman and Thomas H. Coode, *In the Eye of the Great Depression: New Deal Reporters and the Agony of the American People* (DeKalb: Northern Illinois University Press, 1988), have taken a close look at those reporters who were hired, especially by Harry Hopkins, to provide firsthand information to federal officials on the state of American communities. Social reporting took many forms across the political spectrum. Among those contemporary books and later collections that gather useful batches of such reporting, the following provide a sampling of types and viewpoints: Edmund Wilson, *The American Jitters: A Year of the Slump* (New York: Charles Scribner's Sons, 1932); Sherwood Anderson, *Puzzled America* (New York: Charles Scribner's Sons, 1935); Joseph North, ed., *"New Masses": An Anthology of the Rebel Thirties* (New York: International Publishers, 1969); Harvey Swados, ed., *The American Writer and the Great Depression* (Indianapolis: Bobbs-Merrill, 1966); Malcolm Cowley, *Think Back on Us . . . A Contemporary Chronicle of the 1930s: The Social Record*, ed. Henry Dan Piper (Carbondale: Southern Illinois University Press, 1967); David Nichols, ed., *Ernie's America: The Best of Ernie Pyle's 1930s Travel Dispatches* (New York: Random House, 1989); and Richard Lowitt and Maurine Beasley, eds., *One*

*Third of a Nation: Lorena Hickok Reports on the Great Depression* (Urbana: University of Illinois Press, 1981).

The best sense of the American Guide Series can be gained from the pages of the guides themselves, which continue to carry a kind of information and interest not found in the standard travel guides of the present. The contemporary commentaries on the project and the guides as they appeared remain lively cultural documents in themselves. These include Mabel S. Ulrich, "Salvaging Culture for the WPA," *Harper's* 178 (May 1939): 653–64; Katherine Kellock, "The WPA Writers: Portraitists of the United States," *American Scholar* 9 (Autumn 1940): 473–82; Lewis Mumford, "Writers' Project," *New Republic* 92 (20 October 1937): 306–7; and Robert Cantwell, "America and the Writers' Project," *New Republic* 98 (26 April 1939): 323–25. The larger federal relief effort for writers of which the guide series was a part is examined in Monte N. Penkower, *The Federal Writers' Project: A Study in Government Patronage of the Arts* (Urbana: University of Illinois Press, 1977), and Jerre Mangione, *The Dream and the Deal: The Federal Writers' Project, 1935–1943* (Boston: Little, Brown, and Co., 1972).

The public significance and use of photography climbed to new levels in the 1930s; the change was evident in the Luce magazines *Fortune* and *Life*, as it was in the thousands of photographs taken under federal auspices, in particular for the Farm Security Administration. In Erskine Caldwell and Margaret Bourke-White, *You Have Seen Their Faces* (New York: Modern Age Books, 1937), the photographs come from Bourke-White, the most successful commercial photographer in the Luce ranks. In Dorothea Lange and Paul Schuster Taylor, *An American Exodus: A Record of Human Erosion* (New York: Reynal and Hitchcock, 1939), the photographs belong to the former portrait photographer and then FSA employee Lange. Both books seek to combine photographs with text to comment on social conditions, though at times with a different spirit. On the federal photography program, see Forrest Jack Hurley, *Portrait of a Decade: Roy Stryker and the Development of Documentary Photographs in the Thirties* (Baton Rouge: Louisiana State University Press, 1972). Two recent efforts to provide new views of FSA photography may be found in James Curtis, *Mind's Eye, Mind's Truth: FSA Photography Reconsidered* (Philadelphia: Temple University Press, 1989), and Nicholas Natanson, *The Black Image in the New Deal: The Politics of FSA Photography* (Knoxville: University of Tennessee Press, 1992).

Edward A. Purcell, Jr.'s, *The Crisis of Democratic Theory: Scientific Naturalism and the Problem of Value* (Lexington: University Press of Kentucky, 1973) explores within a broad intellectual context the difficulties that arose when arguments for relativistic thinking ran up against the need to define adequate reasons for opposing fascism. Robert Maynard Hutchins, *The Higher Learning in America* (1936; New Haven, Conn.: Yale University Press, 1962), launched an attack on relativism, vocationalism, and unanchored values that became the focus of heated debate during the later thirties. David A. Hollinger inquires into the tensions over ideas and values within universities in "Two NYUs and 'The Obligation of Universities to the Social Order' in the Great Depression," in *The University and the City: From Medieval Origins to the Present*, ed. Thomas Bender (New York: Oxford University Press, 1988). Robert Bannister's *Sociology and Scientism: The American Quest for Objectivity, 1880–1940* (Chapel Hill: University of North Carolina Press, 1987) situates intellectual developments within sociology during the 1930s against a longer history. Contemporary works that suggested strategies for redefining the essential nature of democracy or its American workings included John Dewey, *Freedom and Culture* (1939; New York: Capricorn Books, 1963); Pendleton Herring, *The Politics of Democracy: American Parties in Action* (New York: Rinehart and Co., 1940); John Chamberlain, *The American Stakes* (New York: Carrick and Evans, 1940); and Jacques Barzun, *Of Human Freedom* (Boston: Little, Brown and Co., 1939).

The Federal Art Project is chronicled in Richard D. McKinzie, *The New Deal for Artists* (Princeton, N.J.: Princeton University Press, 1973). Karal Ann Marling provides a creative reading of one major strain of New Deal art in *Wall-to-Wall America*. Barbara Rose, *American Art since 1900*, rev. ed. (New York: Praeger, 1975), combines the general perspective of an art historian with some sharply stated opinions. Many more studies concentrate on individual artists who were active during the 1930s. The Federal Theater Project receives due attention in Jane DeHart Mathews, *The Federal Theater, 1935–1939: Plays, Relief, and Politics* (Princeton, N.J.: Princeton University Press, 1973). The most prominent of earlier 1930s efforts to bring an element of politics to the stage, the Group Theater, is described in Harold Clurman's excellent memoir, *The Fervent Years* (New York: Alfred A. Knopf, 1945). Francis V. O'Connor, ed., *The New Deal Art Projects: An Anthology of Memoirs* (Washington, D.C.: Smithsonian Institution Press, 1972), collects additional recollections. Barbara Melosh looks selectively at the art projects with gender as an interpretive concern in *Engendering Culture: Manhood and Womanhood in New Deal Public Art and Theater* (Washington, D.C.: Smithsonian Institution Press, 1991).

Joseph Horowitz seeks splendidly to examine how the public image of one musician was crafted to fit and to foster cultural expectation in the late 1930s and early 1940s in *Understanding Toscanini: How He Became an American Culture-God and Helped Create a New Audience for Old Music* (New York: Alfred A. Knopf, 1987; Minneapolis: University of Minnesota Press, 1988). Henry Cowell, ed., *American Composers on American Music* (Palo Alto: Stanford University Press, 1933; New York: Frederick Ungar, 1962), contains an important set of contemporary essays on musical directions in the 1930s. Lawrence Starr offers a provocative perspective deserving wider application in "Gershwin's 'Bess, You Is My Woman Now': The Sophistication and Subtlety of a Great Tune," *Musical Quarterly* 72 (1986): 429–48. Several general histories of American music comment substantively on music in the 1930s: H.

Wiley Hitchcock, *Music in the United States: A Historical Introduction*, 3d ed. (Englewood Cliffs, N.J.: Prentice-Hall, 1988); Charles Hamm, *Music in the New World* (New York: W. W. Norton, 1983); Wilfred Mellers, *Music in a New Found Land: Themes and Developments in the History of American Music* (London, 1964; New York: Oxford University Press, 1987); and Barbara Tischler, *An American Music: The Search for an American Musical Identity* (New York: Oxford University Press, 1986). In a study organized differently from this one, jazz and blues music might have claimed a significant place. Paul Oliver, Max Harrison, and William Balcom, *The New Grove Gospel, Blues and Jazz with Spirituals and Ragtime* (New York: W. W. Norton, 1980, 1986), provides a reliable place to begin an exploration of this music and a useful bibliography. Leonard B. Meyer, *Music, the Arts, and Ideas: Patterns and Predictions in Twentieth-Century Culture* (Chicago: University of Chicago Press, 1967), can help lift the level of thinking about aesthetic and intellectual issues above their most immediate context.

# Index

# The Author

Terry A. Cooney serves as professor of history at the University of Puget Sound in Tacoma, Washington. Since 1989 he has also been the associate academic dean. He has previously published *The Rise of the New York Intellectuals: "Partisan Review" and Its Circle* (1986), a study of the literary and political evolution of an important group of intellectuals on the left from the early 1930s through 1945, as well as a number of essays and reviews. He has received a Graves Award in the Humanities and held two National Endowment for the Humanities research fellowships and the Regester Lectureship at the University of Puget Sound. He lives in Tacoma with his wife, Denise Von Glahn Cooney, and their children, Haynes and Evan.